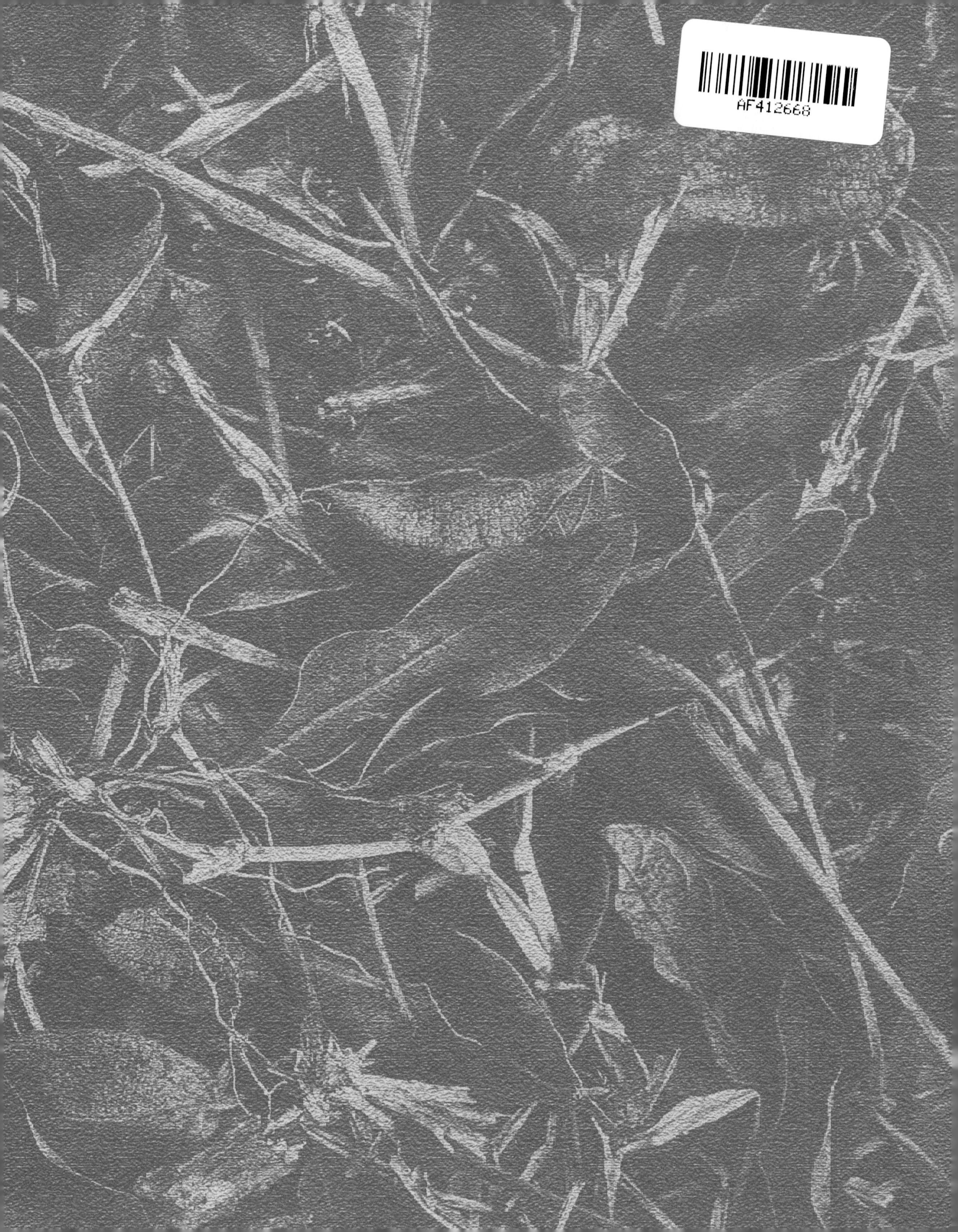
AF412668

AFRICAN TREES

A photographic exploration

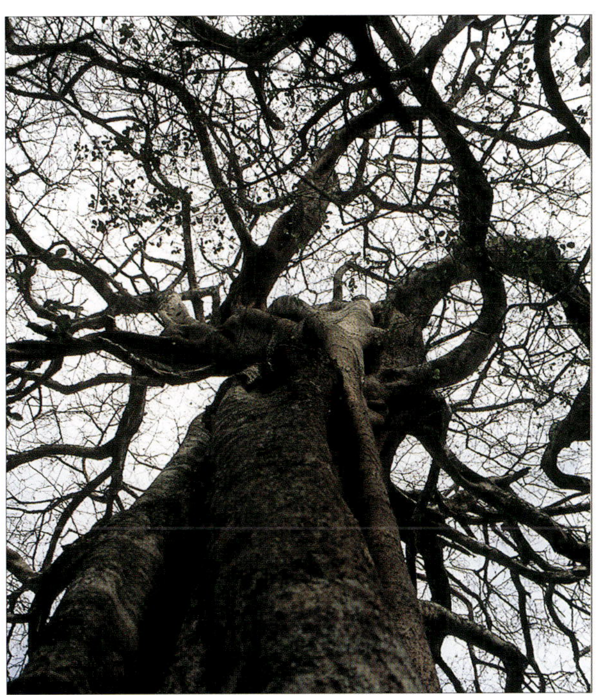

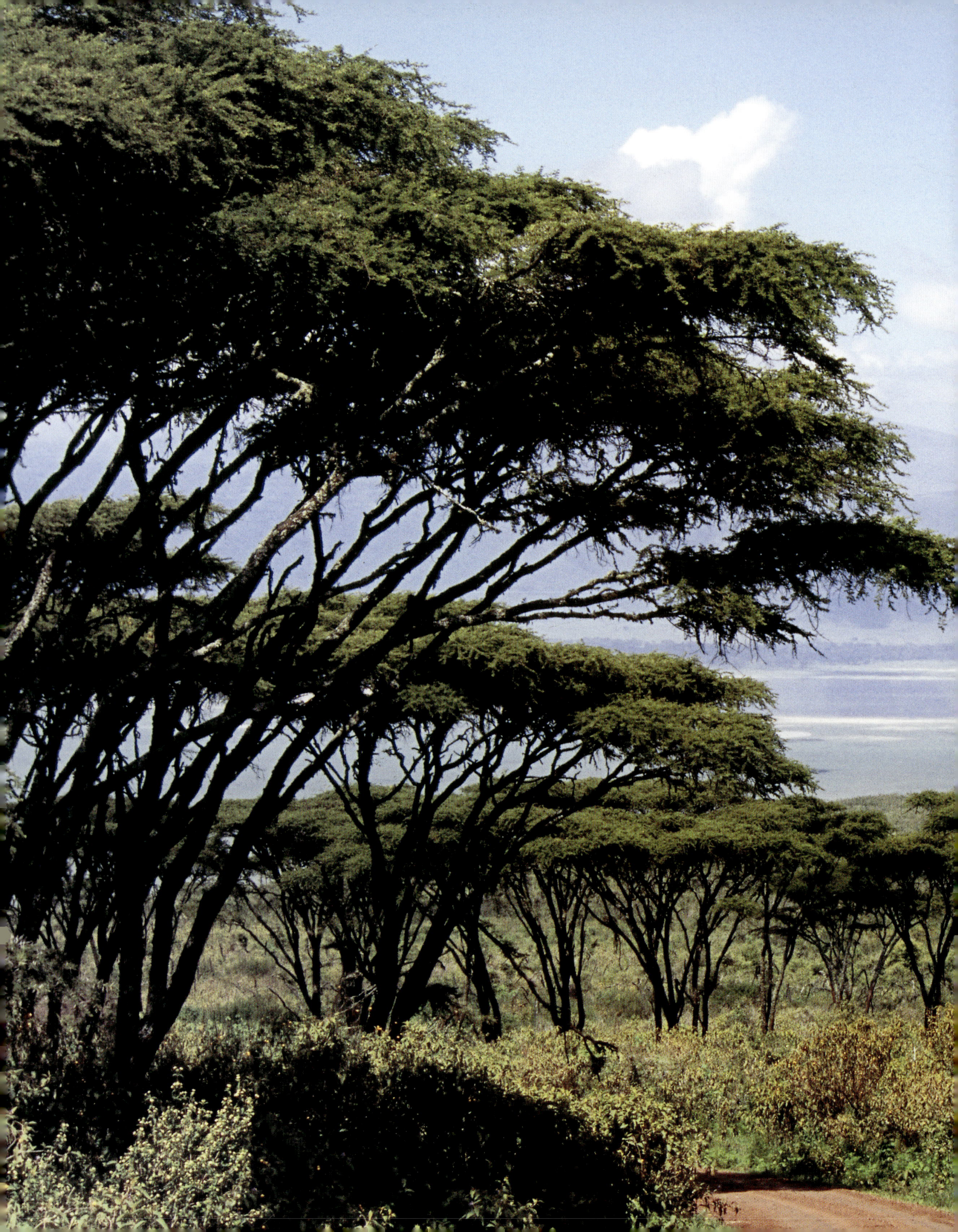

AFRICAN TREES

A photographic exploration

Text and photography by
Charles Bryant and Brita Lomba

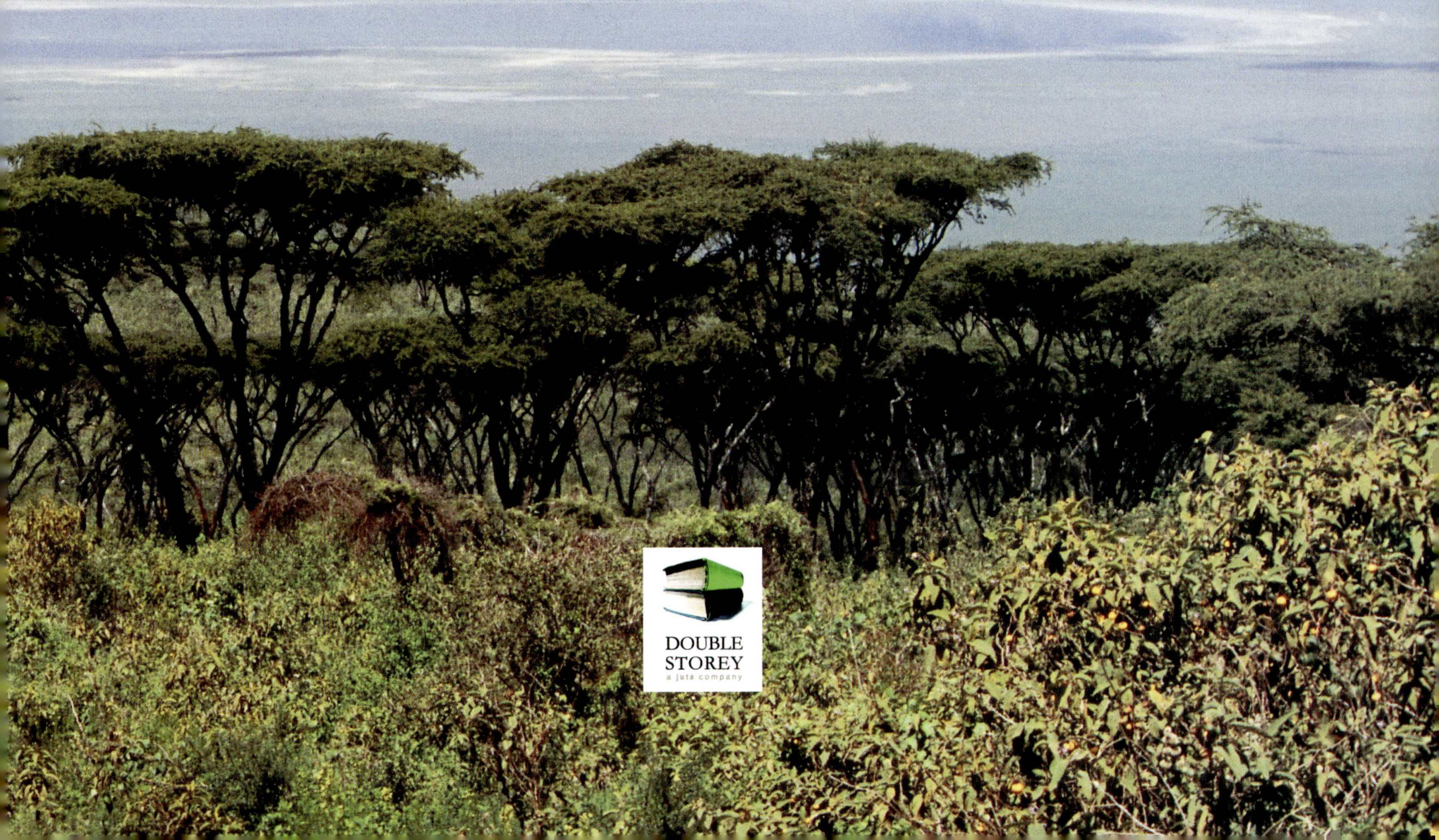

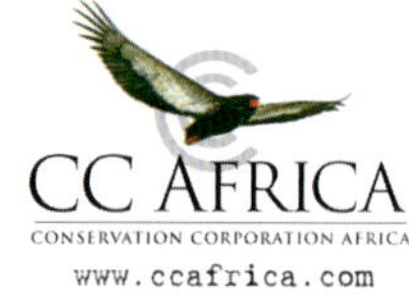

This book would not have been possible without the positive attitude of the directors and staff of CC Africa. 'We have some of the most beautiful trees in Africa' was their opening statement and, with our desire to photograph them, this book was given life. They opened up their reserves and lodges to us, and gave us access to their rangers who willingly shared their knowledge as they drove us, chasing the best light, to their landmark trees.

We were impressed by what they did and how they did it. One senses an ethos of excellence permeating the company – not only to its guests, but also to its staff, the land and the communities living on the fringes of the reserves. Over time, we saw the strength of its model of sustainable ecotourism benefiting neighbouring communities, while having a low impact on the land's resources.

CC Africa also founded the Africa Foundation of which Archbishop Desmond Tutu is a patron. The foundation is an independent, non-profit organisation focusing on education, health care and income generation, and has implemented many successful community empowerment projects across the African continent.

First published 2004 in southern Africa
by Double Storey Books
a division of Juta & Co. Ltd
Mercury Crescent, Wetton
Cape Town, South Africa
www.doublestorey.com
Reg. no. 1919/001812/06

ISBN 1-919930-76-0

Cover and text design by Abdul Amien
Edited by Hilda Hermann
Map by Anne Westoby
Project management by Douglas van der Horst
Reproduction by Virtual Colour, Cape Town
Printing and binding by Tien Wah Press, Singapore

HALF TITLE PAGE: Baobab (*Adansonia digitata*).

PREVIOUS PAGES: Red Thorn Acacia (*Acacia lahai*).

RIGHT: The crater rim setting at Ngororgoro Crater lodge.

OPPOSITE: Ana Tree (*Faedherbia albida*).

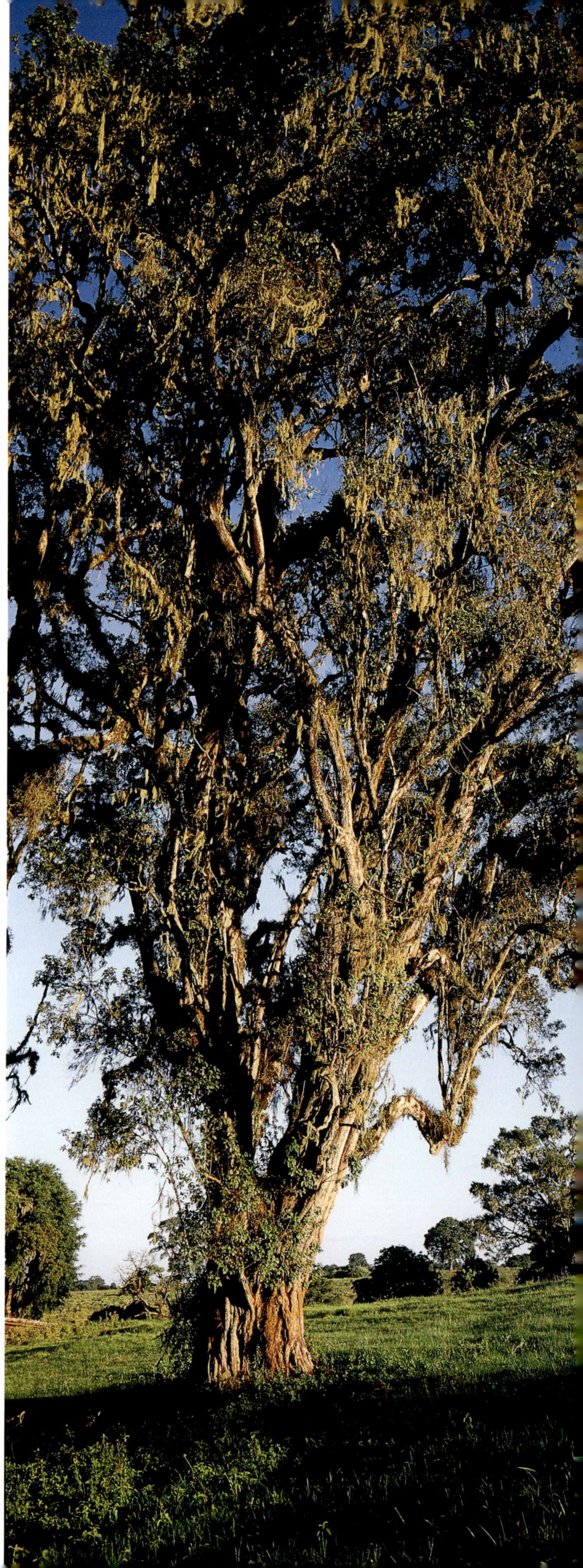

Contents

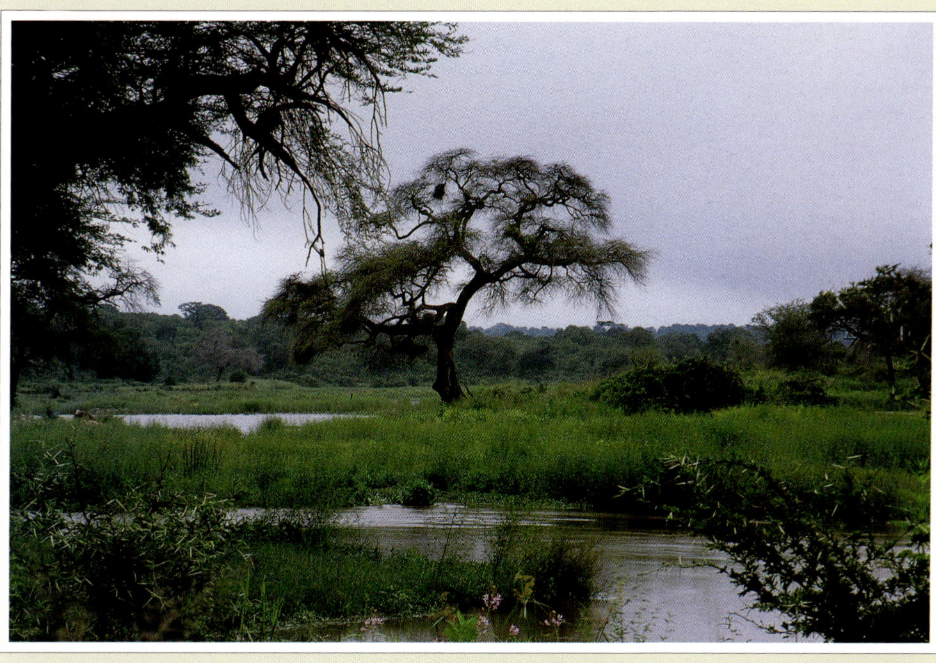

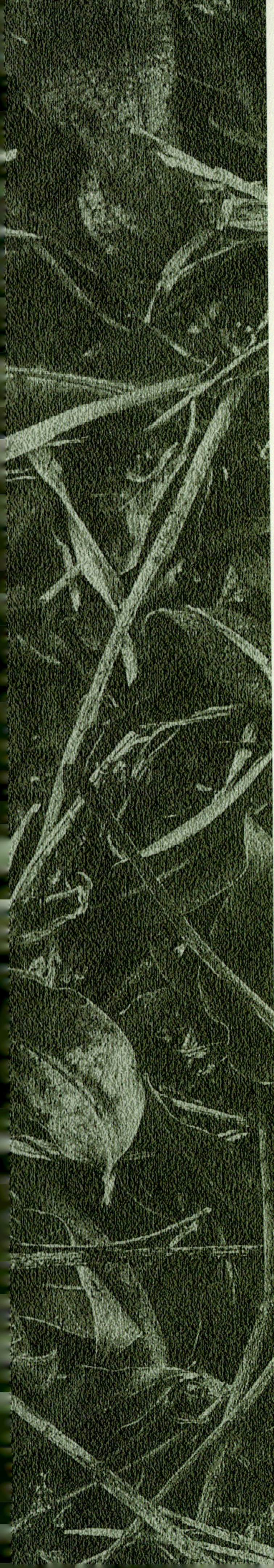

Dedication

To David, Kate, Nikki and Kim

Acknowledgements

The publication of this book would not have been possible without the enthusiastic assistance of numerous people. We would like to thank the following; should anyone have been omitted inadvertently, we apologise for the oversight.

Nicky and Steve Fitzgerald, Duncan Butchart, Shayne Richardson, Martine Karpes, Valerie Senekal, Shona Bagley, Archbishop Desmond Tutu, Chris Ahrends, Inger Ellis, Bridget Impey, Russell Martin, Douglas van der Horst, Hilda Hermann, Abdul Amien, Bottomley Ngwenya, Pieter Ascham, James Hendry and his trainees of 2003, Brett Pearson, Alistair Kilpin, Vitalis Chingo, Vernon Swanepoel, Emiel Mkwizu, Ludovic Saronga, Martin Lucas, Salim Ally Lesian, Peter Dunning, Didas Godfrey, Justice Narika, Rajabu Alute, Phillip Keyter, Gavin Lautenbach, Hamole Sebetwane, Mark Swafield, Milka Kerubo, Lisa Shawe

We would also like to thank CC Africa. They embraced our ideas and opened the world of trees to our lenses. This flora snapshot of the African continent covers seventeen of their lodge destinations.

And thanks to our fathers, John Ellis and Richard Bryant, for putting cameras and inspiration into our hands.

Bibliography

Baldus, R.D. & Siege, L. 2002. *Selous Game Reserve – The Travel Guide.* Michael Landrey, East African Movies Ltd, Dar es Salaam, Tanzania.

Butchart, D. 2000-2003. *Ecological Journal.* CC Africa, Johannesburg.

Butchart, D. 2003. *CC Africa Ecoguides.* CC Africa, Johannesburg.

Coates Palgrave, K. 2002. *Trees of Southern Africa,* 3rd edition. Struik Publishers, Cape Town.

Dale, I. & Greenway. P.J. 1961. *Kenya Trees and Shrubs.* Hatchards, London.

Funston, M. 1993. *Bushveld Trees, Lifeblood of the Transvaal Lowveld.* Fernwood Press, Cape Town.

Johnson, P. (ed.). 2000. *Ruaha.* African Publishing Group, Zimbabwe.

Ngorongoro Book of Life. 2000. African Publishing Group, Zimbabwe.

Noad, T. & Birnie, A. 1989. *Trees of Kenya.* T.C. Noad & A Birnie. Nairobi, Kenya.

Palmer, E. & Pitman, N. 1993. *Trees of Southern Africa.* Balkema, Cape Town.

Roodt, V. 1998. *Shell Field Guide to the Common Trees of the Okavango and Moremi Game Rerserve.* Shell Oil, Botswana.

Smit, N. 1999. *Acacias of Southern Africa.* Briza Publications, Pretoria.

Van Wyk, P. 1974. *Trees of the Kruger National Park.* Purnell, Johannesburg.

Van Wyk, B.E. & Gericke, N. 2000. *People's Plants*: A *Guide to Useful Plants of Southern Africa.* Briza Publications, Pretoria.

Van Wyk, B. & Van Wyk, P. 1997. *Field Guide to Trees of Southern Africa.* Struik Publishers, Cape Town.

Foreword

We who are Africans live in an astonishingly beautiful part of the world. The colonialisation of Africa blinded so many of us to the countless natural wonders that our ancestors in their freedom appreciated.

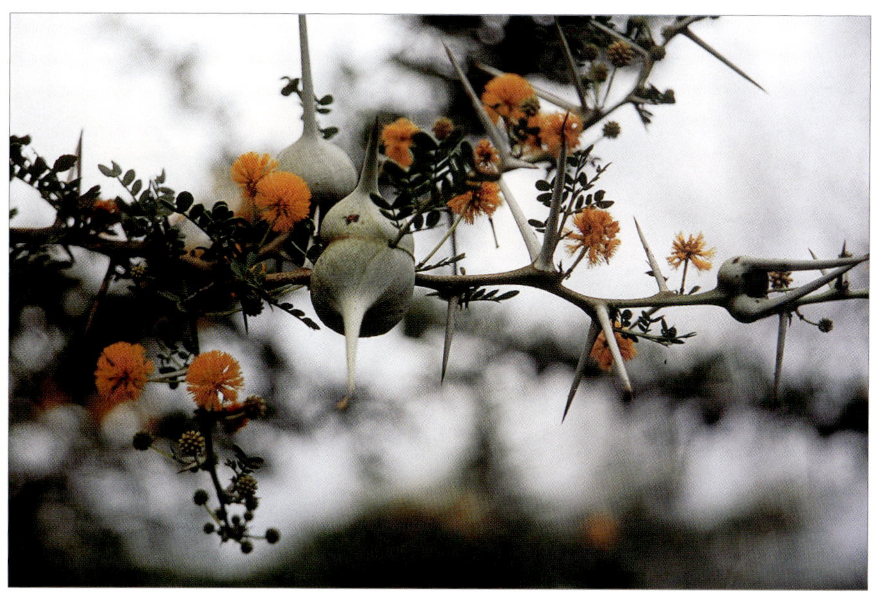

ABOVE: Whistling Thorn (*Acacia drepanolobium*).

In the sacred scriptures, the story of the Garden of Eden is a wonderful metaphor describing the human community living in perfect harmony with nature. This story reminds us that the material universe has a high calling and we, the human family, as viceroys of creation, are called upon to be its stewards not its plunderers.

Our new South African Constitution suggests that environmental rights and human rights are of equal importance. What this means is that we should recognise that all of life is sacred. Our ancestors knew this. They lived fully aware of the delicate network of interdependence that exists between the human community and the natural environment. They understood the sanctity of all living things and recognised that all of life is, in truth, religious.

This beautiful book of photographs and stories about the majestic and diverse trees of southern and eastern Africa calls us to reaffirm this way of life, this understanding of interdependency. The trees and those who live under them are of equal importance as both are bound together within the sacred created order, needing each other in order to survive.

As we strive for the renewal of Africa, we take heart from those like Brita and Charles, who have spent considerable time and effort to reawaken us to the beauty, majesty and wonder of our world.

The trees of southern and eastern Africa, so intimately tied to so many inspiring African stories and myths, have presided for hundreds of years over African history. In them we see the steadfastness and the patience of nature. From them we draw inspiration to live more sensitively within our environment, to strive all the harder to protect it, and to work tirelessly to share it with all who live in the shelter and shadows of the great trees of Africa.

God bless Africa, her wonderful natural beauty and all her people.

DESMOND M. TUTU, ARCHBISHOP EMERITUS

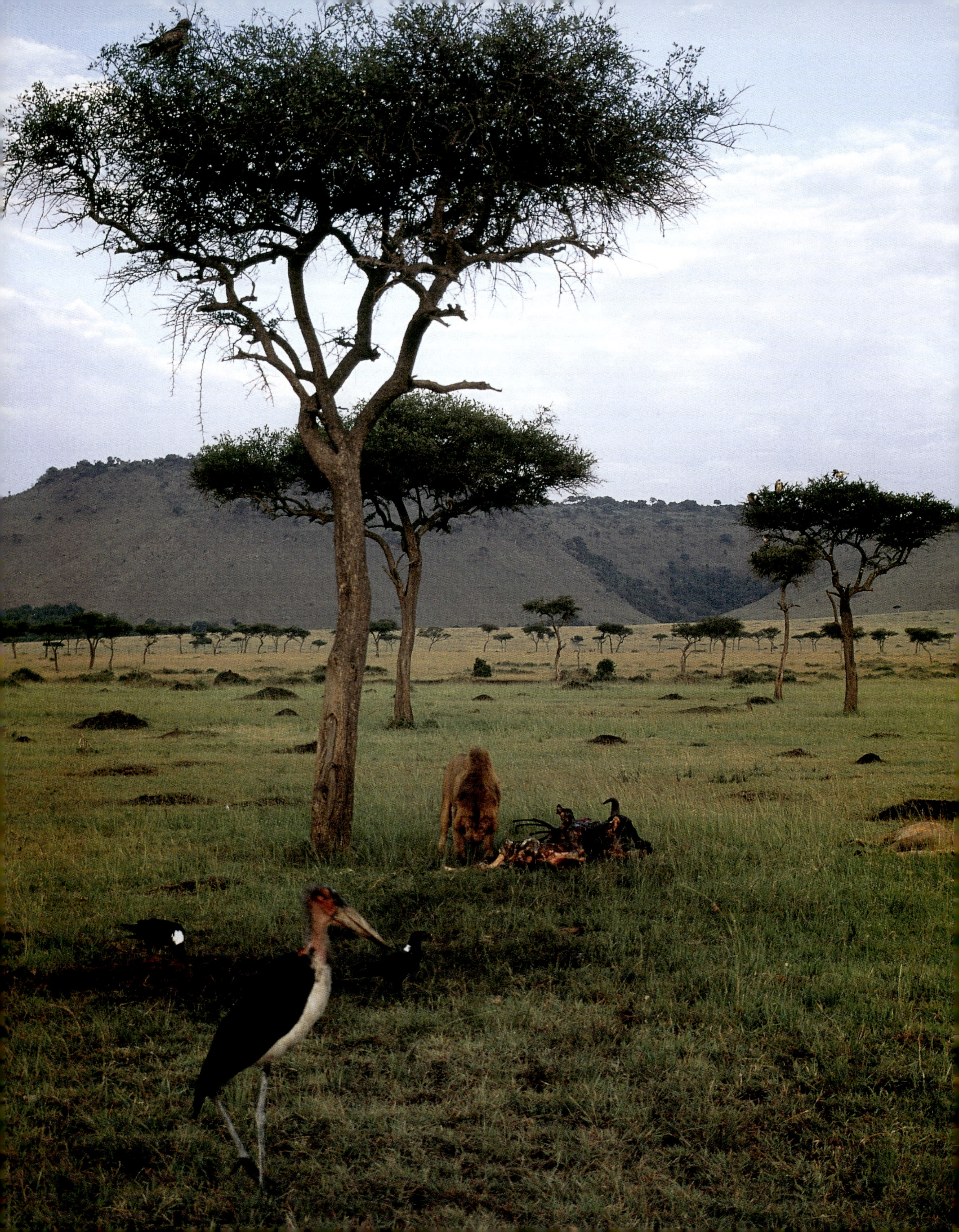

Introduction

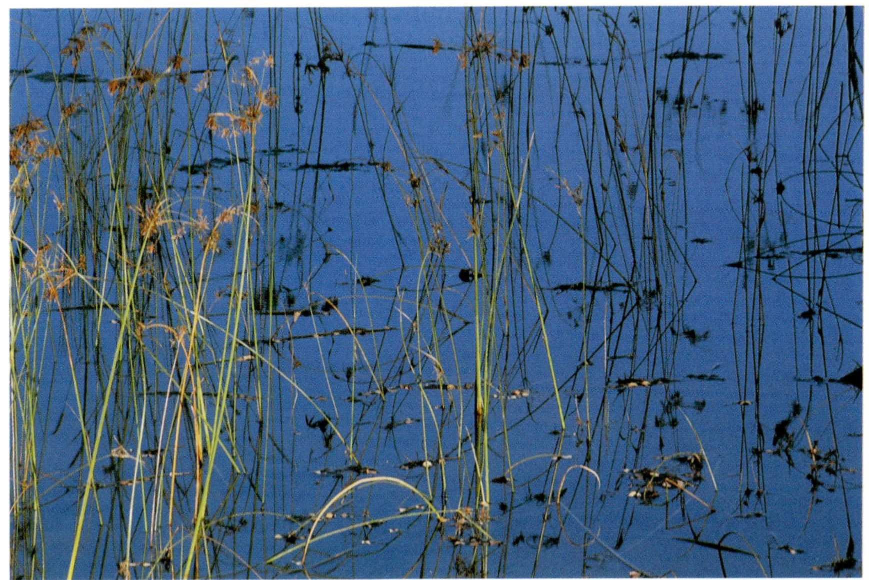

ABOVE: The favourite habitat of the tiny painted reed frog.

One Sunday morning in spring we decided to turn our passion for nature and photography into something more finite than a stream of endless ideas based in Cape Town. We chose to do it through trees, the only plant life that outlives the oldest elephant or human, and the life-givers and supporters of all living creatures. Our idea ran away with its own enthusiasm to develop into this book.

The colours of Africa run through our veins. Its sounds and shapes infiltrate our dreams. We share, with so many, a profound appreciation of undisturbed places where there is a sense of time to contemplate the surrounding beauty that puts everything into perspective.

We love trees because they transport us out of the world of concrete and other material things into a time warp that bonds the soil to the stars. Trees tell us about the Earth and the atmosphere. They are immensely humanising because it is impossible to imagine a planet without them. They are the doctors for the people of Africa and survivors of the continent's extremes.

Jan Smuts once said, 'When nature provides us with more than we can take, we turn to art.' Our journey took us further than we could ever have imagined. In search of nature's true art, we touched the tip of extensive fields of study that would take several lifetimes to learn and absorb: taxonomy, archaeology, anthropology, botany, geology and medicine. We met many wonderful people who were willing to impart their hidden knowledge with painstaking patience to two beginners, and Africa gripped us with a new sense of wonder.

Above all, our story is about light. To do justice to the magnificent shapes and colours of trees in photographs the light had to be perfect. In nature, light is ever-changing with the time of day and the time of year. In the dynamics of change, nature taught us to appreciate the fine art of light's spectrum and disciplined us not to expect perfect tones throughout our journey. Our challenge was to exploit the artistry of any given light to do credit to our subjects.

CHARLES BRYANT & BRITA LOMBA

OPPOSITE: A maribou stork patiently awaits the afterfeast under a Desert Date (*Balanites aegyptiaca*).

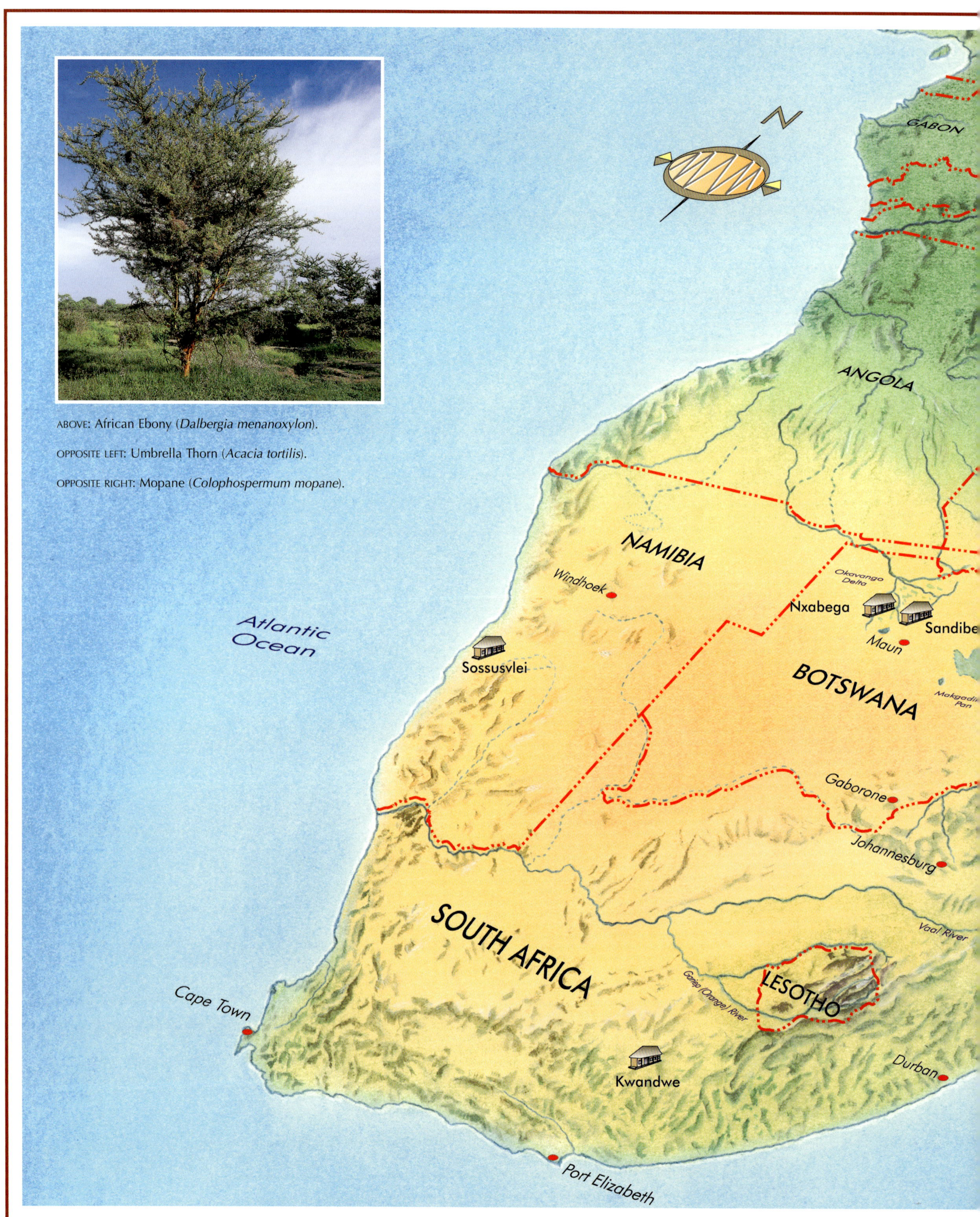

ABOVE: African Ebony (*Dalbergia menanoxylon*).

OPPOSITE LEFT: Umbrella Thorn (*Acacia tortilis*).

OPPOSITE RIGHT: Mopane (*Colophospermum mopane*).

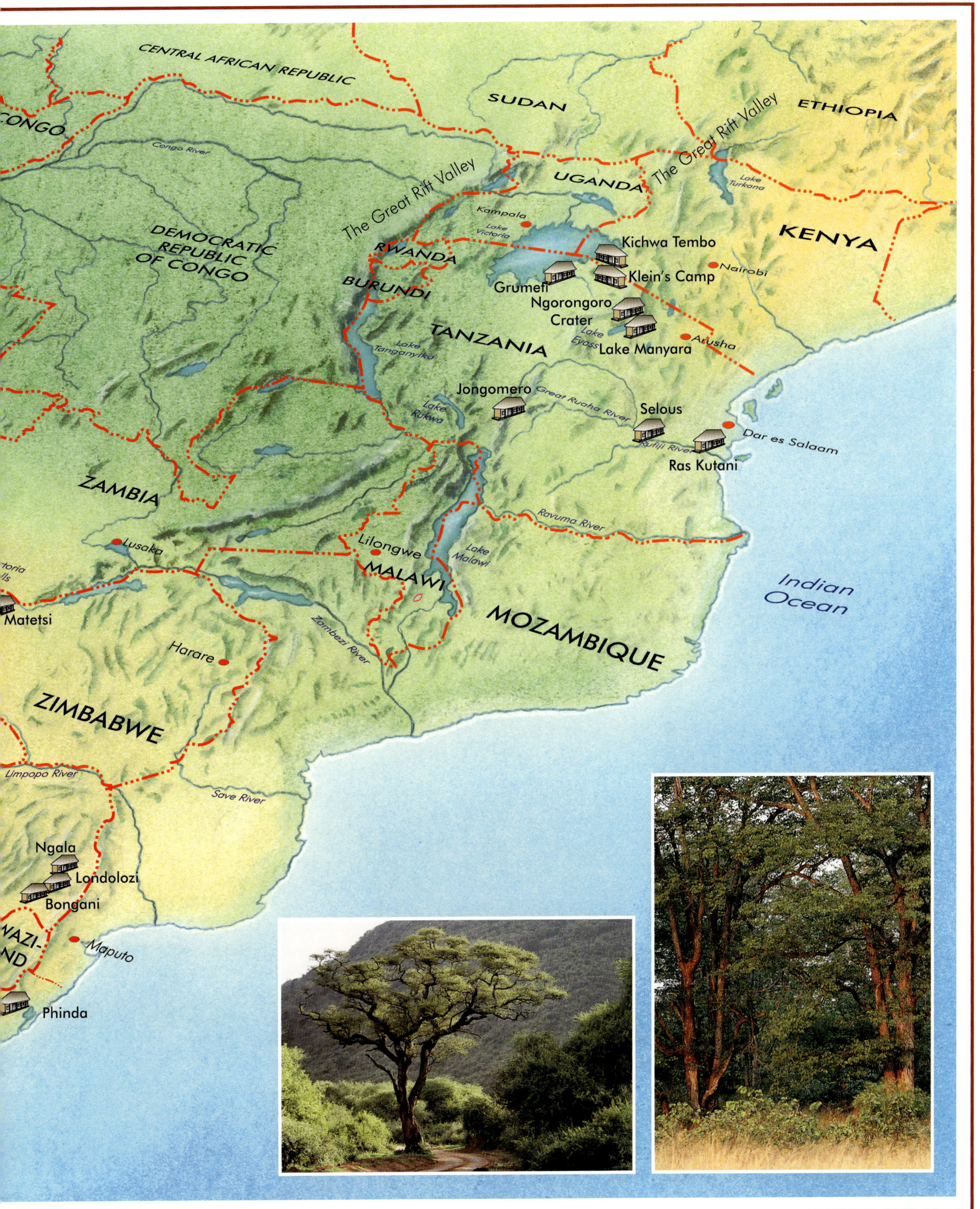

CENTRAL AFRICAN REPUBLIC
CONGO
SUDAN
ETHIOPIA
Congo River
The Great Rift Valley
UGANDA
The Great Rift Valley
Lake Turkana
DEMOCRATIC REPUBLIC OF CONGO
Kampala
Lake Victoria
KENYA
RWANDA
Kichwa Tembo
BURUNDI
Grumeti
Klein's Camp
Nairobi
Ngorongoro Crater
TANZANIA
Lake Eyasi
Lake Manyara
Arusha
Lake Tanganyika
Jongomero
Great Ruaha River
Selous
Lake Rukwa
Rufiji River
Dar es Salaam
Ras Kutani
ZAMBIA
Ruvuma River
Lusaka
Lilongwe
MALAWI
Lake Malawi
Indian Ocean
Victoria Falls
MOZAMBIQUE
Matetsi
Harare
Zambezi River
ZIMBABWE
Limpopo River
Save River
Ngala
Londolozi
Bongani
SWAZILAND
Maputo
Phinda

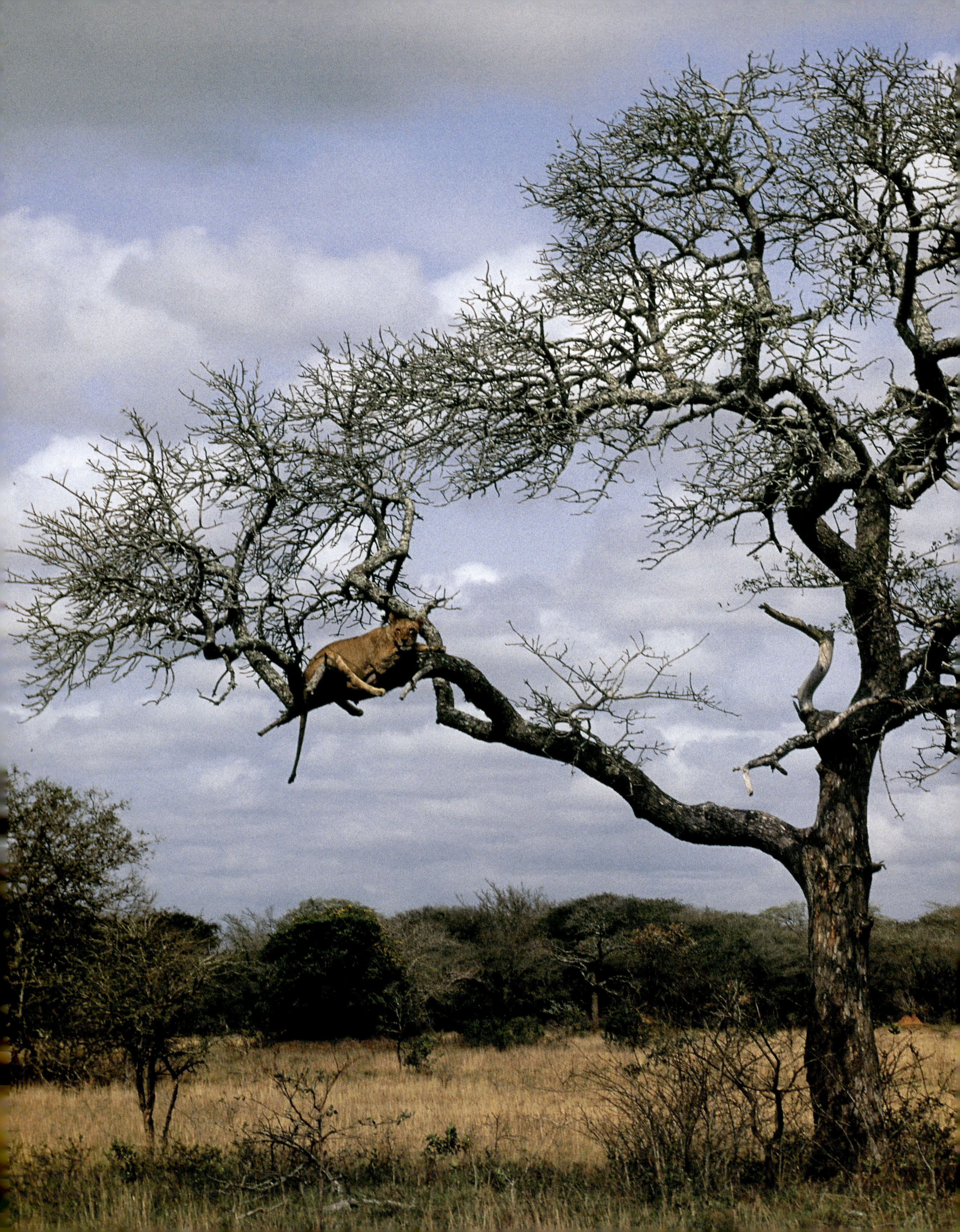

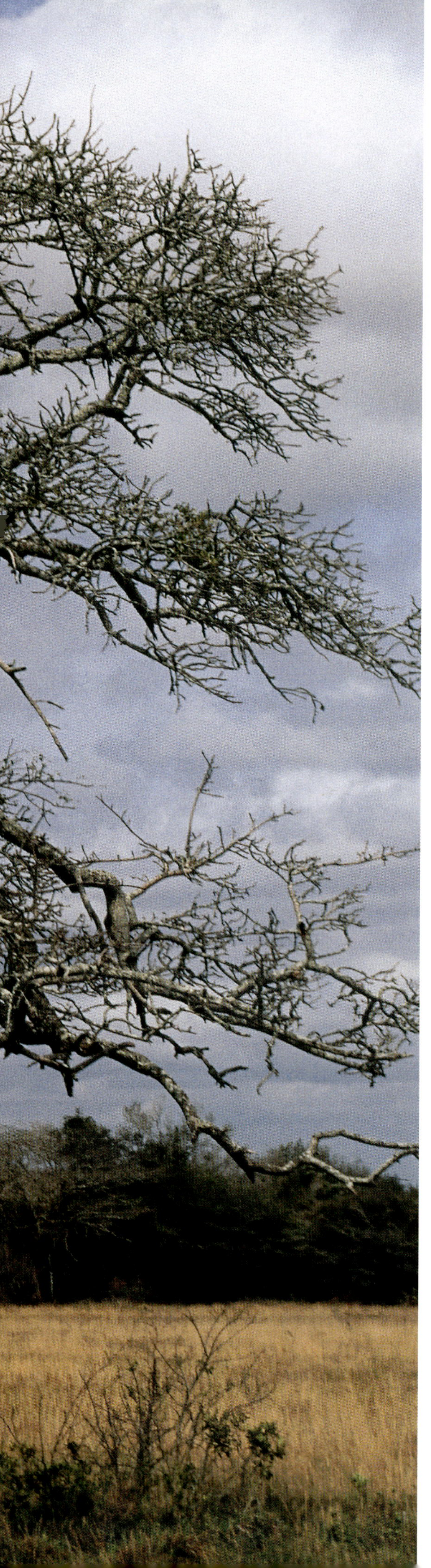

ALLOWING NATURE TO RETURN

The northern tip of Zululand is a wonderland of forest, waterways, marshes, lakes and white sand beaches. It is a fragile area, hotly contested by farming enterprises, property developers, mining companies, recreational and ecotourism activities, and community growth. Sandwiched between the World Heritage Site of Lake St Lucia and the Lebombo mountains is an extraordinary conservation initiative that has become a sustainable model for ecotourism. Here, in the heart of Maputaland, the land has been restored to wildlife, free to roam the forest and savanna biomes – the beginnings of the Greater St Lucia Wetland Reserve.

LEFT: Marula (*Sclerocarya birrea*) with lion. The tree's nut-like kernels are very small and taste like walnuts, while its fruit is used to make jelly and a liqueur. According to archaeological research, Marula trees have been widely used as a source of food and shelter since the days of the early Bushmen. In summer, some of the trees are stripped of their leaves by caterpillars that cover the tree with a beautiful silvery web.

Phinda Private Game Reserve
Maputaland South Africa

A hunger for land during the twentieth century caused severe habitat destruction in Maputaland, at the southern end of the great East African coastal plain. This is the southernmost point at which many tropical species of trees are found. In between two verdant wetlands, the 14 000 hectare reserve of Phinda is an example of how nature responds to conservation. Given the chance, nature returns.

In 1917 the whole of Maputaland was opened to hunters. Apart from the wholesale slaughter of game, people were moved from cool, well-watered hills to lower lying areas. This led to rural poverty and choking ecosystems in the midst of great tracts of land ploughed to enrich farmers who feed the world sugar.

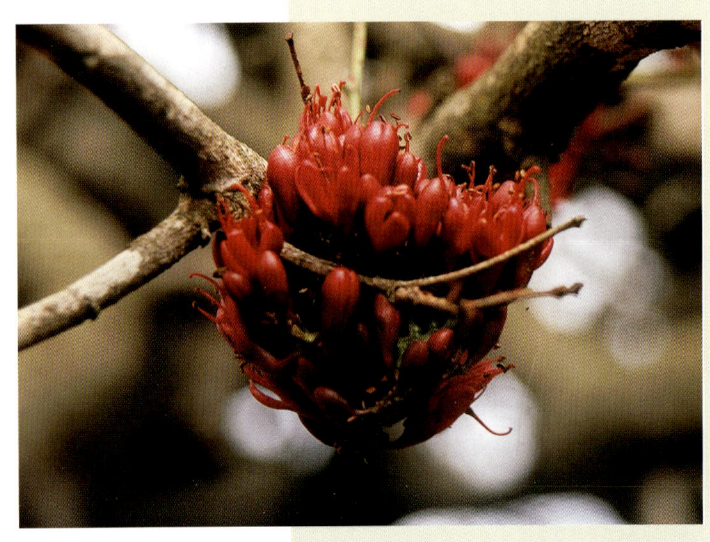

The sand forest at Phinda is an exciting and mysterious place to visit. There are numerous species of trees and plants confined to its infertile, deep grey sand, where everything that grows is brittle and dry. Yet the Sandveld Newtonia (*Newtonia hildebrandtii*), Green Thorn (*Balanites maughamii*) and False Tamboti (*Cleistanthus schlechteri*) are both impressive and ancient. In the depth of the forest, there is a Newtonia estimated to be over 1 000 years old. Unfortunately it was impossible to photograph as it was surrounded by smaller trees and covered in epiphytic orchids and lichen. One disturbing discovery about Newtonia is that there are no young saplings growing in the forest. After three years of research only three young trees were found.

In the sand forest we were shown the only indigenous cactus (*Rhipsalis baccifera*) in southern Africa. This epiphyte is so special, yet so tiny and leafless that it is most often overlooked.

On the fringes of the forest, thriving in tropical conditions from Mozambique and the warm Agulhas current, is a broad-leaved woodland comprising mainly spectacular Flat-crown Albizia (*Albizia adianthifolia*), River Thorn (*Acacia robusta*), Silver Cluster-leaf (*Terminalia sericea*) and Black Monkey Oranges (*Strychnos madagascariensis*). The defining line between woodland and forest is grass; in a true forest there is no grass.

ABOVE: Weeping Boerbean (*Schotia brachypetala*). These beautiful flowers attract sunbirds and a mass of insects with their sweet nectar.

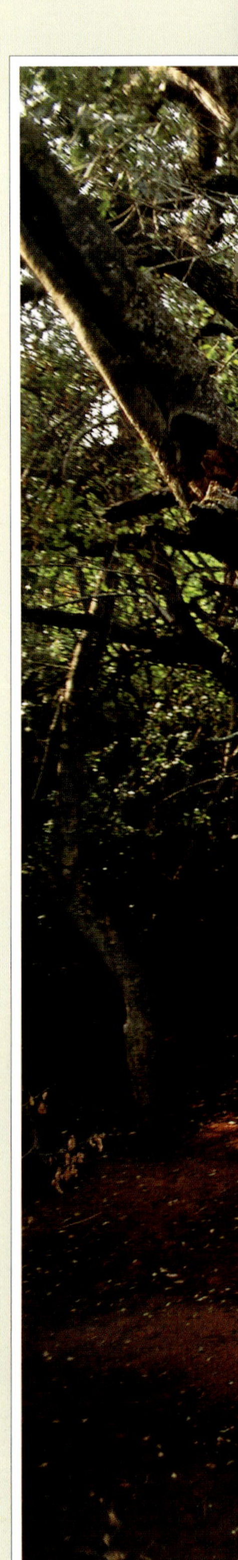

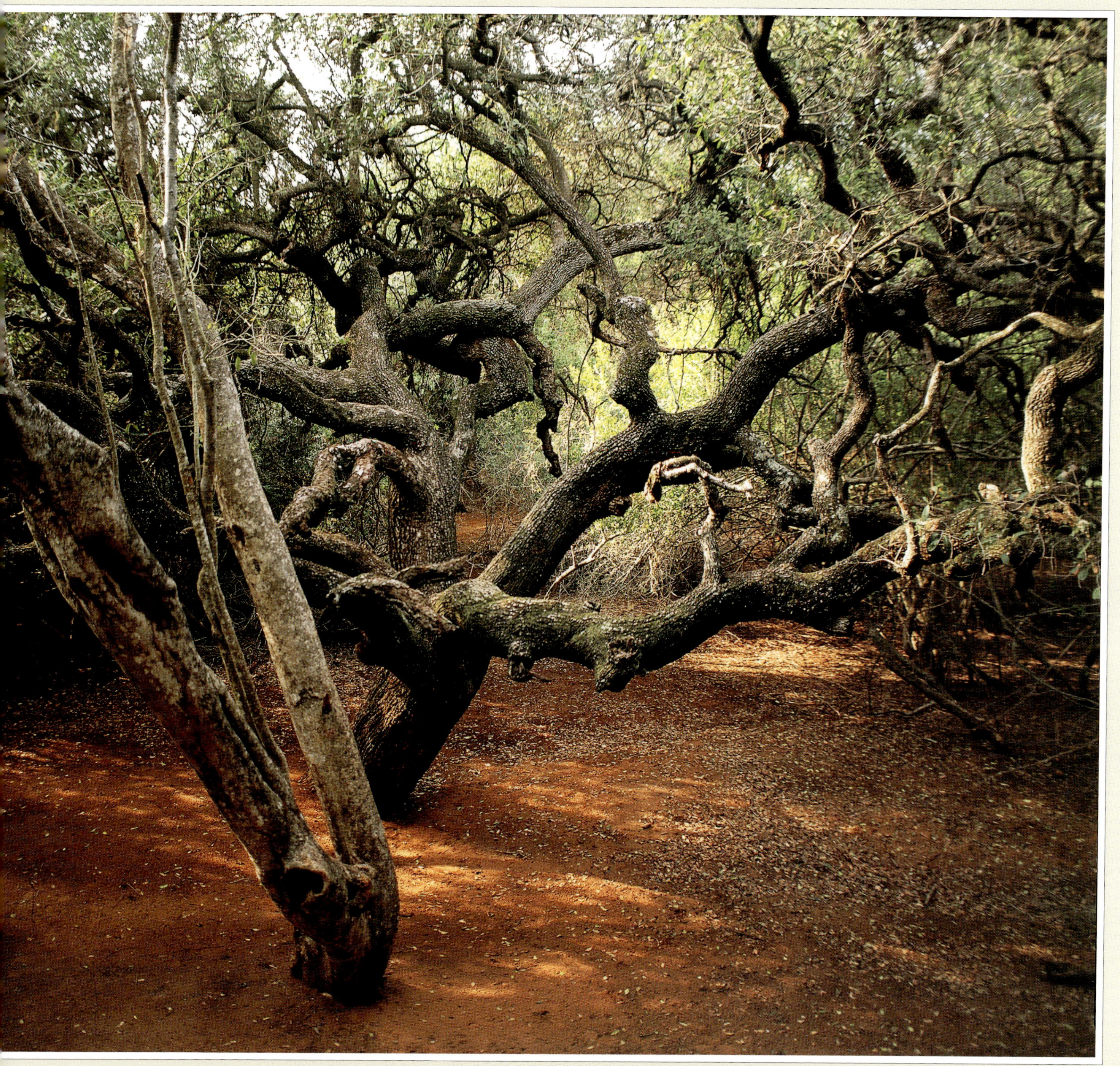

BELOW: Milkwood (*Sideroxylon inerme*). The bark and roots are used to heal broken bones and to treat fevers. The fine-grained wood is used for fence posts and boat building.

With ever-changing colours through the different seasons, we loved the deep purple pod of the Stink Bushwillow (*Pteleopsis myrtifolia*) in May and the crimson flowers of the Weeping Boerbean (*Schotia brachypetala*) in September. From August to December the nectar literally weeps from these beautiful flowers. In the past, the Voortrekkers roasted its beans for a snack.

In the flat sandy areas to the north of Phinda there is coastal bushveld grassland, also known as Palmveld. In May 1994, during the total eclipse of the moon, we felt eerily close to the universe while we watched the changing moon shaped by the Earth's shadow light up huge fan-leaved Lala Palms (*Hyphaene coriacea*).

Another haunting area near the Mzinene River is the flood plain filled with Fever Trees (*Acacia xanthophloea*). Under rain-laden clouds, their golden lime trunks gave a warm light in the dampness. They are among the most distinctive acacias in Africa and thrive in muddy soil. Their Zulu name *umHlosinga* means 'the tree that shines from afar'.

The list of trees and shrubs in this part of Maputaland runs to over 730 specimens. This magical place, with marshes, rivers and flood plains, as well as rocky hillsides, savanna and sand forest, is a popular place of learning for game rangers and trackers. Taking a rest from photography, we became absorbed in the rigorous training of future guides, eager to conquer the vast wealth of knowledge of those who have helped to create this twenty-first century model to rehabilitate land.

RIGHT: Marula (*Sclerocarya birrea*) is protected by law and custom in many rural areas.

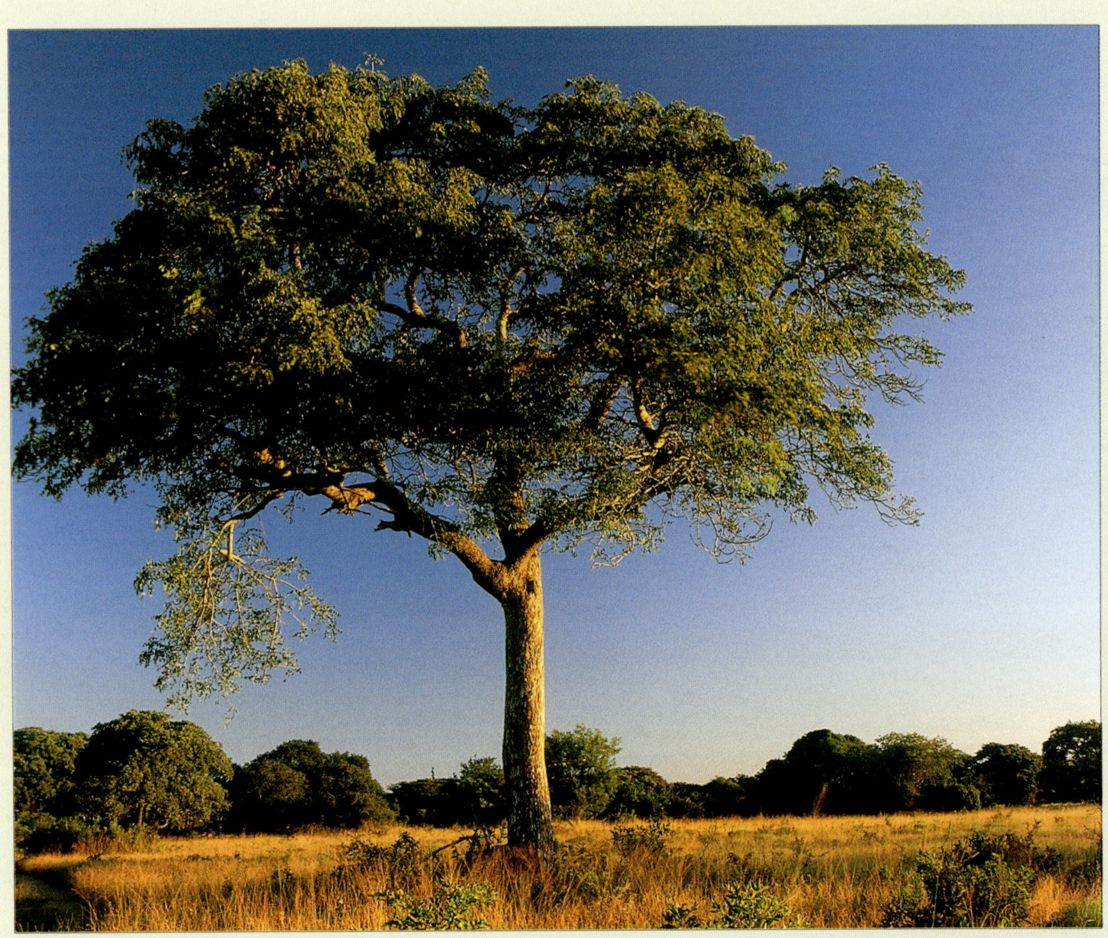

BELOW: Fever Tree (*Acacia xanthophloea*). The main stems and large branches are used to fence out hippo from fields on the Pongola floodplain. The timber is used for boxwood and the bark is used to treat eye complaints and fevers.

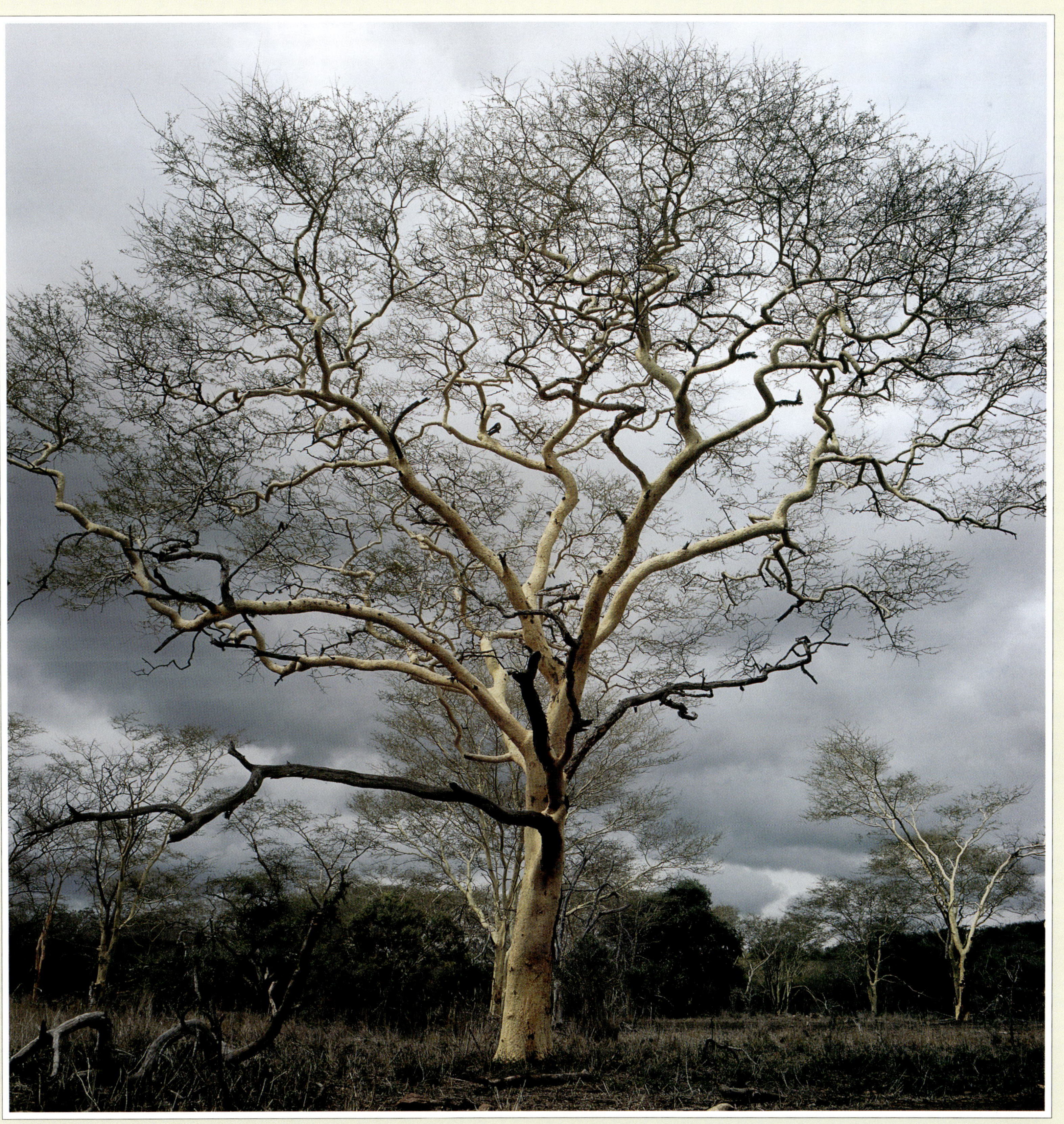

BELOW AND OPPOSITE: Lala Palm (*Hyphaene coriacea*). The tapping of palm sap has become a large industry in Maputaland. Both this and the weaving of baskets from young palm leaves are a source of income for local communities. The popular, nutritious and intoxicating wine made from the palm is called *ubusulu*. The palm heart is also edible.

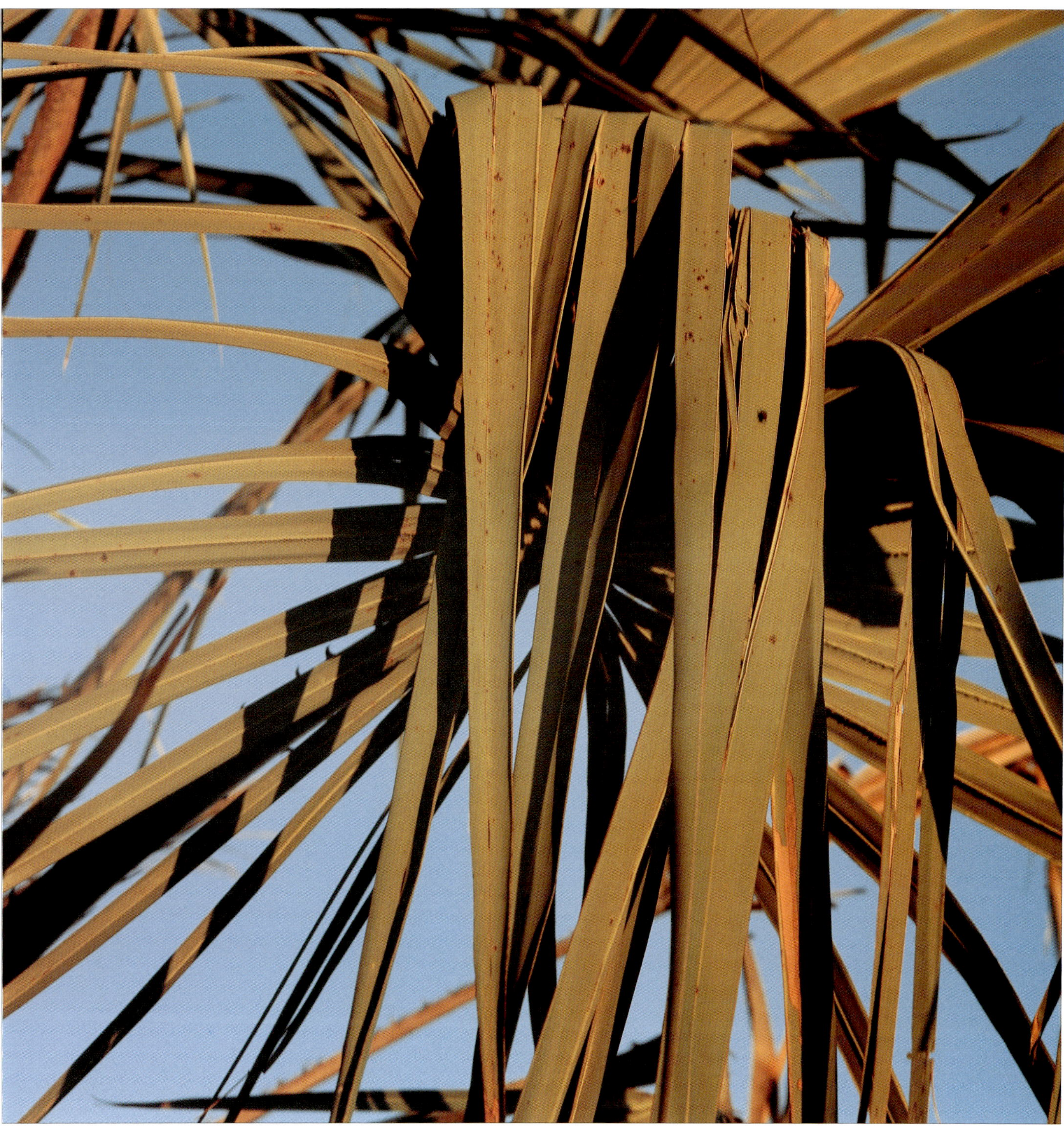

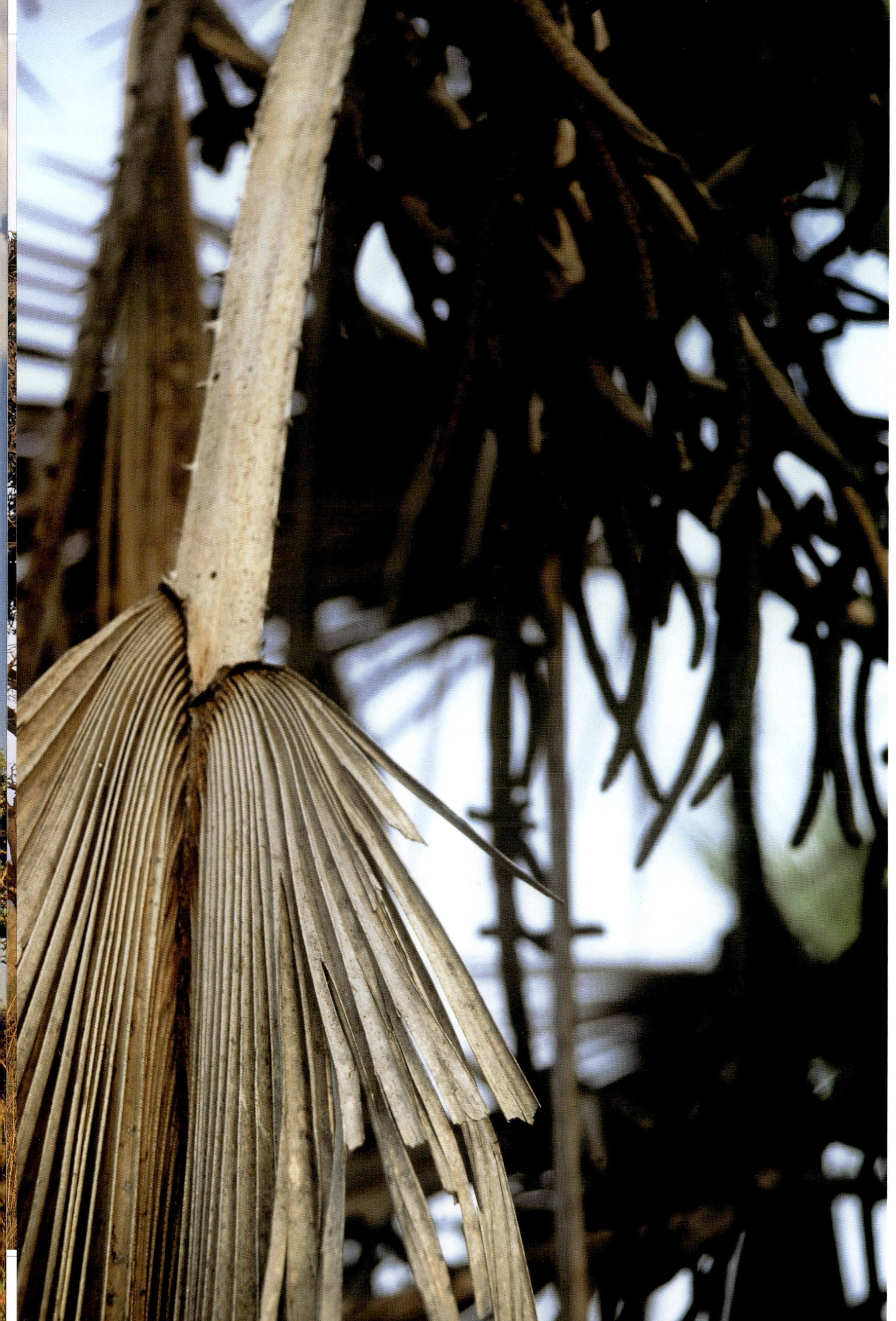

We were treated to a spectacular Eastern Cape sunrise. We crossed the Great Fish River and drove to a slope where every inch was covered in prehistoric-looking Honey Euphorbia (*Euphorbia tetragona*), belonging to a habitat known as tall succulent thicket. The pink-and-orange light washed these trees resembling Mexican cacti to life. While the two families are unrelated, their similar forms are due to 'convergent evolution', whereby similar climates and ecological circumstances have resulted in common structural designs. Most animals, with the exception of black rhino, avoid browsing Euphorbia because of its poisonous latex and spiky thorns. Sneezewood (*Ptaeroxylon obliquum*) is also found in this area and along the river cliffs.

Returning to the deeply incised Great Fish River, we were interested to learn that it is artificially filled from the Orange River, enabling it to flow throughout the year.

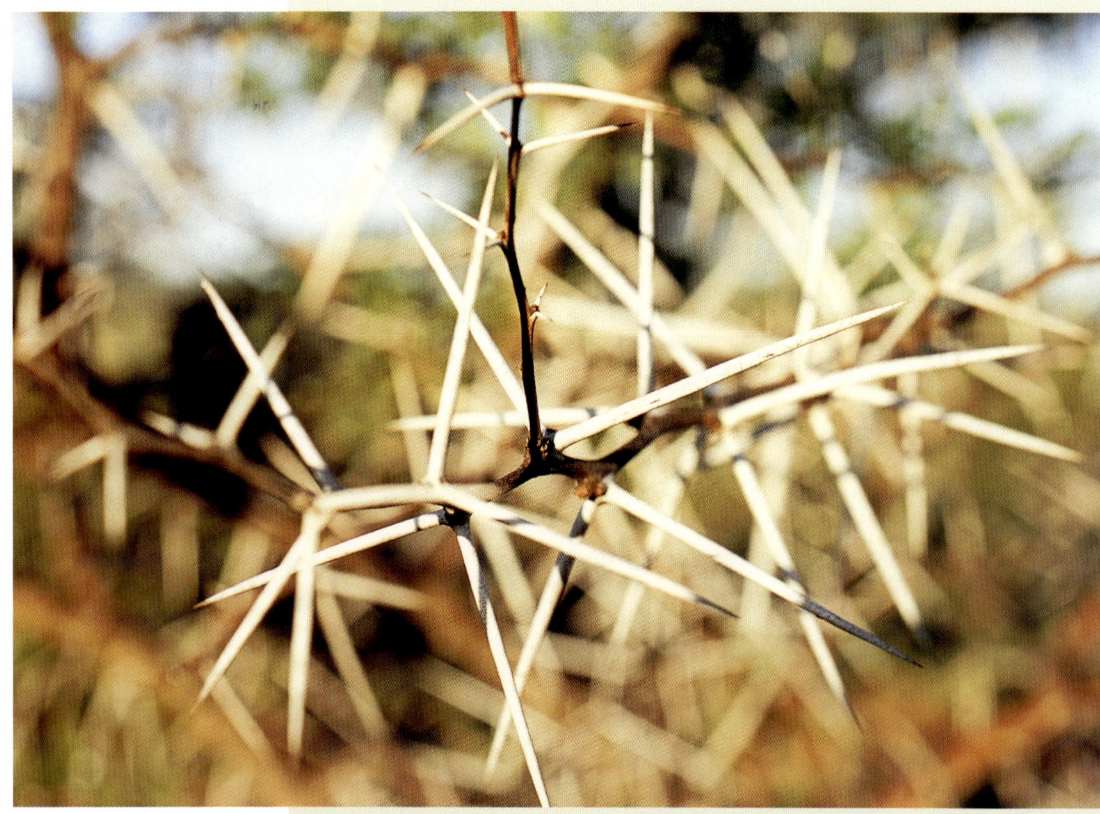

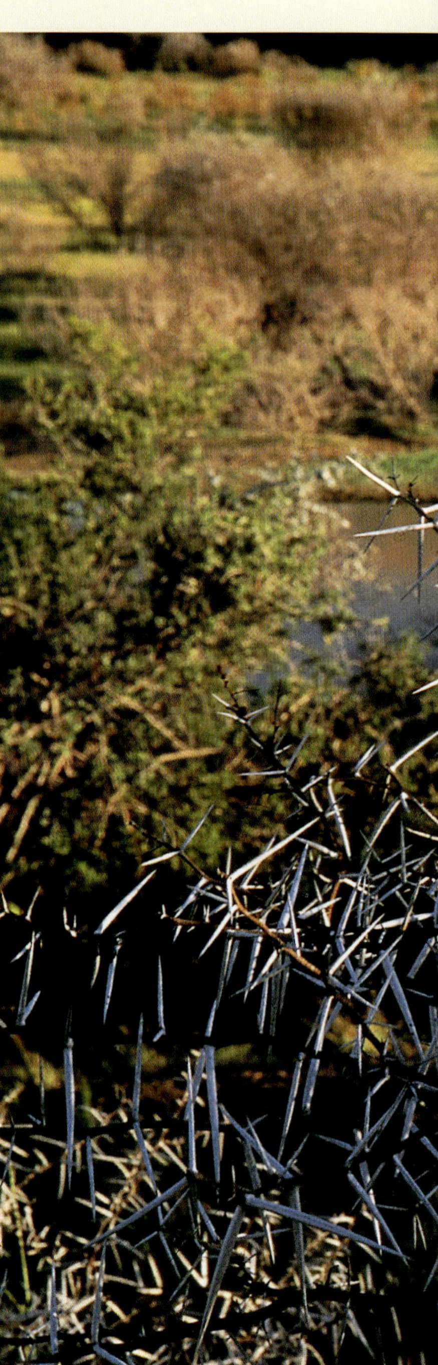

ABOVE: Sweet Thorn (*Acacia karroo*). These trees are good indicators of where to find water in arid areas. They are normally surrounded by sweet grasses, which are good for cattle grazing. It is a very good 'bee tree' and important in the production of honey.

The river banks are lined with Cape Bushwillow (*Combretum caffrum*), Sweet Thorn, Wild Olive (*Olea europaea africana*) and False Olive (*Buddleja saligna*). Many parts of the river are inaccessible because of the steep slopes. The alluvial soil of the former farming land provides better access and stands of Sweet Thorn line the banks.

With Kwandwe only 100 kilometres from the coast, the southern ocean makes its presence felt. South-facing slopes capture the moisture, encouraging denser and taller vegetation. Close inspection of the rocks and plants on these slopes reveals a mass of lichen of all shapes and sizes. Lichen represents a symbiotic partnership between a fungus and algae, with the former providing nutrition and the latter shape. Interestingly, lichens are unable to tolerate air pollution and their presence, or lack thereof, is an important health indicator in cities around the world.

BELOW: Sweet Thorn (*Acacia karroo*). The flowers are rich in pollen, which is rich in protein, and loved by many birds. Ants and other insects abound in these trees, which are favoured foraging sites for warblers, shrikes and other insectivorous birds. Many smaller birds choose to nest in the thorny fortress made by the inter-twined branches.

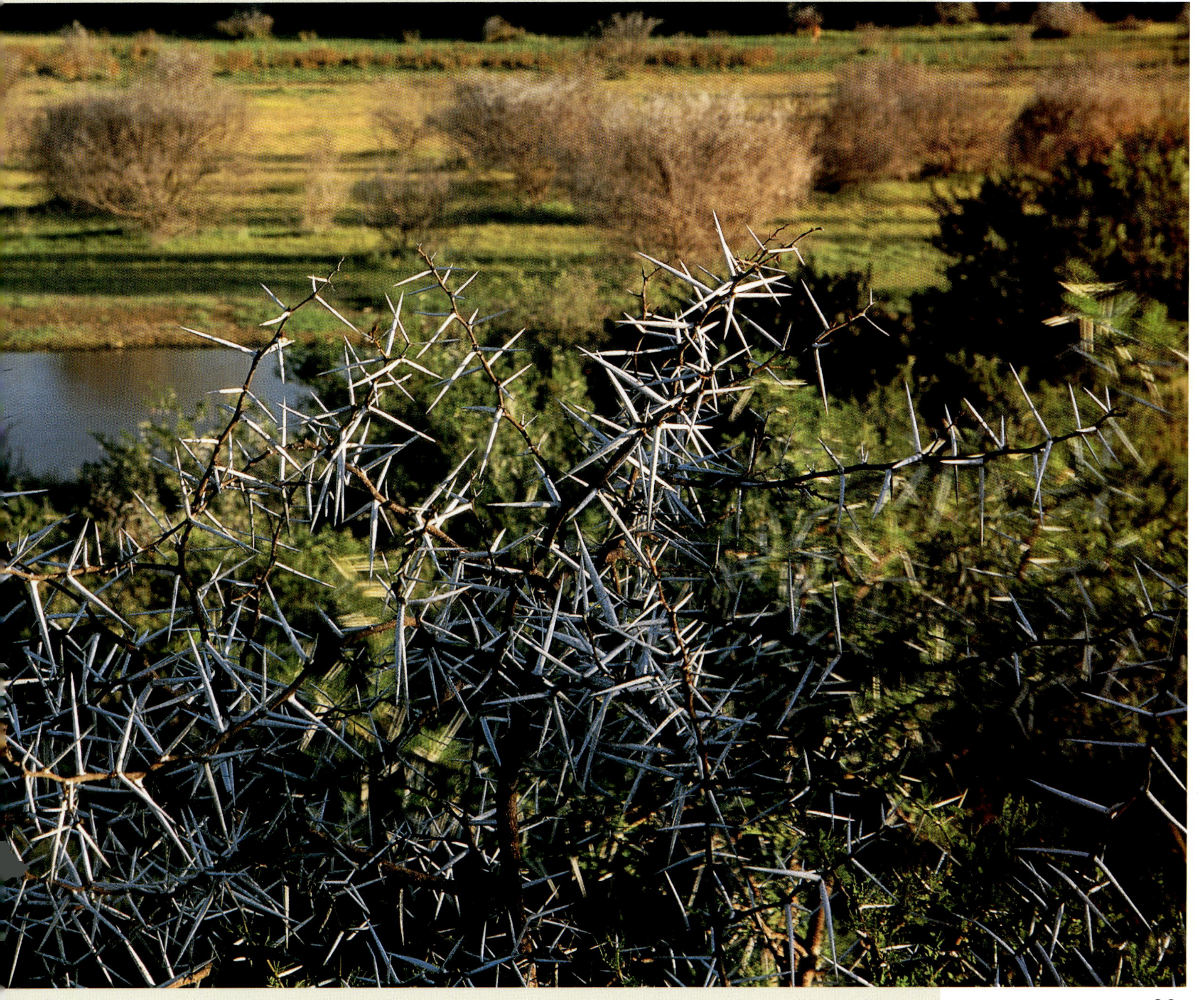

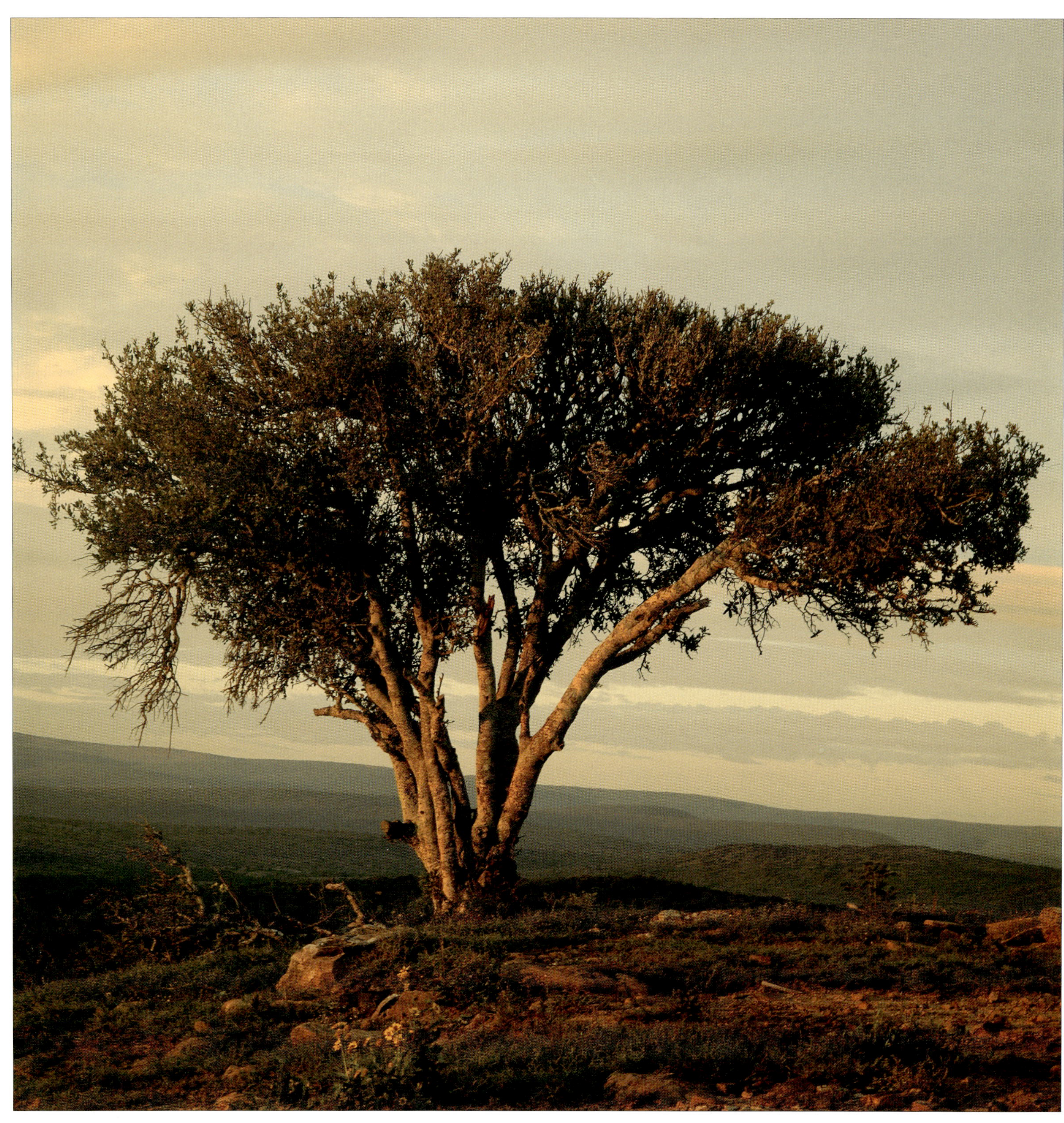

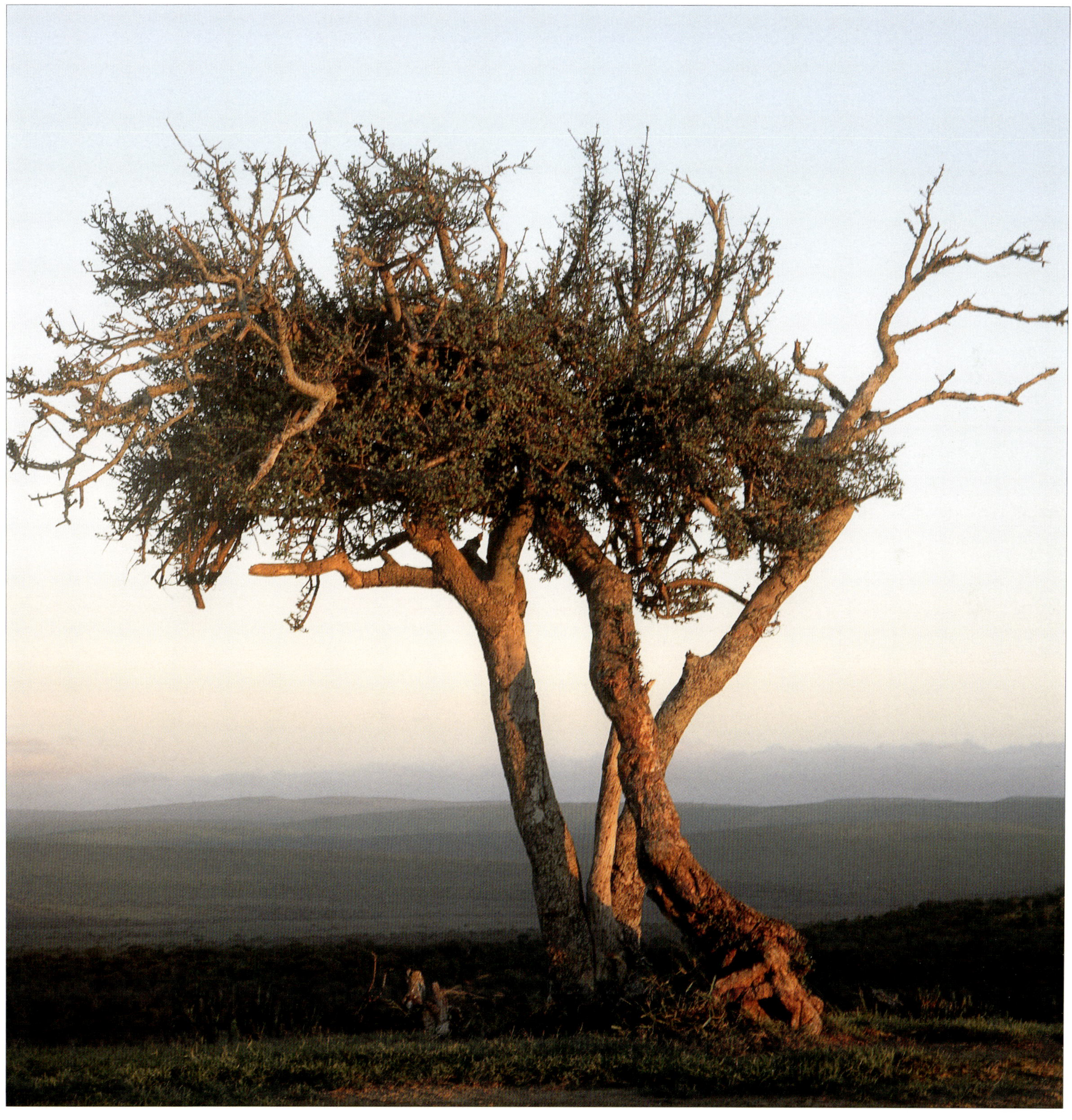

Kwandwe
South Africa

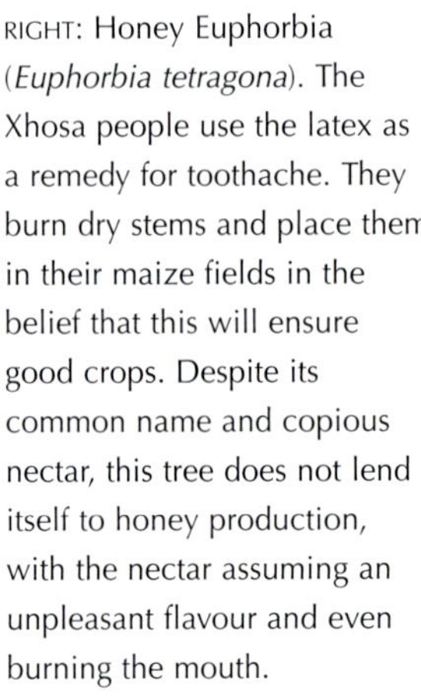

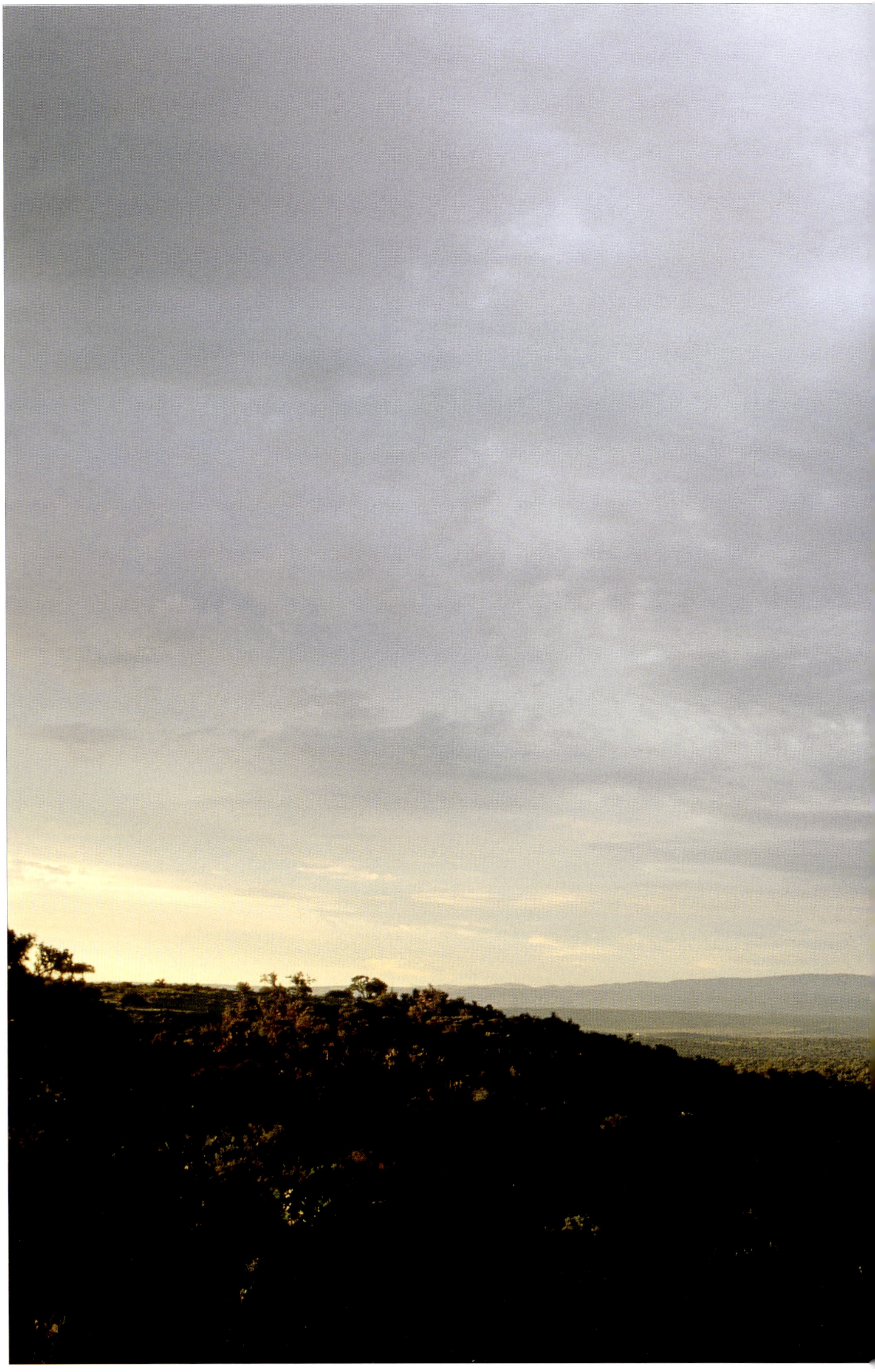

RIGHT: Honey Euphorbia
(*Euphorbia tetragona*). The
Xhosa people use the latex as
a remedy for toothache. They
burn dry stems and place them
in their maize fields in the
belief that this will ensure
good crops. Despite its
common name and copious
nectar, this tree does not lend
itself to honey production,
with the nectar assuming an
unpleasant flavour and even
burning the mouth.

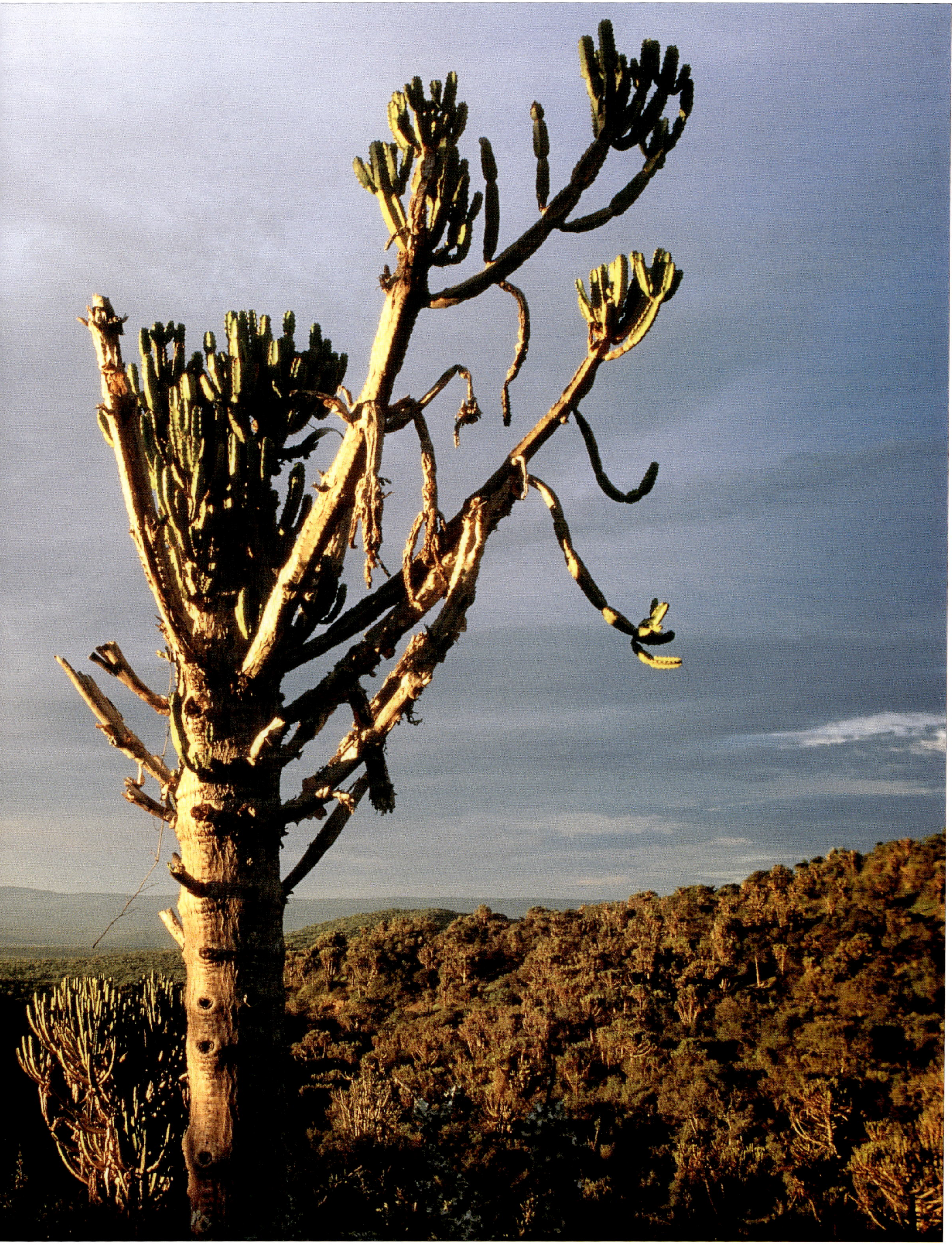

33

RIGHT AND OPPOSITE:
Honey Euphorbia (*Euphorbia
tetragona*).

Kwandwe | South Africa

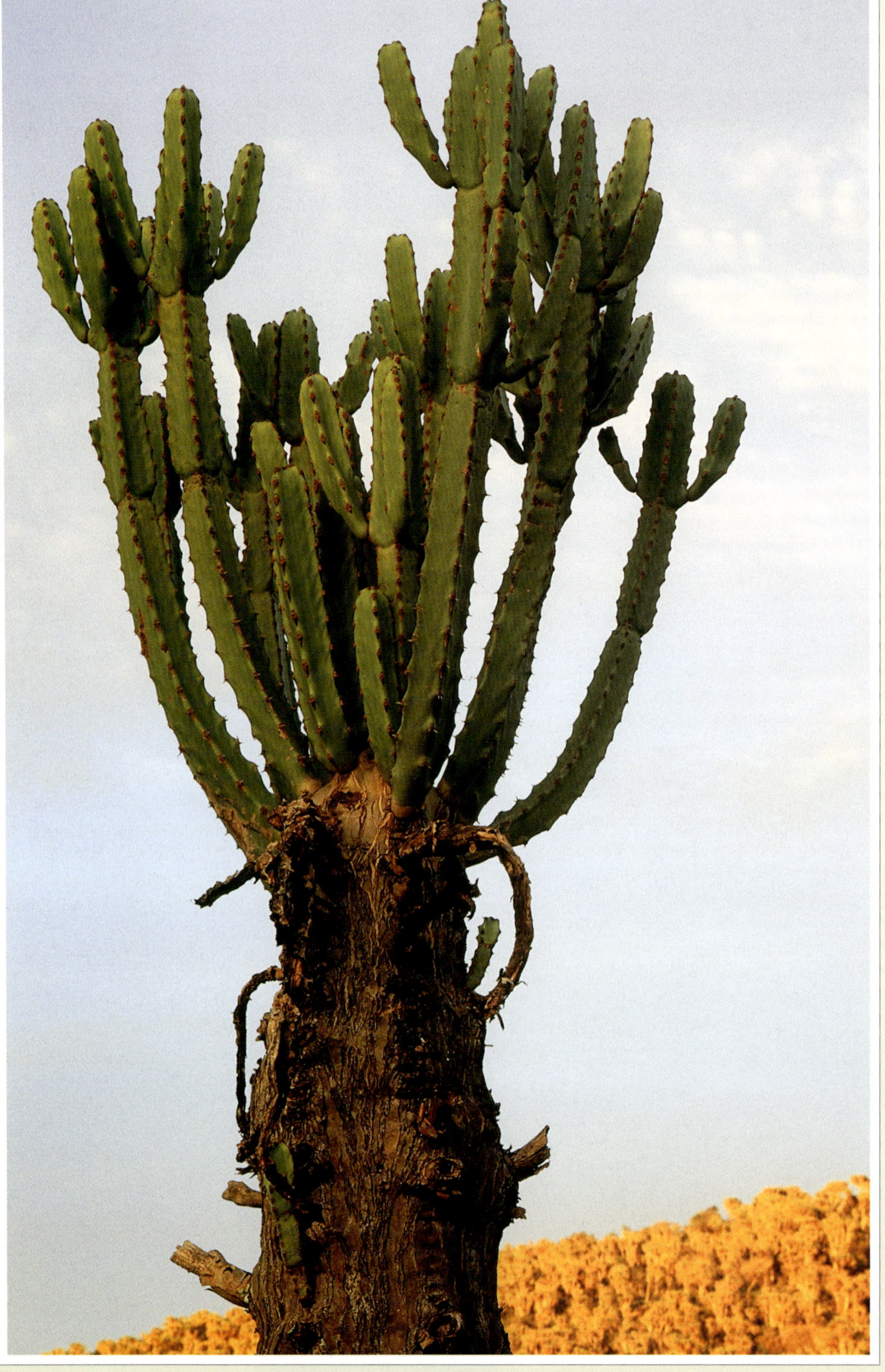

34

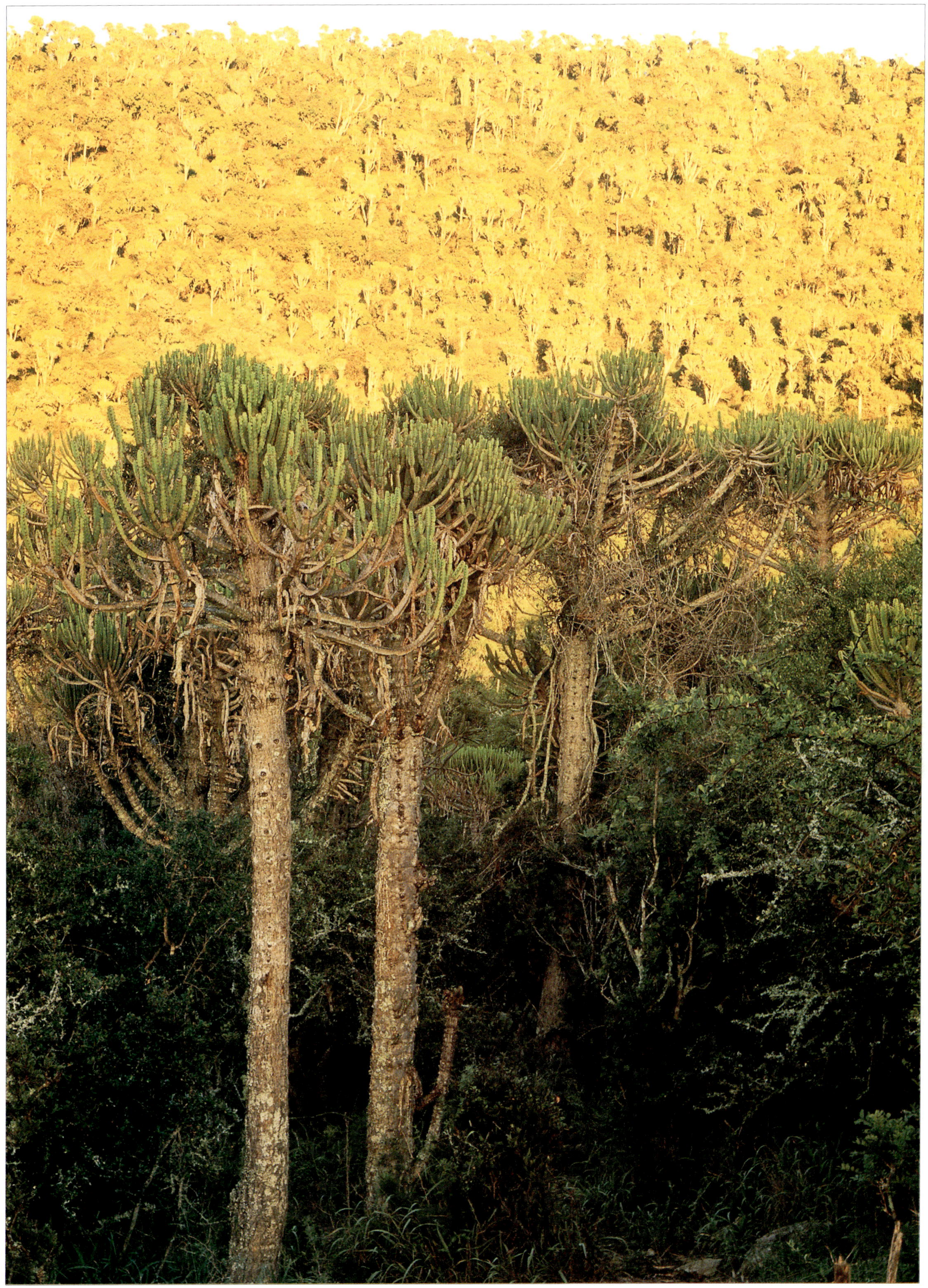

Kwandwe | South Africa

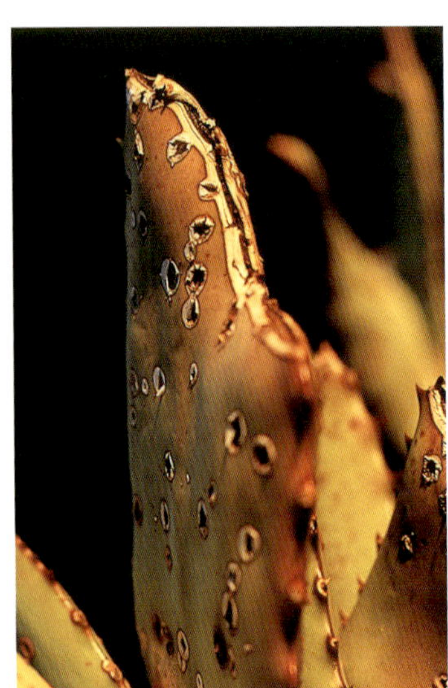

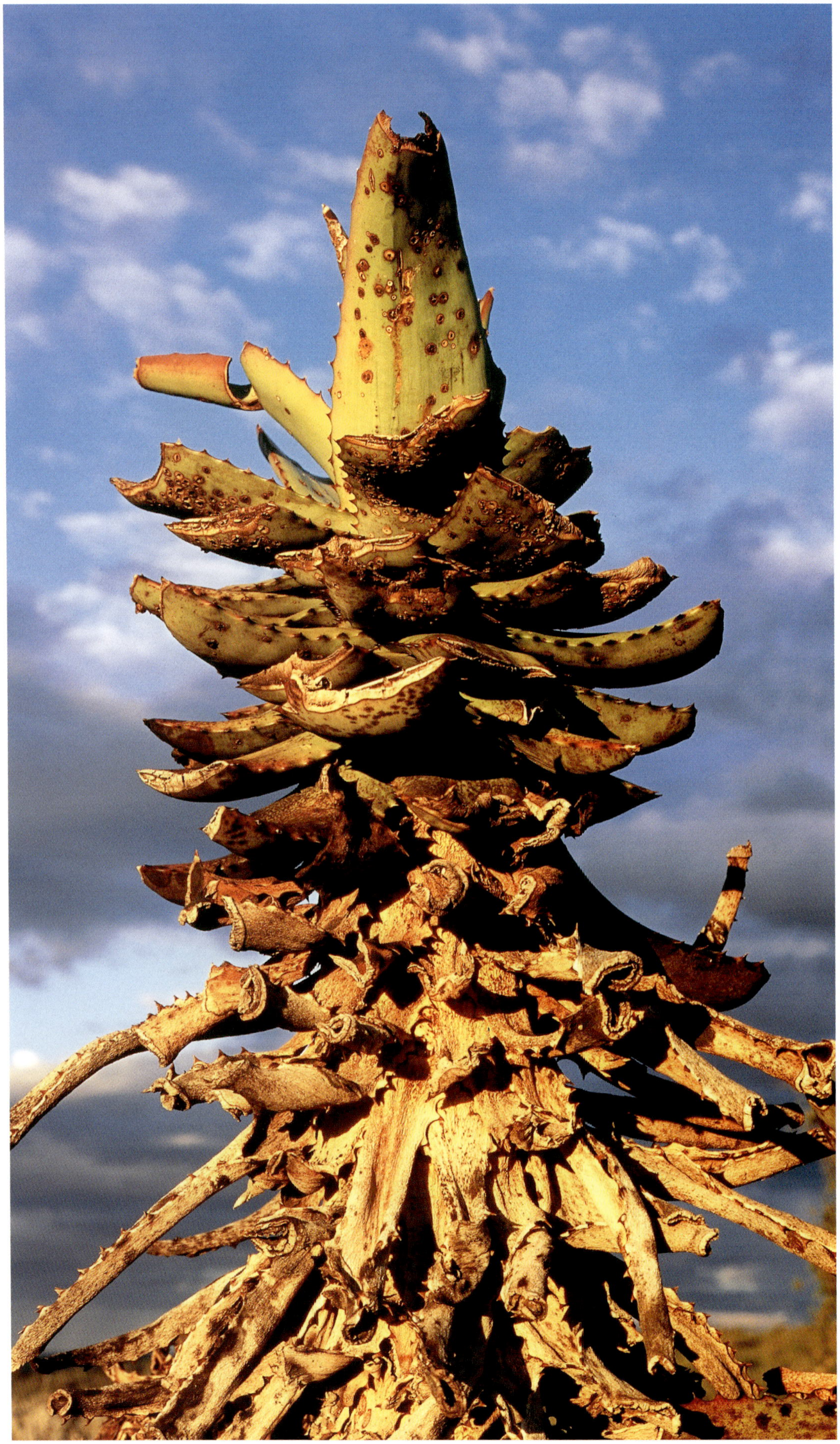

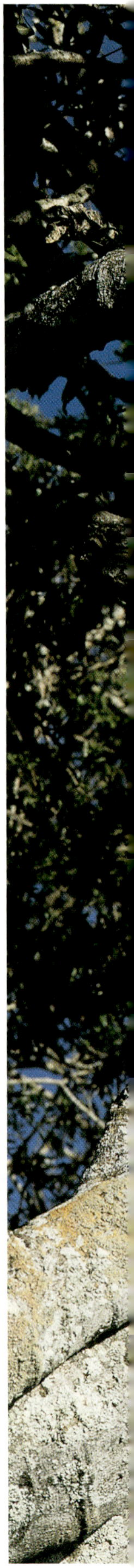

ABOVE AND RIGHT: Bitter Aloe (*Aloe ferox*). A characteristic feature of the Eastern Cape is the circle of aloes planted around cattle kraals. In winter, the striking orange flower spikes attract sunbirds and starlings that feed on the nectar and transfer pollen from one aloe to the next. Bees are also effective pollinating agents. Elephants and eland are partial to the succulent leaves and easily damage the slender plants. The fibrous trunks of larger specimens may be used by acacia pied-barbets to bore out their nest chambers.

OPPOSITE: Karoo Shepherds Tree (*Boscia oleoides*). In the past, part of the root was chopped and roasted to make coffee.

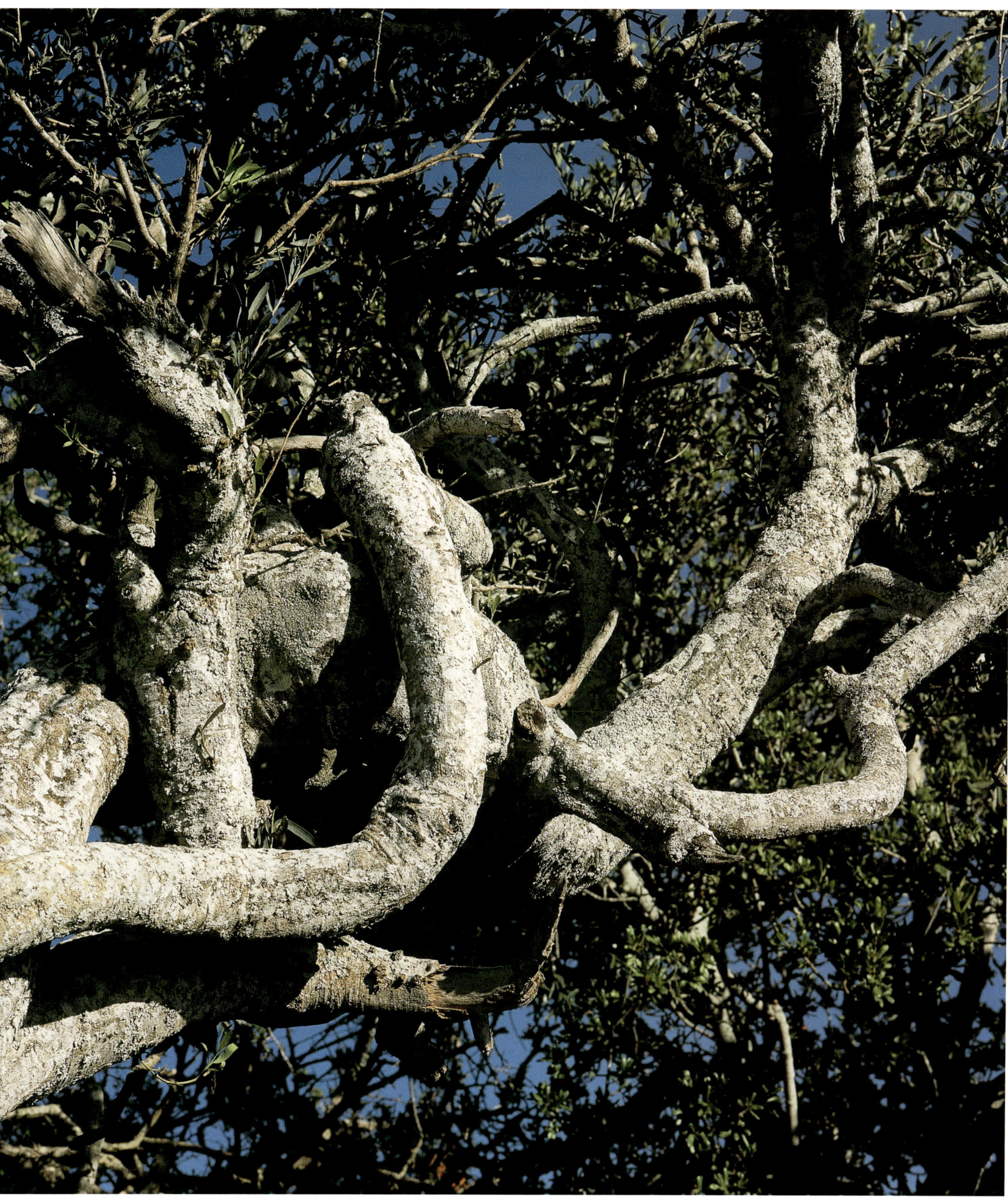
Kwandwe | South Africa

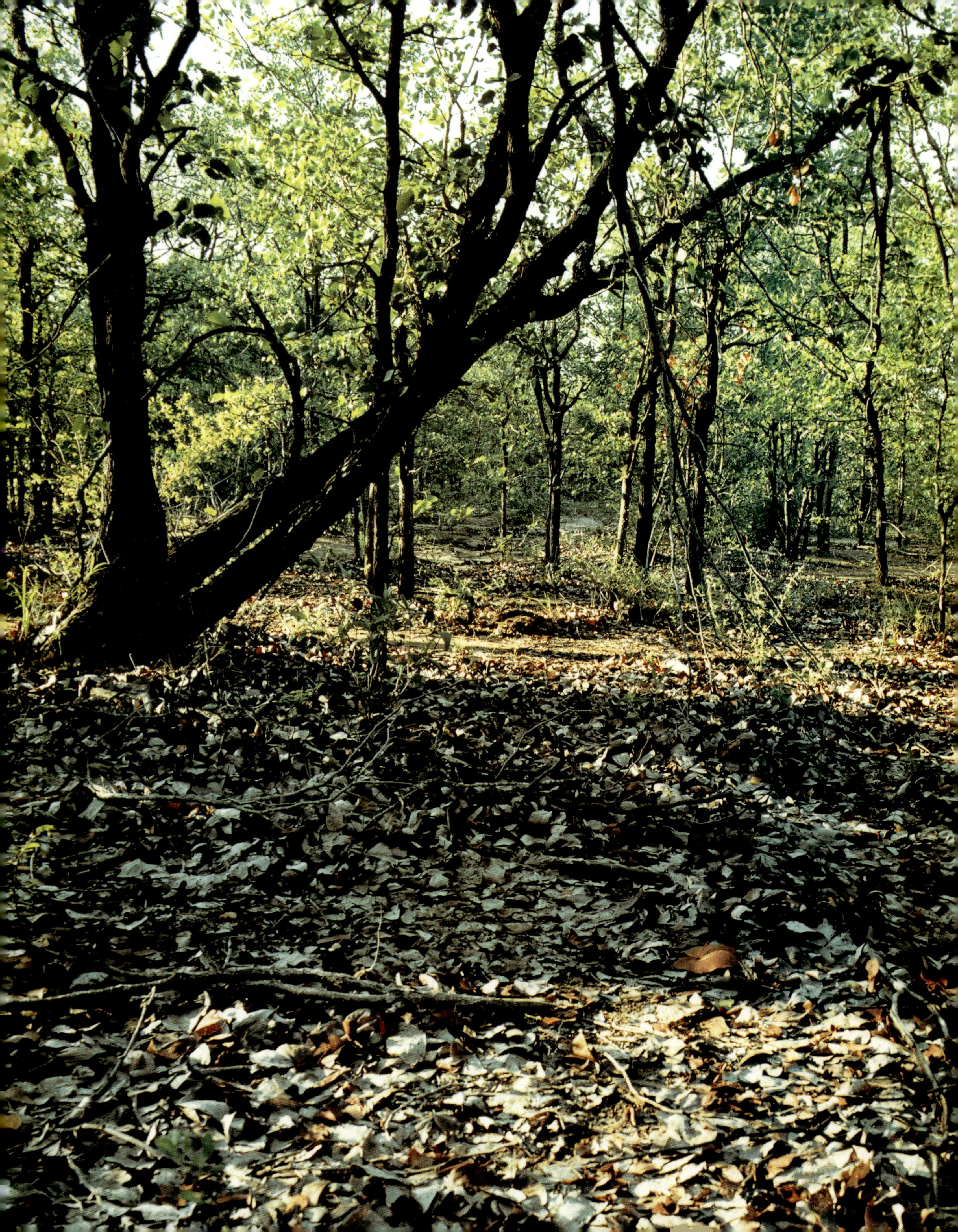

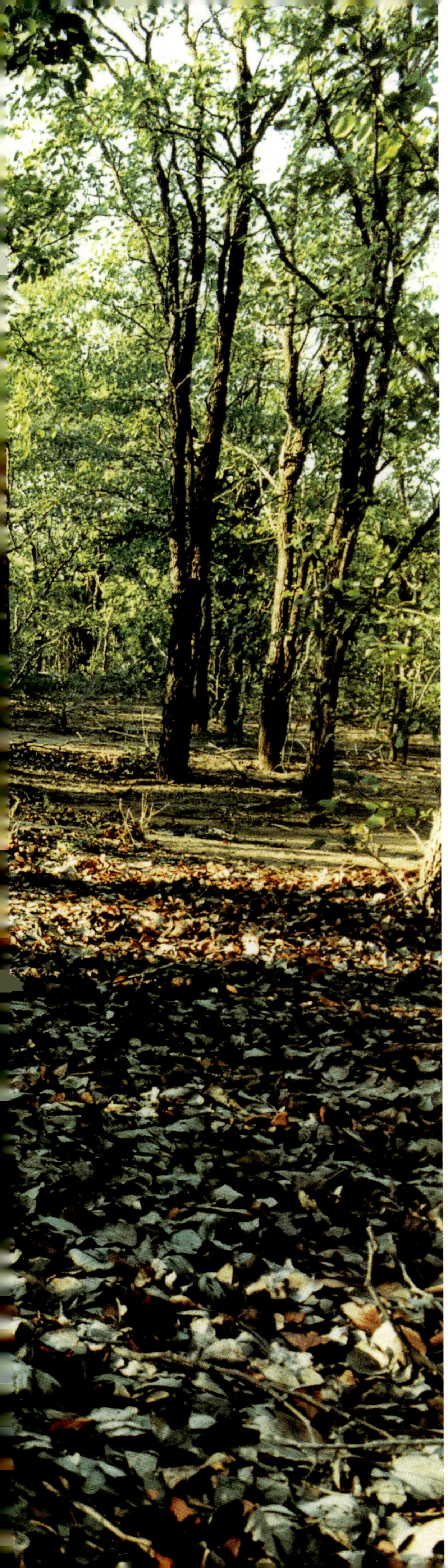

QUINTESSENTIAL BUSHVELD

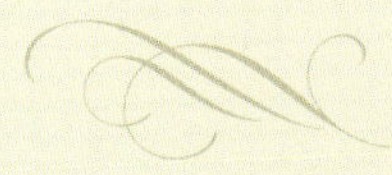

Between the Lebombo mountains, which form the border between South Africa and Mozambique, and the foothills of the Great Escarpment, lies the Lowveld. It is an undulating low-lying savanna that captures the spirit of the bushveld, with the world-famous Kruger National Park as its focus. It is a place of extremes where rivers that run dry for years suddenly flood, where elephant defy human interference, and where the largest and smallest of animals roam a stretch of land that is larger than many small countries of the world.

It has become a place of great vision, where the unity of conservation areas in both Mozambique and Zimbabwe that surround the Lowveld could form a transfrontier reserve close to 95 000 square kilometres in extent.

LEFT: Mopane (*Colophospermum mopane*). The ever-changing colours of the forest floor signal the variations in seasons and rainfall. The taste of the Mopane is enhanced by a small cicada-like insect, the *Arytaina mopani*, which, in its larva stage, has a protective waxy scale rich in sugar that is favoured by baboons.

Ngala Private Game Reserve
South Africa

Ngala Private Game Reserve is situated on the fringe of the Kruger National Park. From the lodge's beautiful setting among Tamboti (*Spirostachys africana*), Weeping Boerbean (*Schotia brachypetala*) and Russet Bushwillow (*Combretum hereroense*), we set off with a band of recently graduated game rangers under the tutorship of head ranger James Hendry. We were privileged to sit among a fascinating case study of human dynamics as James 'tested the team' and encouraged debate over a two-day practical on tree identification. We eagerly jumped aboard this learning curve as we began photographing the trees of the Lowveld plain.

Beginning at the north of Ngala and heading south, the terrain changes from woodland on poorly drained clay soils to bush savanna on coarse sands. Bisecting this area is a riverine thicket along the easterly flowing Timbavati River.

The nutritious Mopane Tree (*Colophospermum mopane*) dominates the north and is relished by elephant that readily break down the trees to get to fresh foliage. There is a general feeling of destruction associated with these trees. The green nutritious leaves of summer bring out the mopane worms, which, in their feeding period of six weeks, can consume more foliage than the elephant. Harvested by the ton, these caterpillars are

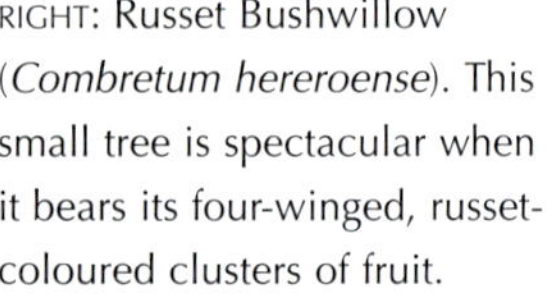

RIGHT: Russet Bushwillow (*Combretum hereroense*). This small tree is spectacular when it bears its four-winged, russet-coloured clusters of fruit.

OPPOSITE: Leadwood (*Combretum imberbe*). Contrary to popular belief, leadwood is not fire resistant and, once alight, can blaze away to complete destruction. The wood burns slowly and is extremely difficult to extinguish.

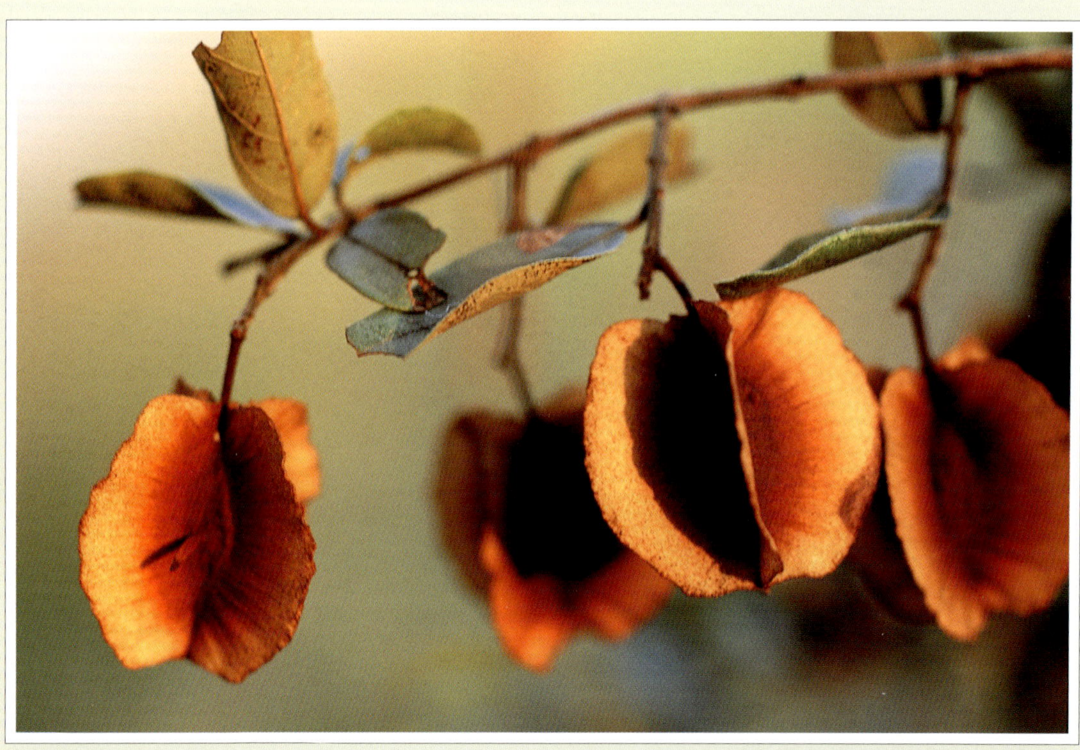

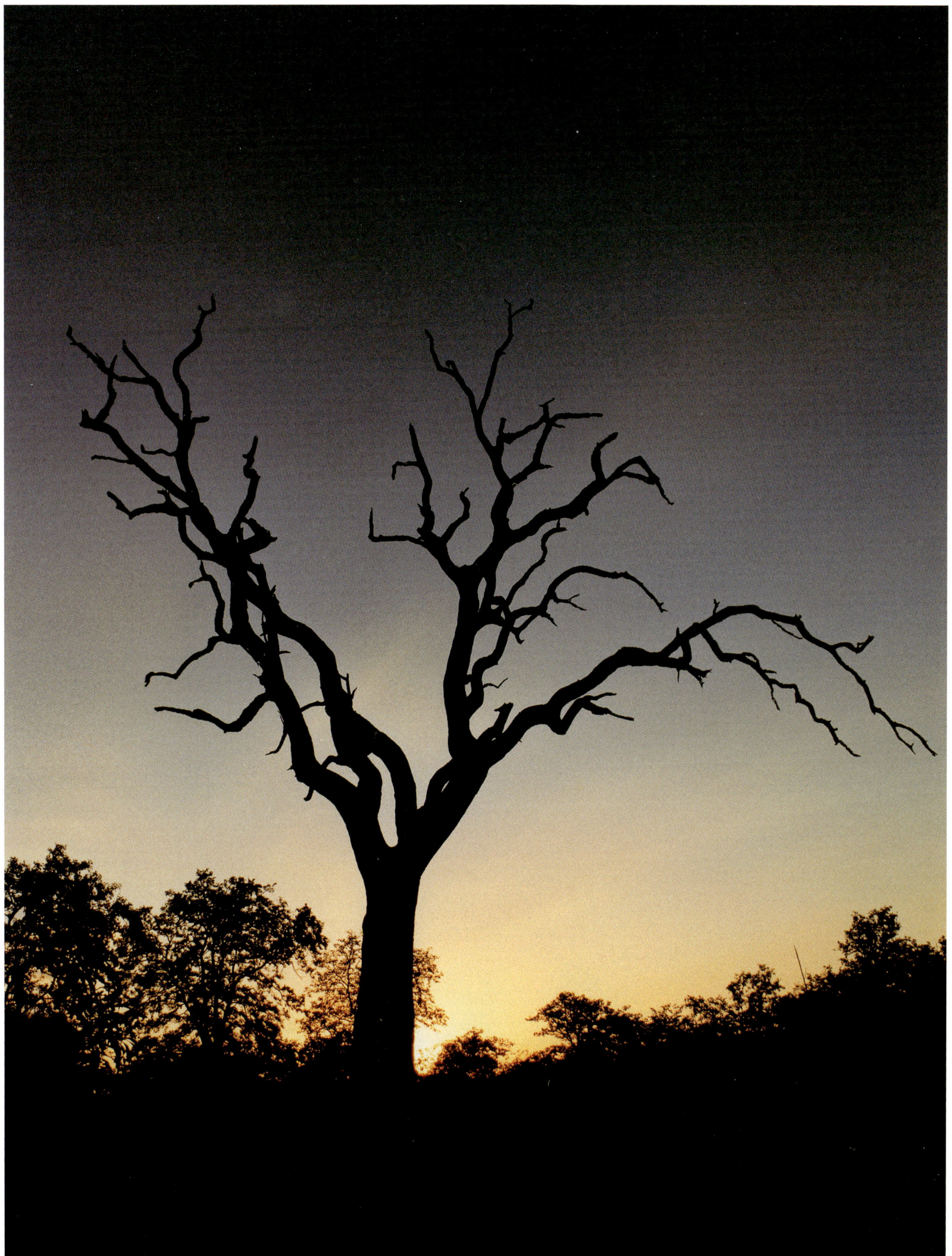

Ngala | South Africa

Ngala | South Africa

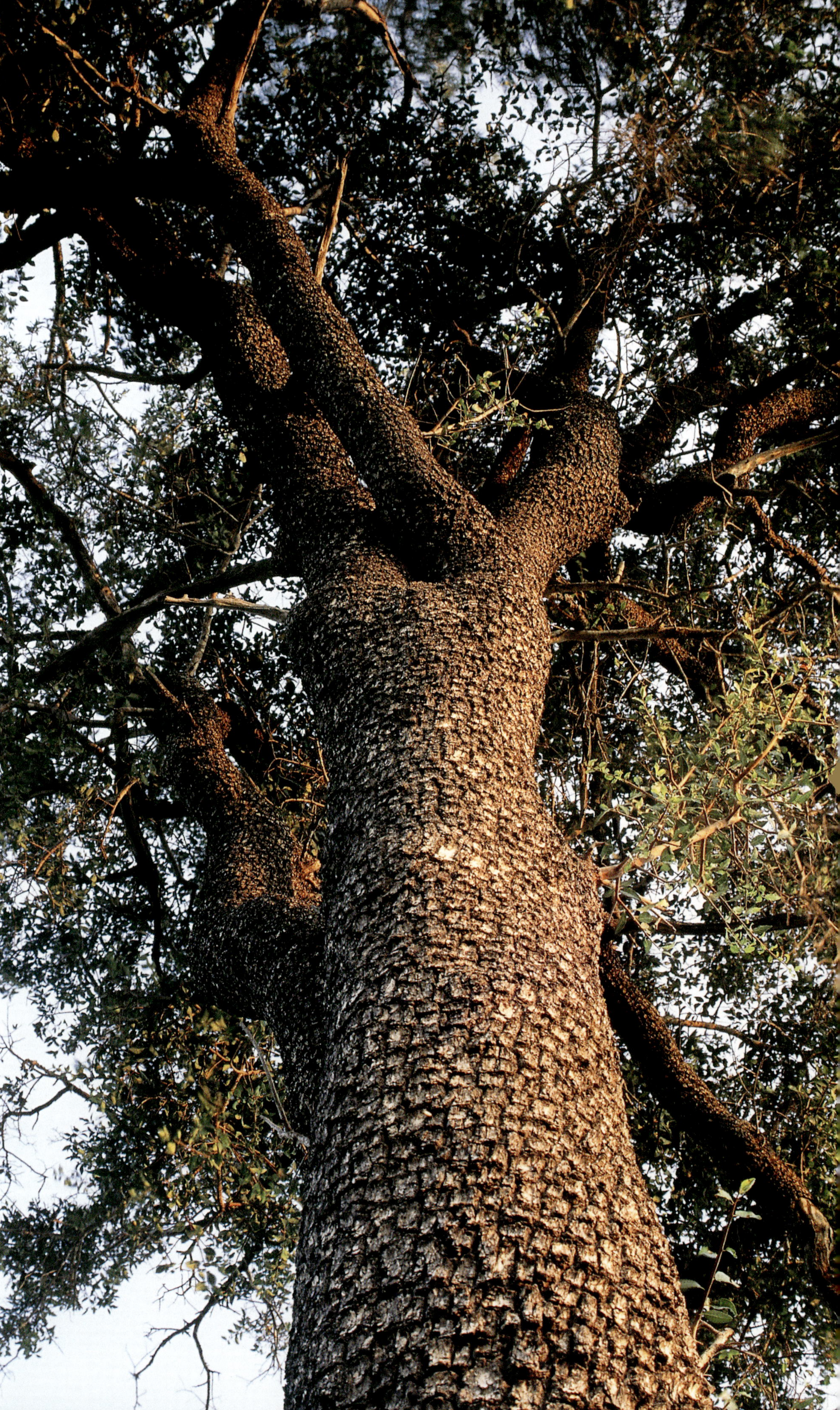

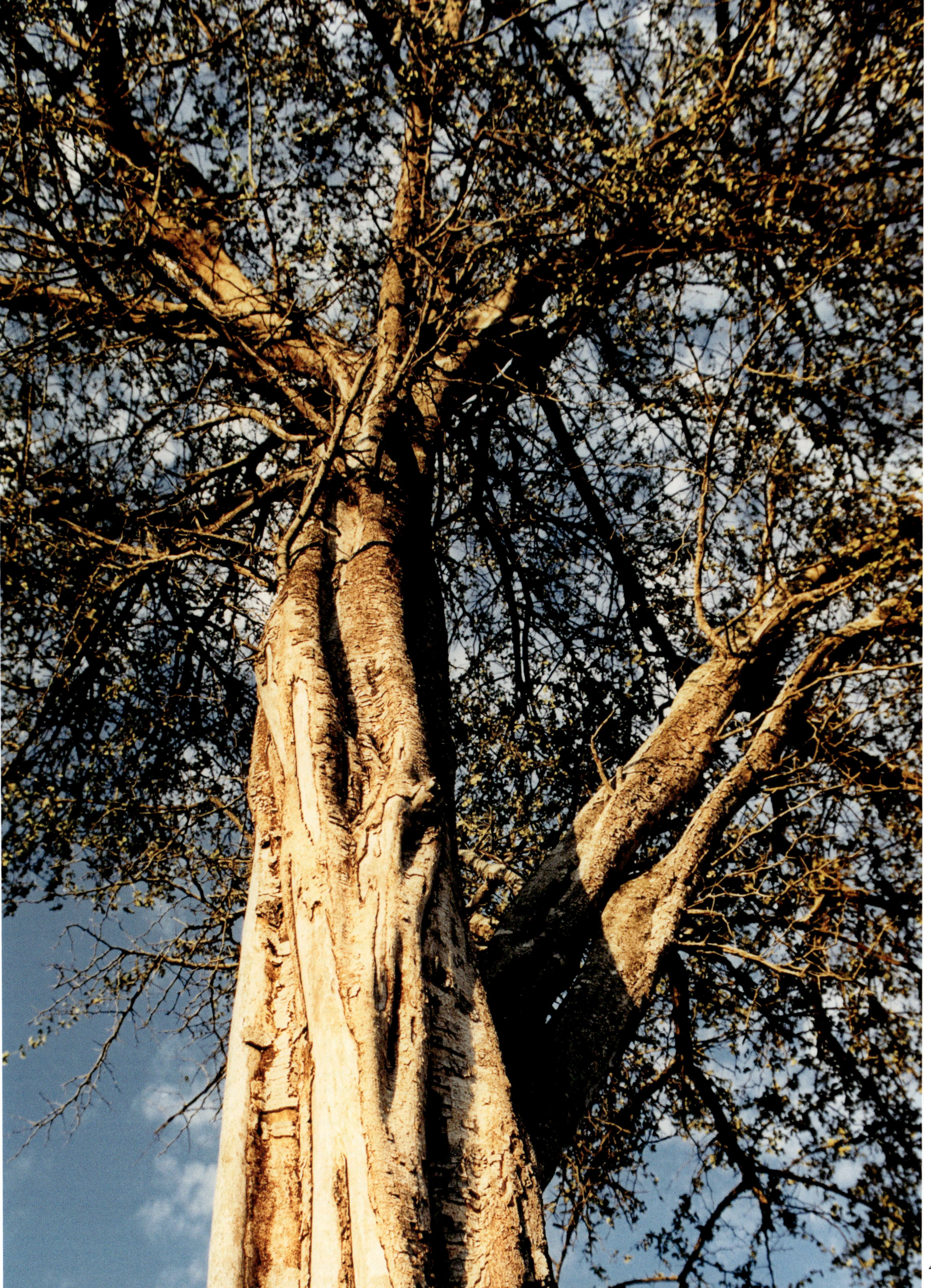

Ngala | South Africa

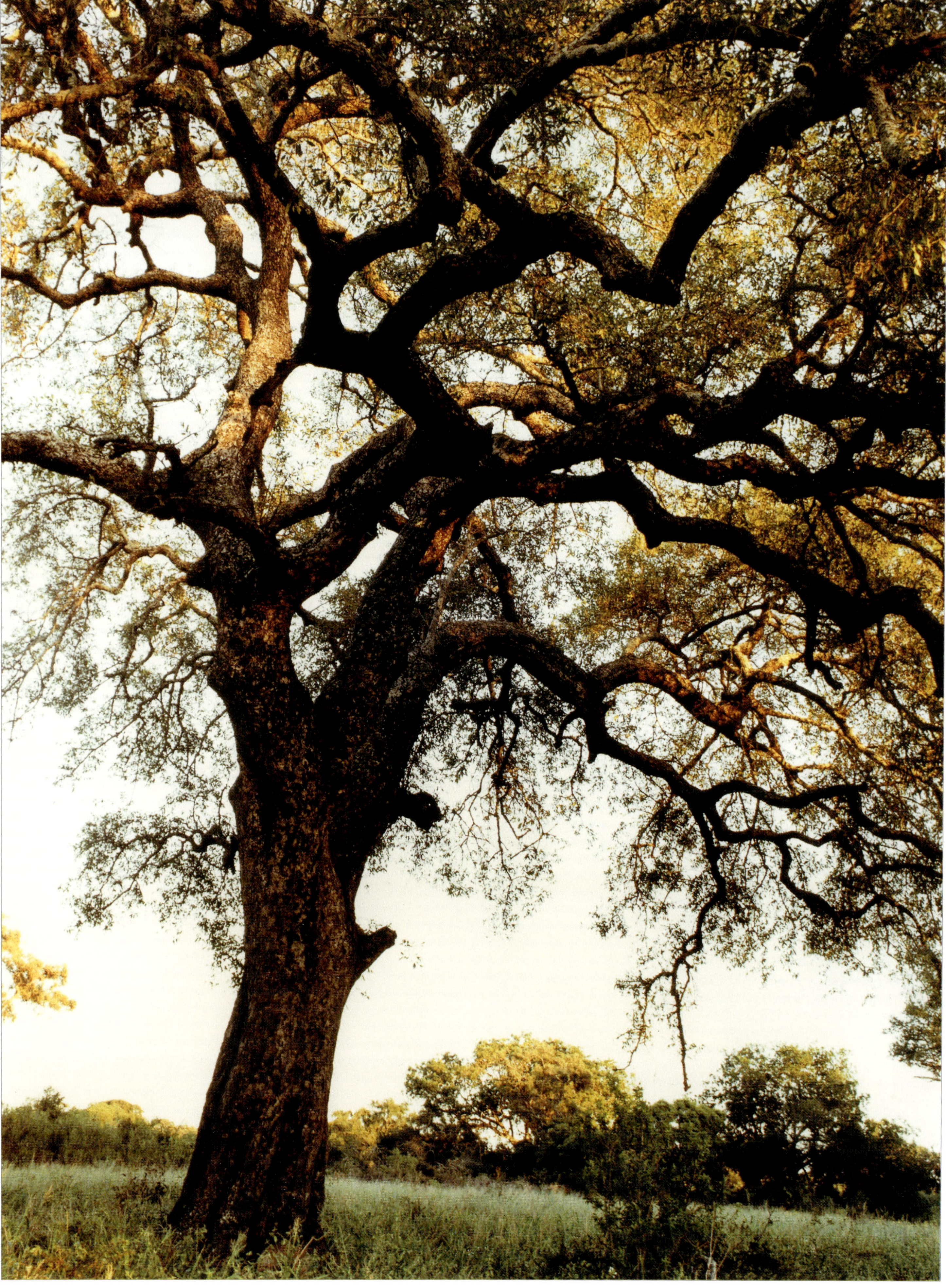
Ngala
South Africa

OPPOSITE: Jackalberry (*Diospyros mespiliformis*).

BELOW: Star Chestnut (*Sterculia rogersii*).

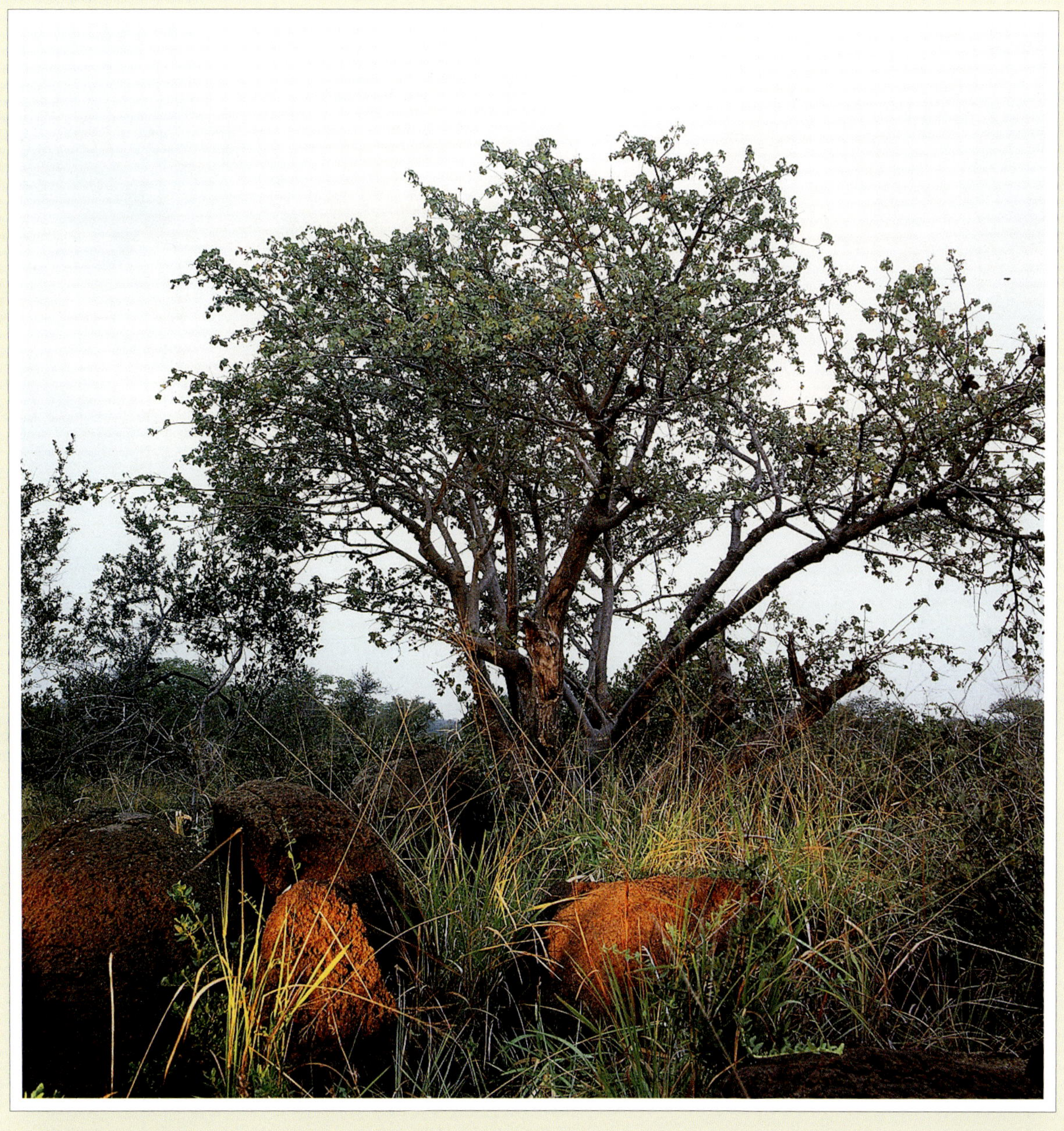

BELOW: Weeping Boerbean (*Schotia brachypetala*).

OPPOSITE: Tree Wisteria (*Bolusanthus speciosus*). The glint and shine of the leaves of this beautiful tree makes it easily identifiable from a distance. It is most captivating in spring when adorned with clusters of delicate violet blossoms.

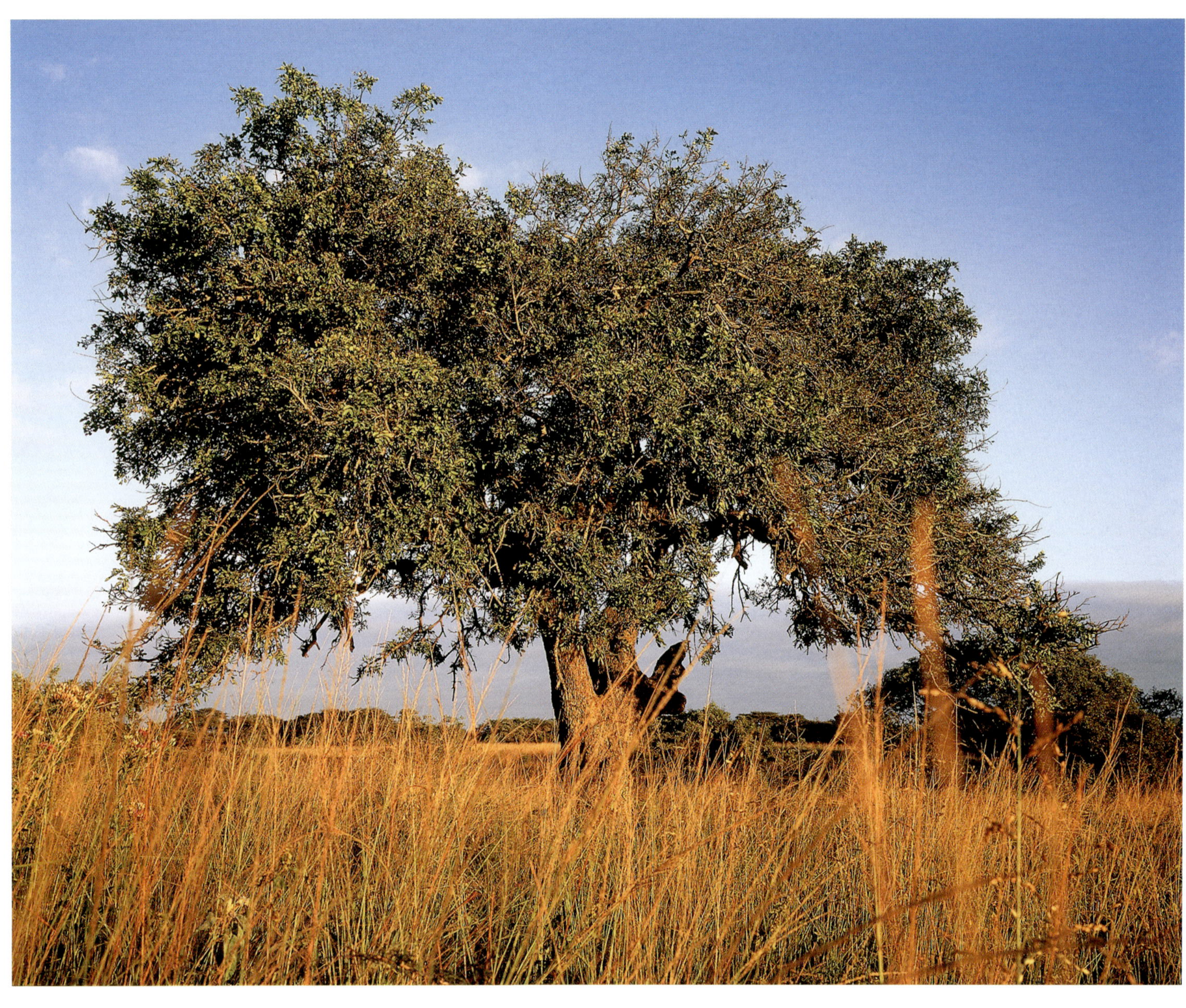

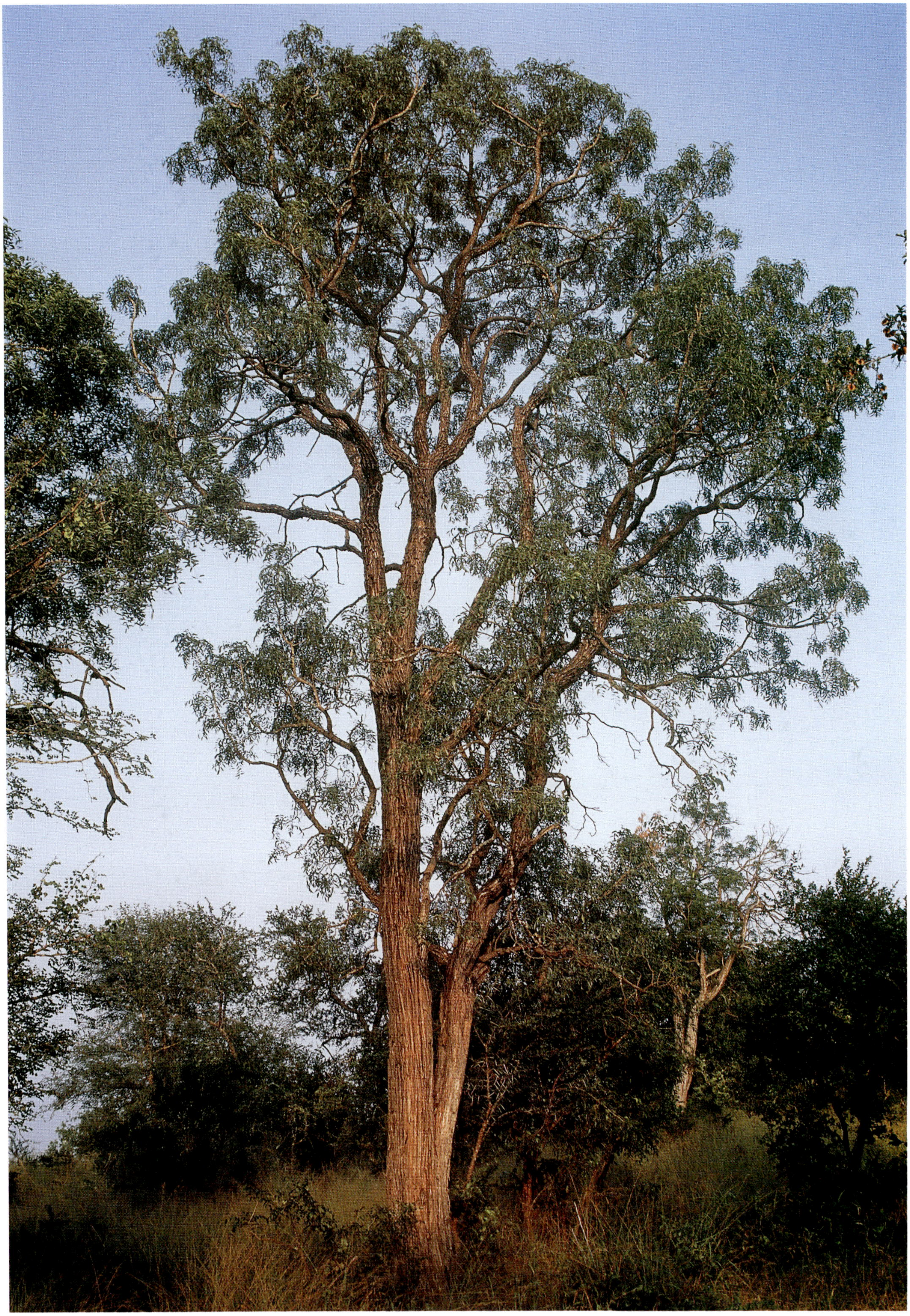

Ngala South Africa

Londolozi Private Game Reserve
Sabi Sand South Africa

t was in pre-dawn light that we gazed over the Sand River from the lodge at Londolozi. The morning mist lay thick over the band of riverine forest cutting the reserve in its southeasterly flow. This area is rich in wildlife, boasting great diversity and an abundance of game. As if to testify to this statement, we watched as guests downed their coffee and literally ran to their game-viewing vehicles so as not to miss the early morning spectacle of leopard, cheetah, lion, elephant and rhino.

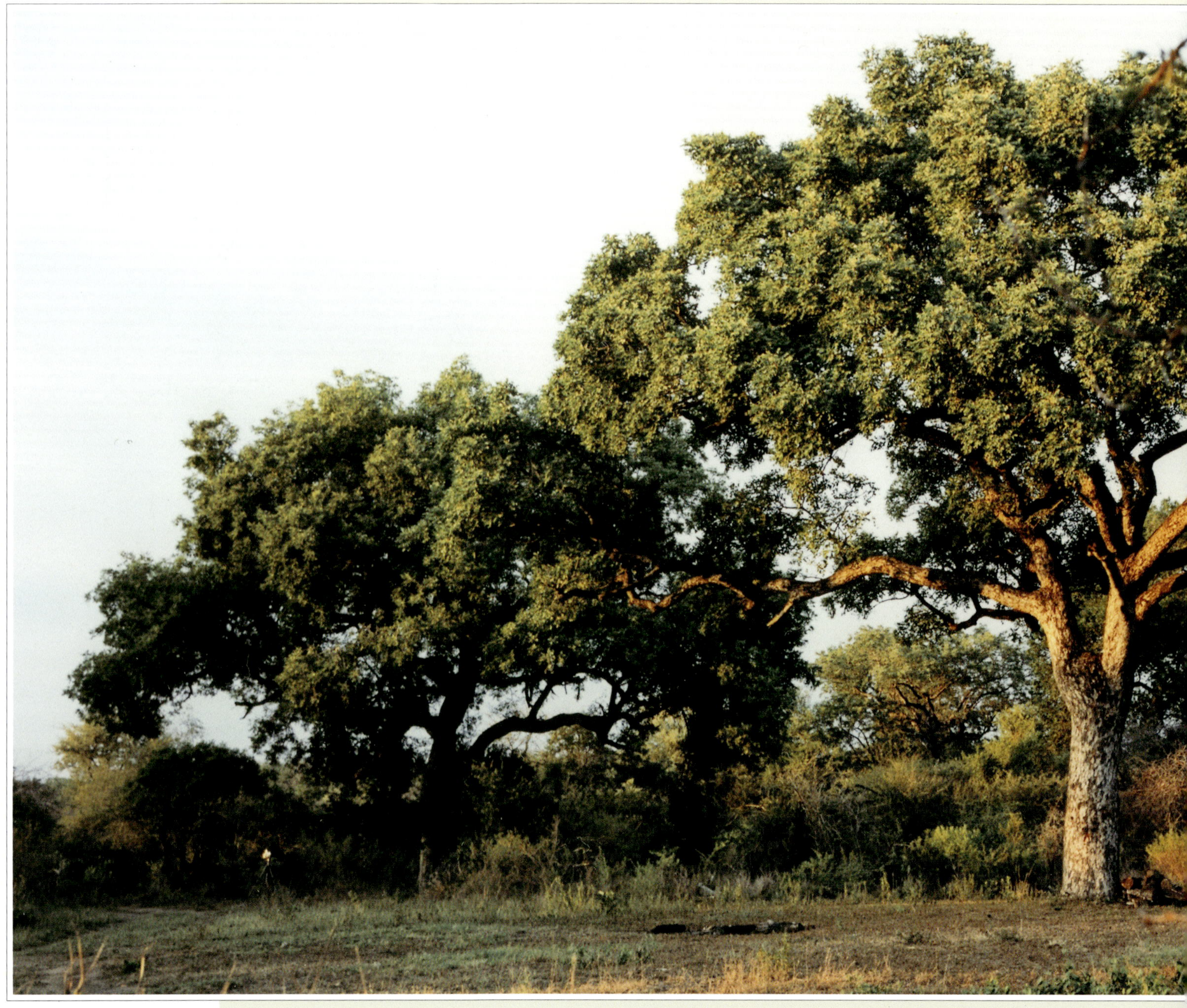

The Sabi Sand reserve came into existence in 1950. Ten years later, a fence was erected between the Kruger National Park and the reserve, blocking the natural flow of large mammals. Ostensibly this was to prevent foot-and-mouth disease between the national park and the cattle areas of the west. The fence remained in place for 30 years, until 1990, when after a hard-fought campaign it was finally removed. We made our way to the Sand River to wait for the sun to burn through the mist and light up an impressive Sycamore Fig (*Ficus sycomorus*).

Passing through the river areas we noticed spectacular Leadwood (*Combretum imberbe*) lining the banks, together with Jackalberry (*Diospyros mespiliformis*), Weeping Boerbean (*Schotia brachypetala*), Tamboti (*Spirostachys africana*) and Knob Thorn (*Acacia nigrescens*). On the fringe of this green ribbon of trees are *Phragmites* reeds and

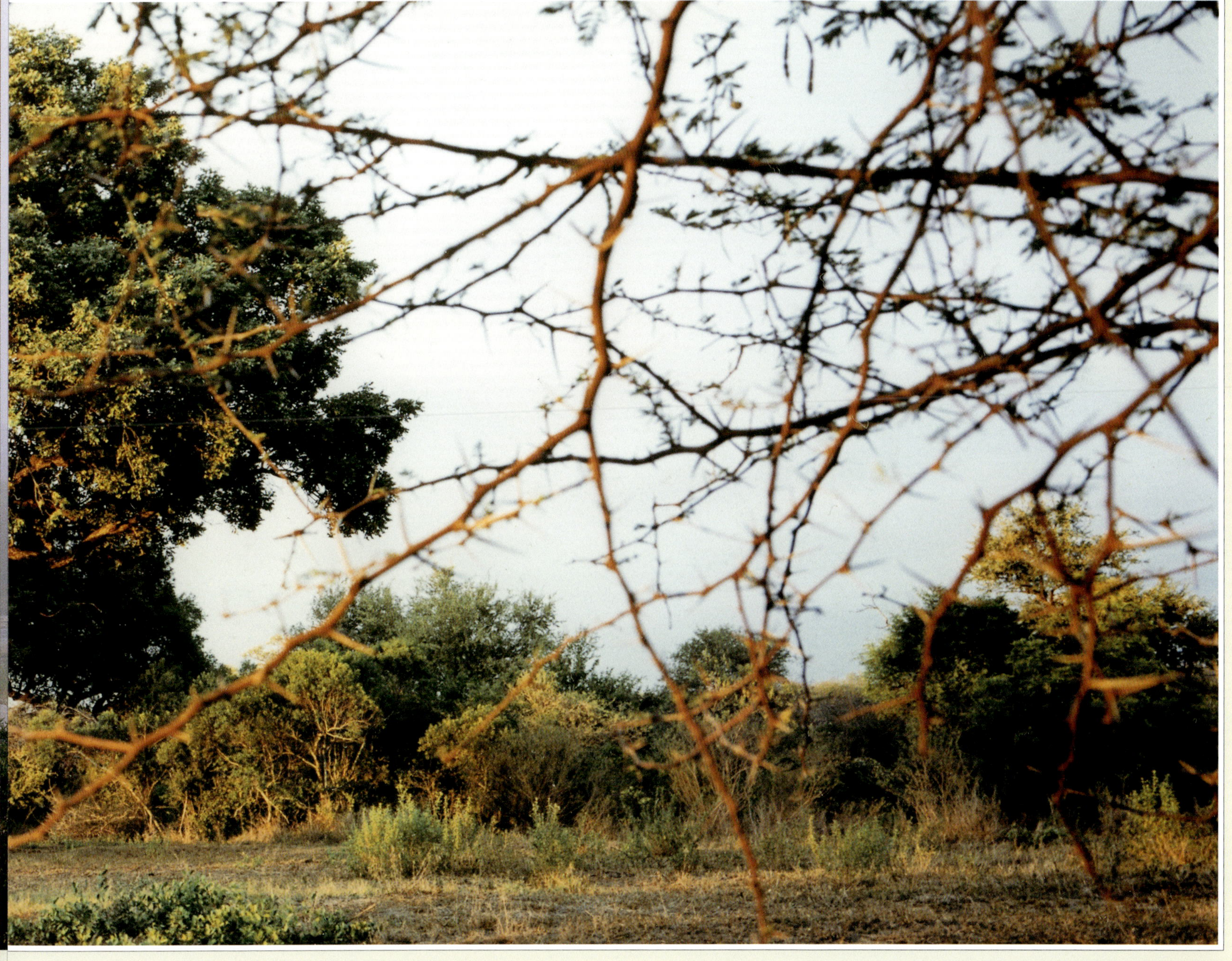

RIGHT: Broad-leaved Coral Tree (*Erythrina latissima*). These trees are very sensitive to damage by fire.

OPPOSITE: Broad-leaved Coral Tree (*Erythrina latissima*).

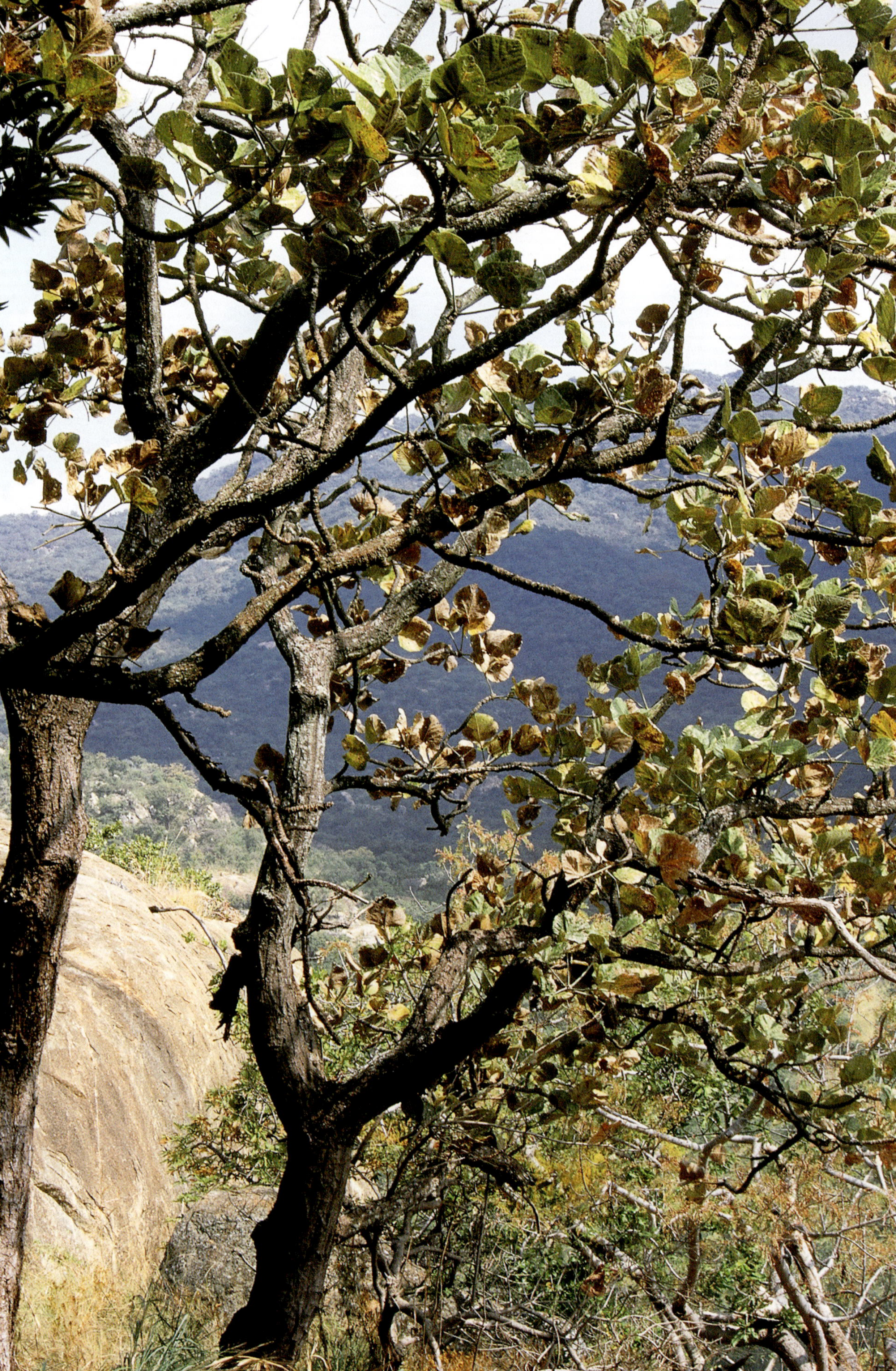

The Sabi Sand reserve came into existence in 1950. Ten years later, a fence was erected between the Kruger National Park and the reserve, blocking the natural flow of large mammals. Ostensibly this was to prevent foot-and-mouth disease between the national park and the cattle areas of the west. The fence remained in place for 30 years, until 1990, when after a hard-fought campaign it was finally removed. We made our way to the Sand River to wait for the sun to burn through the mist and light up an impressive Sycamore Fig (*Ficus sycomorus*).

Passing through the river areas we noticed spectacular Leadwood (*Combretum imberbe*) lining the banks, together with Jackalberry (*Diospyros mespiliformis*), Weeping Boerbean (*Schotia brachypetala*), Tamboti (*Spirostachys africana*) and Knob Thorn (*Acacia nigrescens*). On the fringe of this green ribbon of trees are *Phragmites* reeds and

BELOW: Marula (*Sclerocarya birrea*) The Marula is the tree most valued by indigenous people in the Lowveld. The fruit contains four times more vitamin C than an orange! It is the favoured fruit of elephant, which sometimes push the trees over without foresight of their loss of the valued fruit. Indabas are often held in the shade of a Marula tree, which is believed to be the protector of secrets.

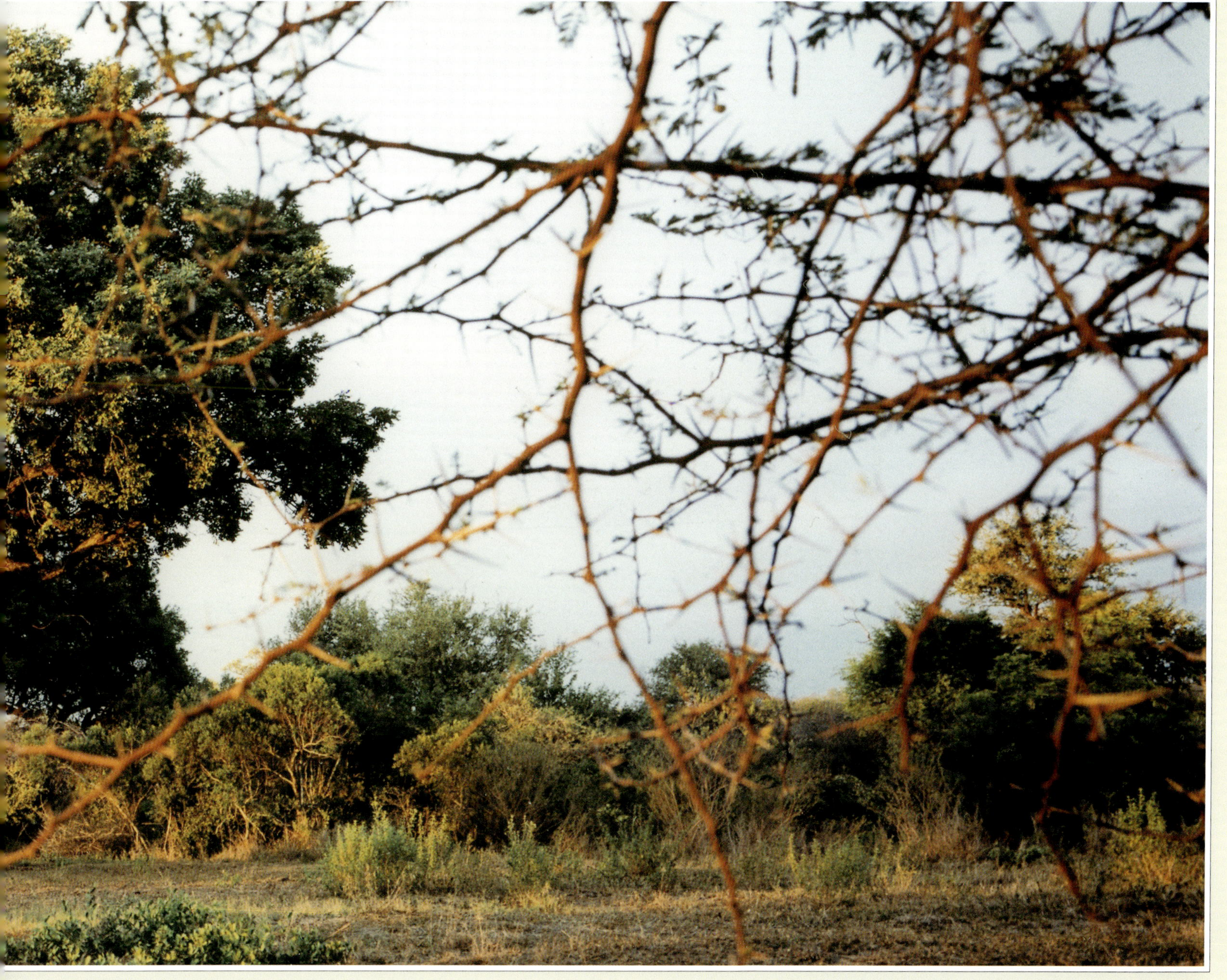

Wild Date Palm (*Phoenix reclinata*). It was winter and the mist took more than two hours to lift. We made our way from the river into the bush savanna, the principal habitat of the Lowveld.

Similar to Ngala, the crests and slopes are dominated by Combretum, while the bottomlands are characterised by fine-leaved trees with acacias such as the Knob Thorn and the Scented Thorn (*Acacia nilotica*). The Leadwoods, purely because of their size, deserve another mention. They are difficult to photograph on their own because they are mostly shaded by other trees. We passed stands of Knob Thorn, impressive for their height and proudly African.

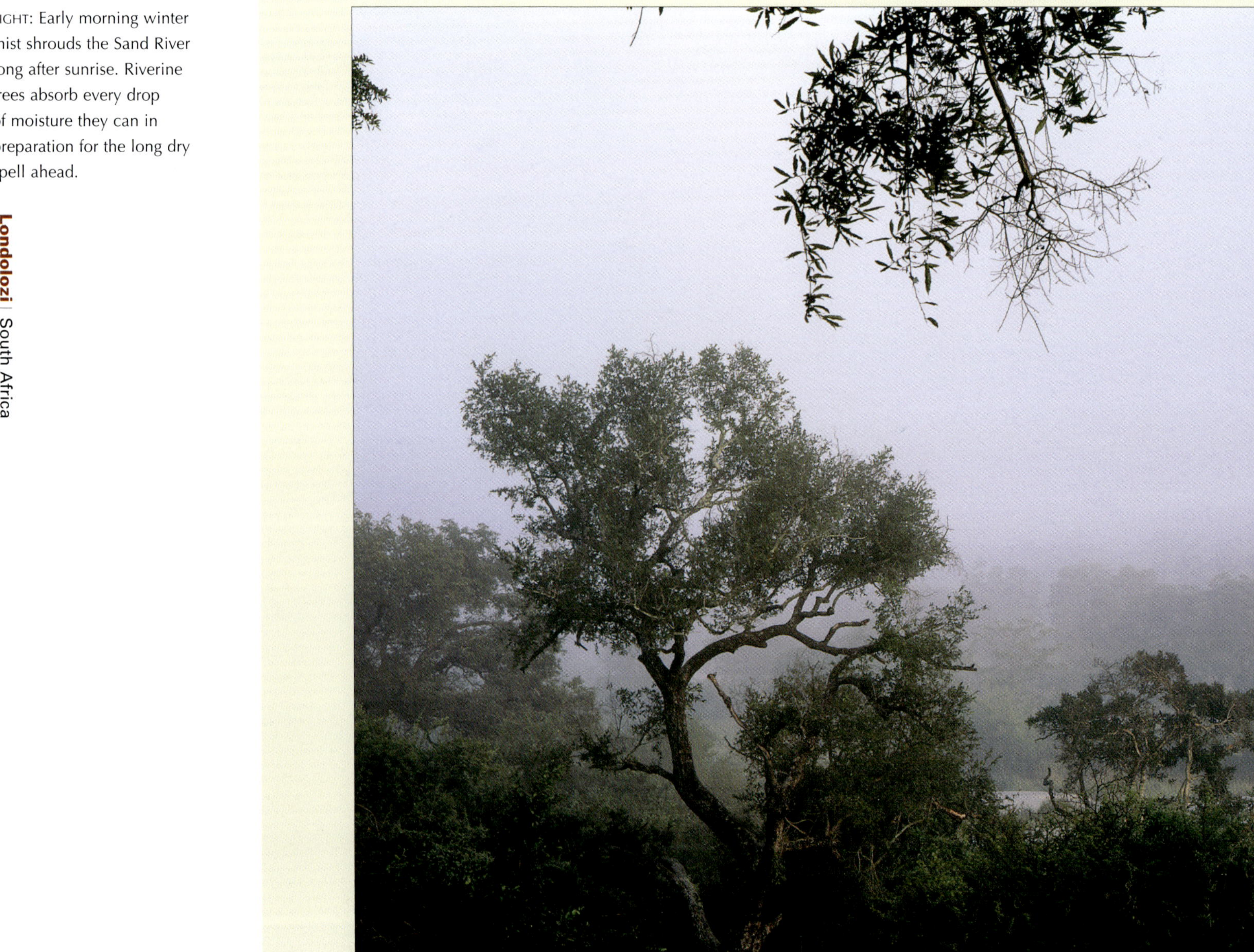

RIGHT: Dead Leadwood
(*Combretum imberbe*).

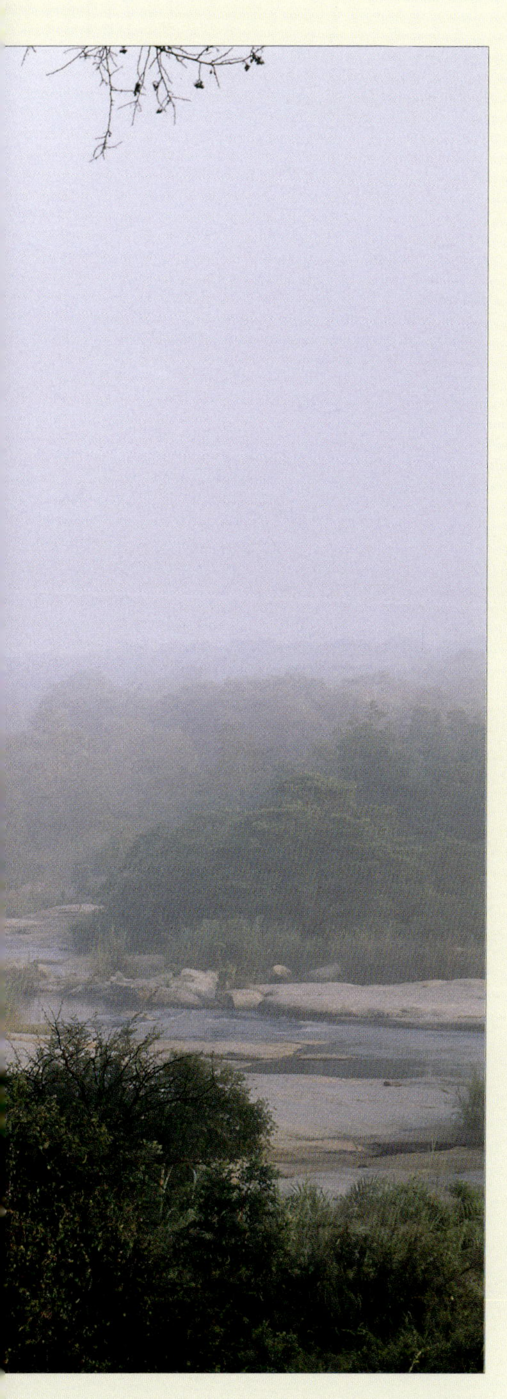

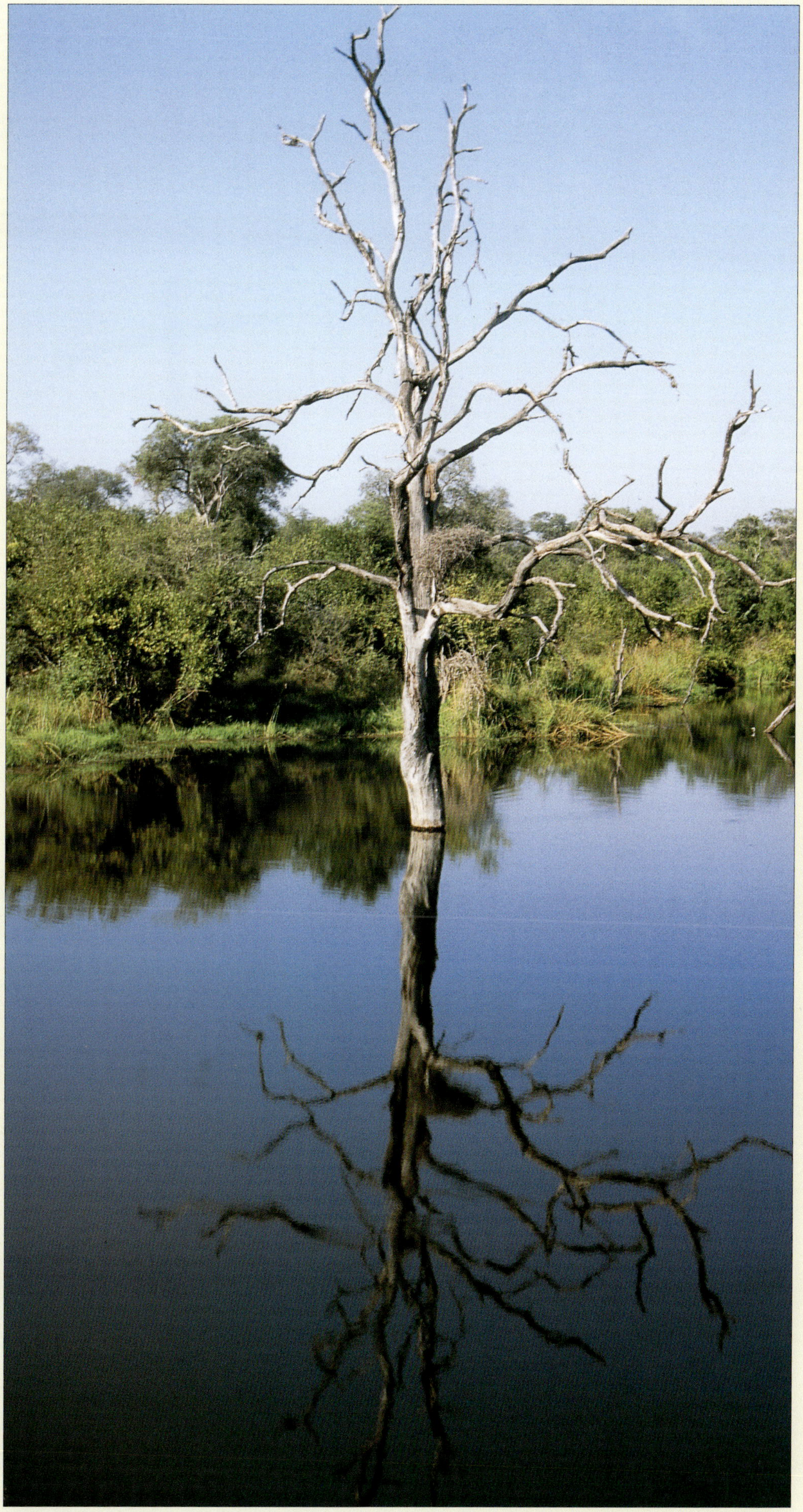

As luck would have it, we spotted a leopard in one of its favoured trees – the Marula (*Sclerocarya birrea*). Of the many trees in the Lowveld, the Marula is highly valued for its juicy fruit, which is high in vitamin C and a key ingredient of a much prized liqueur. Whenever we ask people, not only in the Lowveld but in many parts in Africa, about their favourite tree, the Marula is invariably mentioned. Animals also relish the fruit, especially baboon and elephant, although stories of animals becoming intoxicated are far-fetched. Elephant sometimes push the trees over to get to the moist root system – a short-sighted move considering their love for the fruit.

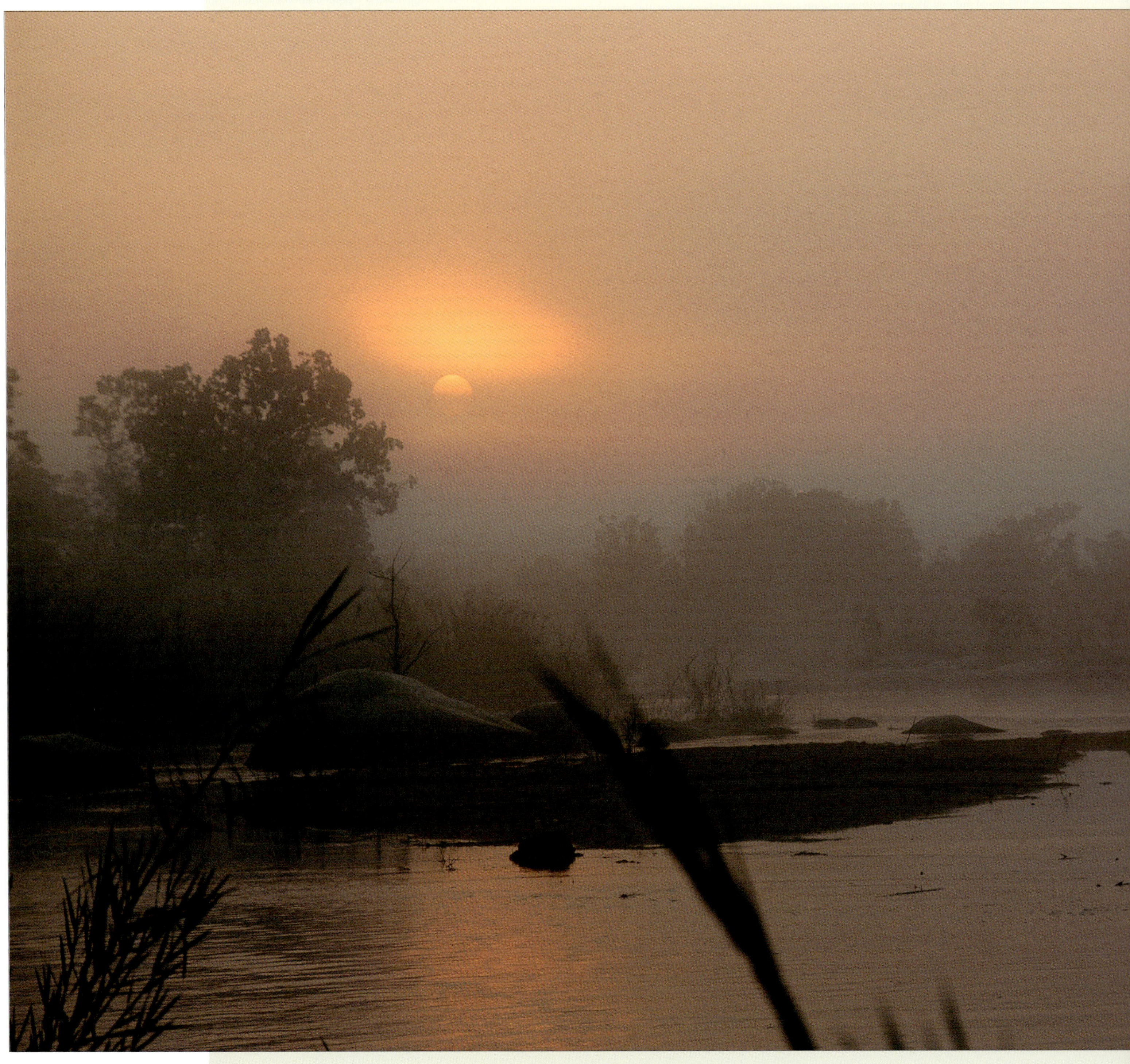

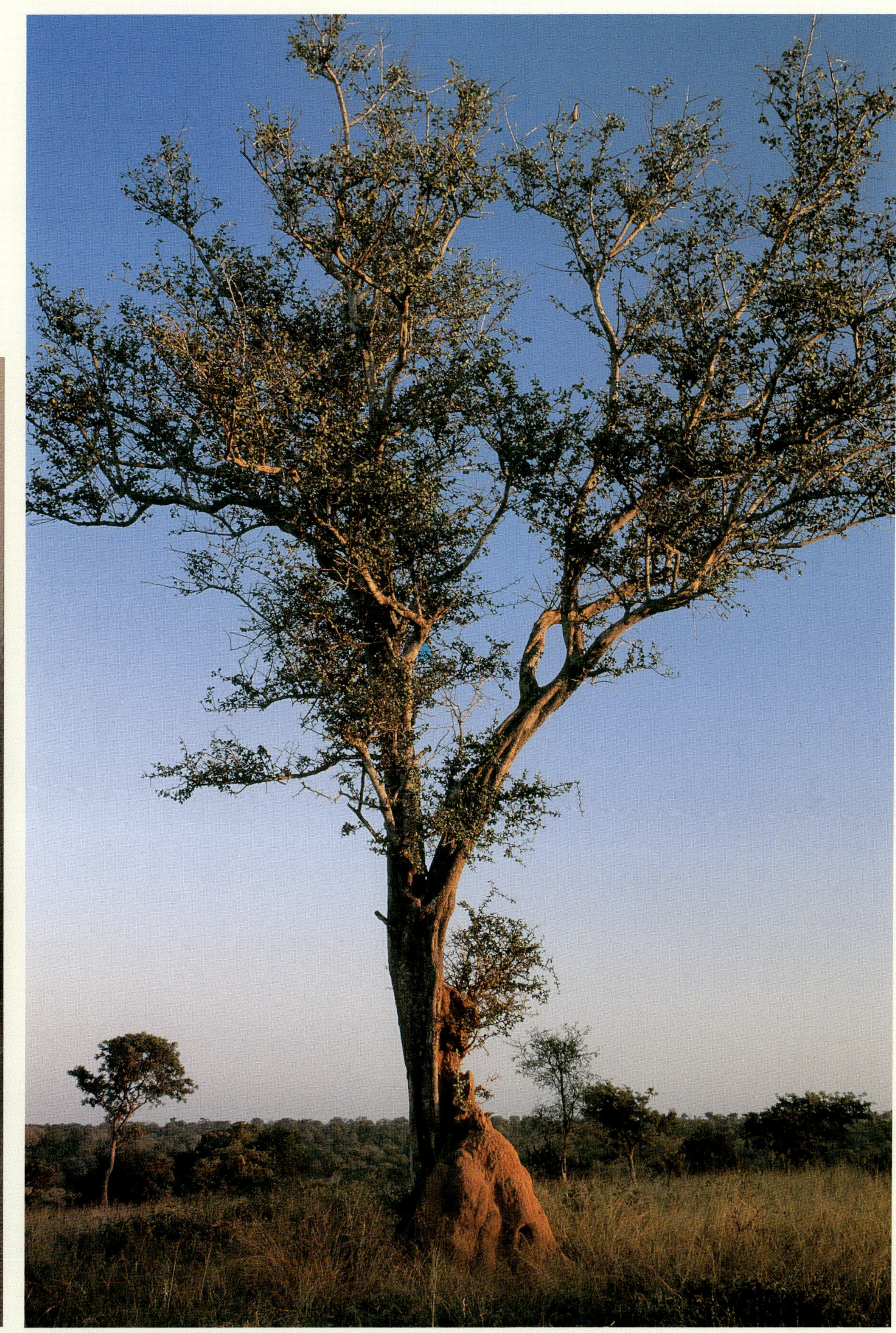

Londolozi | South Africa

BELOW: The ancient autumn colours of the Lowveld.

OPPOSITE: Black Monkey Thorn (*Acacia burkei*). Because of the knobs that form on the trunks with age, these acacias are often confused with the Knob Thorn (*Acacia nigrescens*). However, it has brighter yellow bark than the Knob Thorn and rarely reaches a great size.

Also part of the bush savanna are the seep lines where the sandy slopes and clay bottomlands meet. Rainwater seeping downhill reaches the surface and forms a contour-hugging band of moist ground, where grasses predominate over trees. Under certain conditions, such as the absence of natural bush fires, woody plants have tended to encroach. A bushveld clearing programme keeps these productive grazing zones clear particularly of Sicklebush (*Dichrostachys cinerea*), Round-leaved Kiaat (*Pterocarpus rotundifolius*) and Zebrawood (*Dalbergia melanoxylon*). The result is sometimes an increase in the level of the water table and the obvious restoration of grazing areas for herbivores. Other spin-offs are improved visibility for game viewing and employment opportunities for local communities.

Termitaria thickets grow on the large mounds created by termites, with Weeping Boerbean and Jackalberry often at the centre of these thickets.

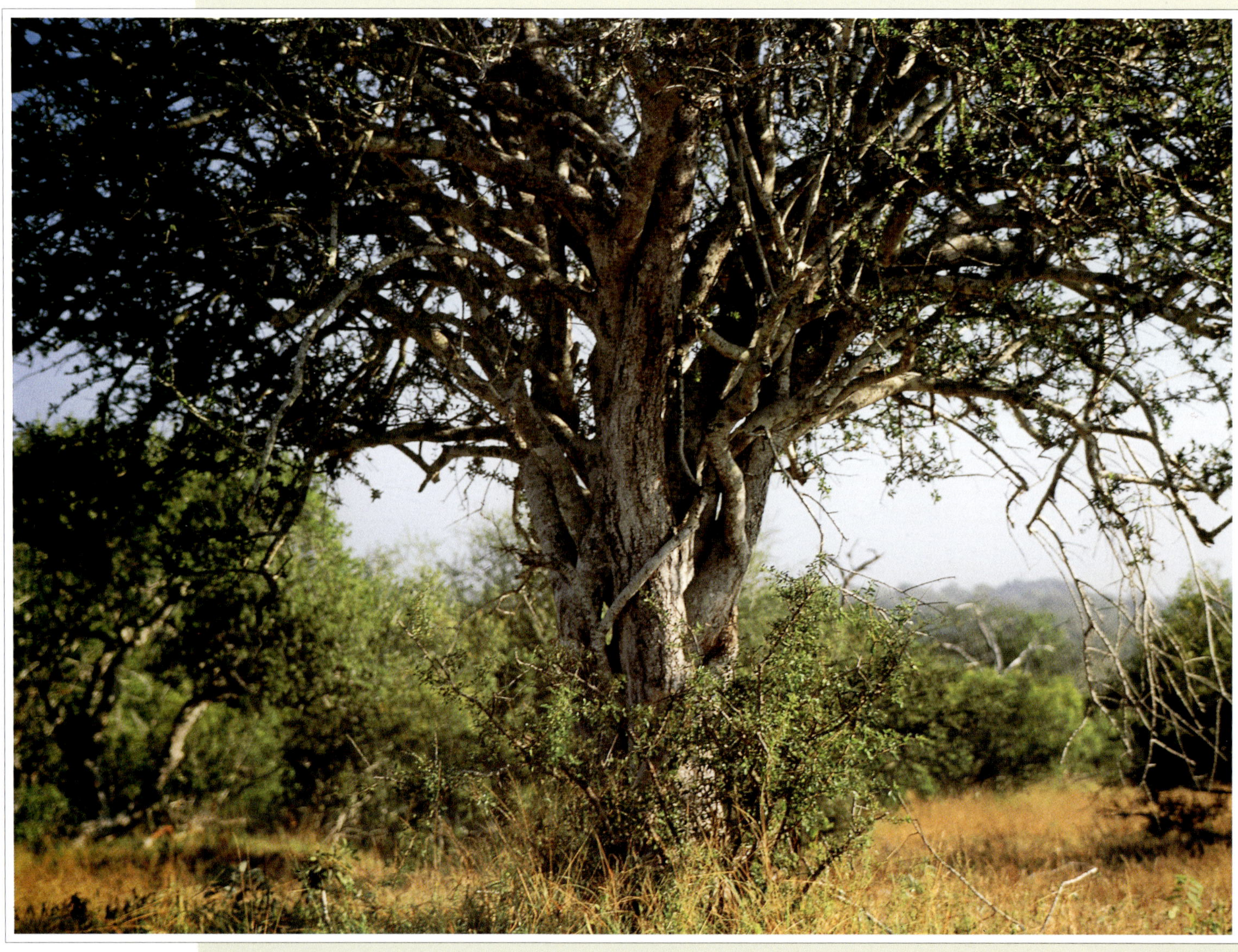

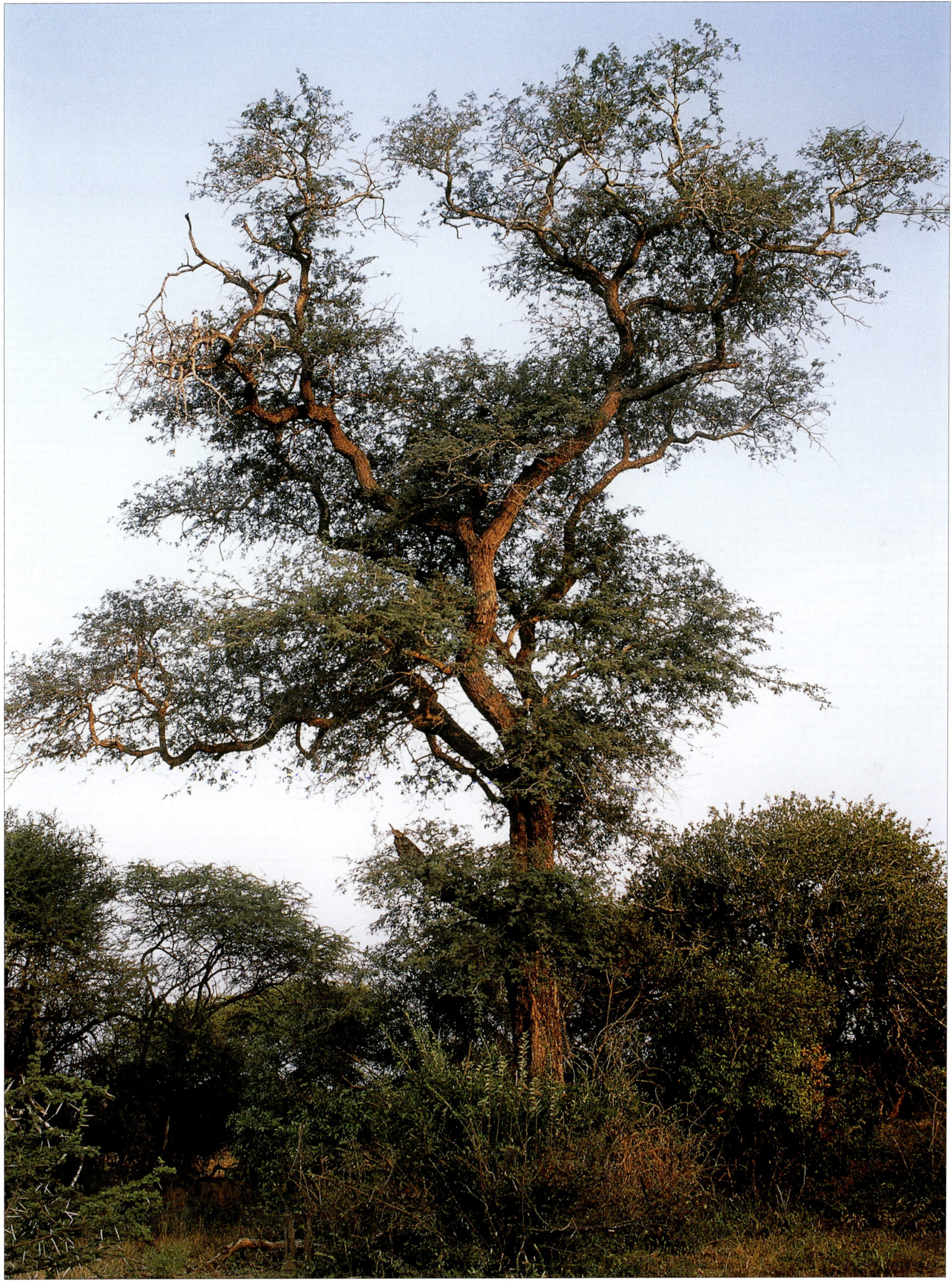

Londolozi | South Africa

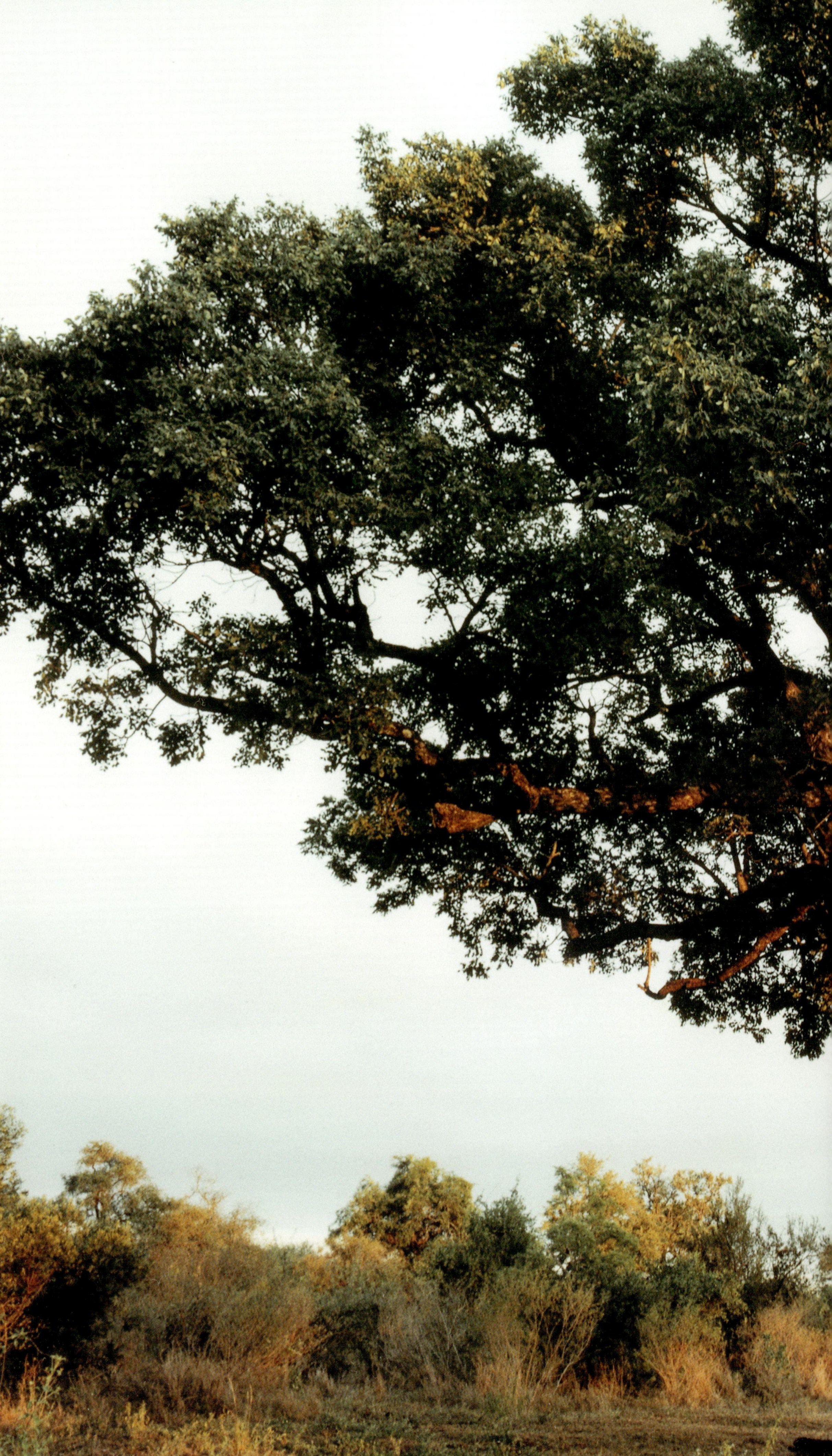

RIGHT: Marula (*Sclerocarya birrea*).

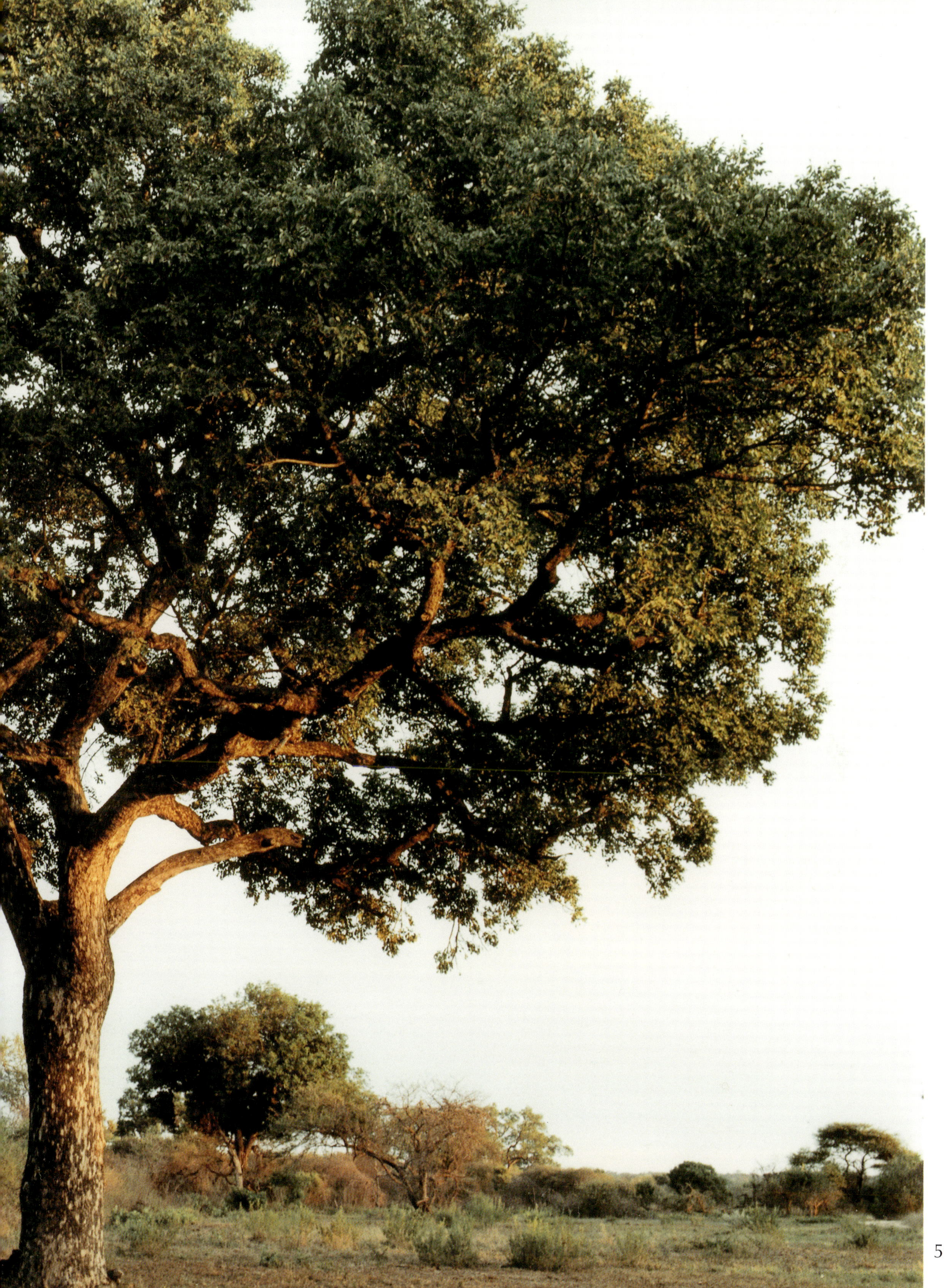

59

Bongani Mountain Lodge
Mthethomusha Game Reserve
South Africa

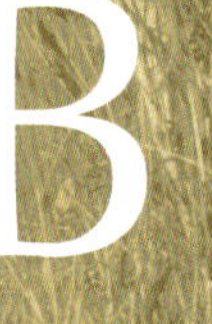

Bongani is set in a hilly topography where the principal habitats are exposed granite outcrops, wooded hillsides and valleys. The highest point is 1 000 metres above sea level and the valley bottoms lie at 488 metres. The Mthethomusha Game Reserve borders the Kruger National Park, with the Nsikazi River forming its eastern border.

We arrived at the gate, ready for the 4X4 climb to the lodge. The roads were good and had to be, for all had variable gradients. The lodge, perched on magnificent granite hilltops, boasts incredible views, worth climbing for on foot.

The Broad-leaved Coral Tree (*Erythrina latissima*), evident at the lodge but scarce elsewhere, has huge leaves divided into three leaflets peppered with prickles. In early winter, leaves shower down after each gust of wind and layer on the ground for months before decomposing. The tree is at its aesthetic best when woolly buds appear on the bare branches and open up. Clusters of scarlet flowers decorate the tree in August and September.

Where rocks are jumbled and relatively deep soil has accumulated, the Lowveld Star Chestnut (*Sterculia murex*) is found. Not great in size, the tree is distinct for its star-like palmate leaves (hence its botanical name) and its spiny seed cases containing seeds that are roasted and relished by the local people. Also found on the granite hilltops are the Mountain Syringa (*Kirkia wilmsii*), Wild Pear (*Dombeya rotundifolia*), and Common Cabbage Tree (*Cussonia spicata*). Growing out of cracks and fissures are Mountain Fig (*Ficus glumosa*) and Large-leaved Rock Fig (*Ficus abutilifolia*).

While the views are impressive, it is only on the descent and looking back that one can appreciate the granite hilltops. The shapes are rounded and weathered, with evidence of onion-like peeling of the rock face. Rocks balance precariously on each other, creating the distinct impression that this geological climate is far from static.

The wooded slopes of the reserve are covered in Weeping Bushwillow (*Combretum collinum*) and Red Bushwillow

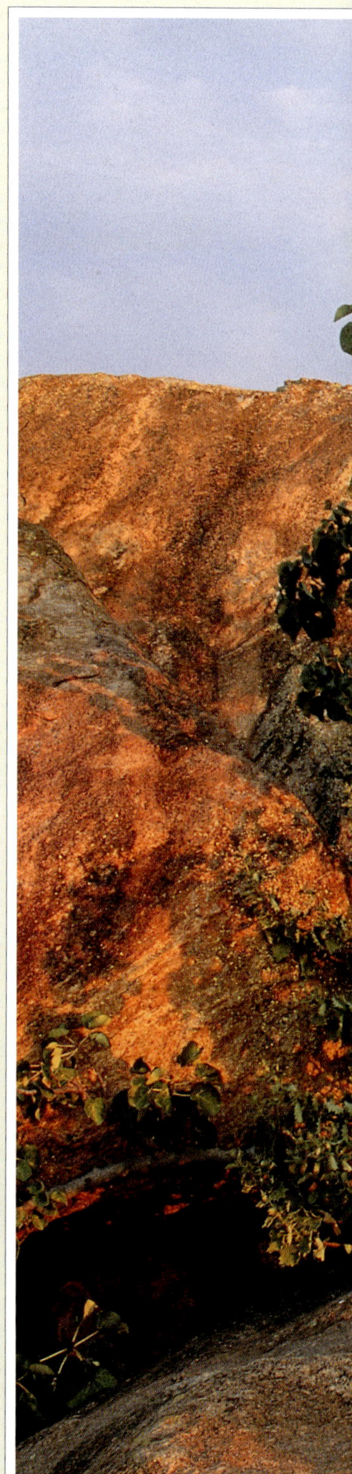

(*Combretum apiculatum*), together with the distinctive Kiaat (*Pterocarpus angolensis*). The Kiaat stands proud on most of the slopes and is easily recognised as one of the bigger and shapelier trees. Between the Lavender Trees (*Heteropyxis natalensis*), Willow Beechwood (*Faurea saligna*) and Marula (*Sclerocarya birrea*) is the scent of Wild Ginger (*Tetradenia riparia*), its white and lilac flowers glistening in the morning light. The common acacias are the Corky Thorn (*Acacia davyi*) and the Common Hook Thorn

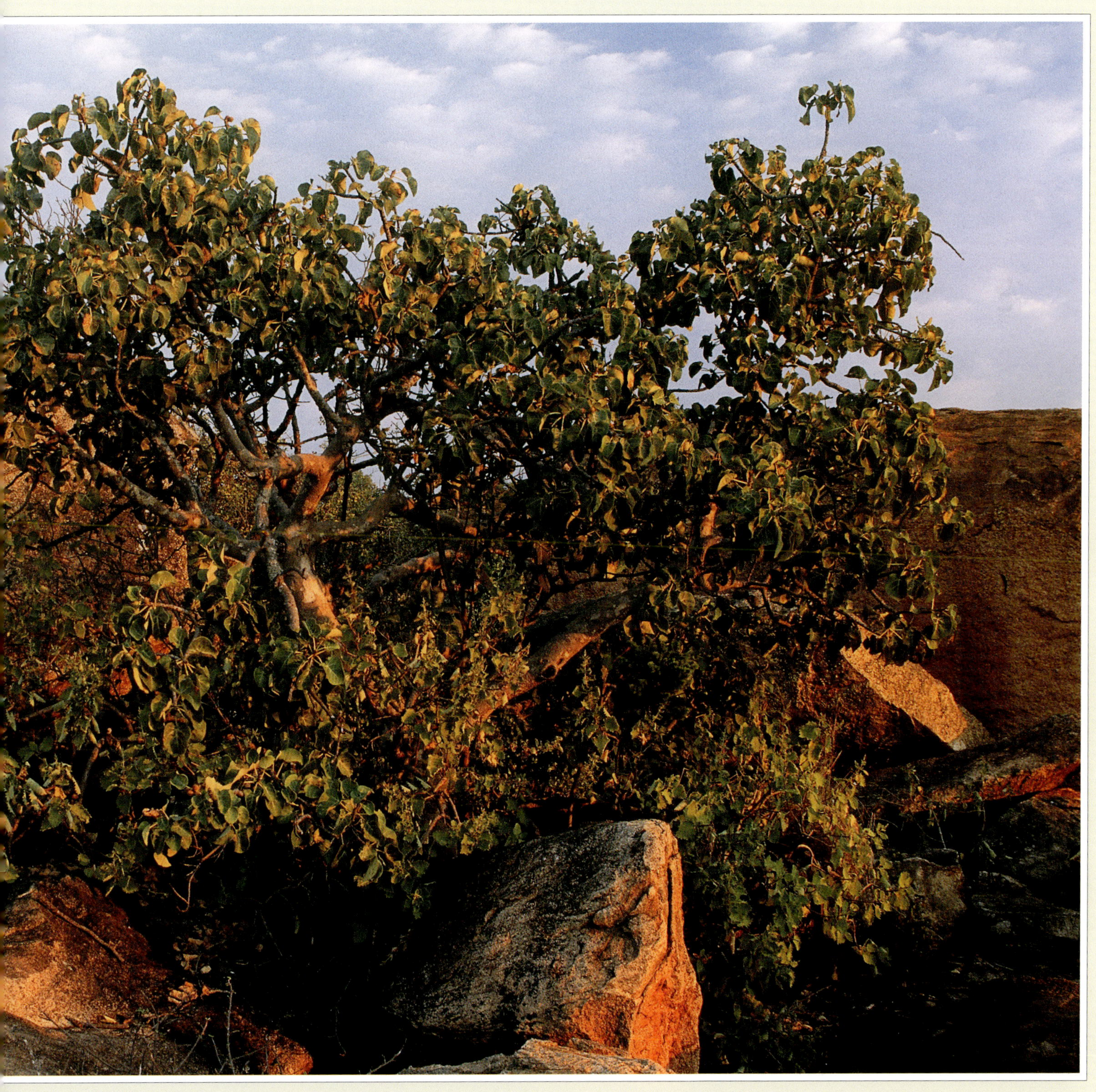

61

BELOW: Sunset over the hills at Bongani.

OPPOSITE: Lowveld Star Chestnut (*Sterculia murex*). These well-foliaged trees can reach up to ten metres in height. They have a very small distribution area, confined mainly to rocky ridges and koppies of the Lowveld.

(*Acacia caffra*). Trees that stand out for their scarcity are the Matumi (*Breonadia salicina*) and the Waterberry (*Syzygium cordatum*), while the presence of Silver Cluster-leaf (*Terminalia sericea*) and the Apple-leaf (*Philenoptera violacea*) indicates a shallow underground water source.

Lower down in the valley one finds not only the more common bushveld and riverine trees, but also the greater numbers of wildlife in the reserve. To mention the Marula, Knob Thorn (*Acacia nigrescens*), Weeping Boerbean (*Schotia brachypetala*), Tamboti (*Spirostachys africana*), Leadwood (*Combretum imberbe*) and Tree Wisteria (*Bolusanthus speciosus*) brings us back to the bushveld trees so common in the Lowveld. The Nsikazi River, which flows into the Crocodile River, diminishes into a series of pools in winter, but there is always water below the surface. Sycamore Fig (*Ficus sycomorus*), Jackalberry (*Diospyros mespiliformis*), Tamboti and Weeping Boerbean provide nourishment for animals in winter when much of the surrounding bush dries out and trees lose their leaves.

Our lasting impression of Bongani was the breathtaking views of the Lebombo mountains. Ripples of purple fading into the distance and the unmistakable silhouette of a Broad-leaved Coral Tree ended our Lowveld experience.

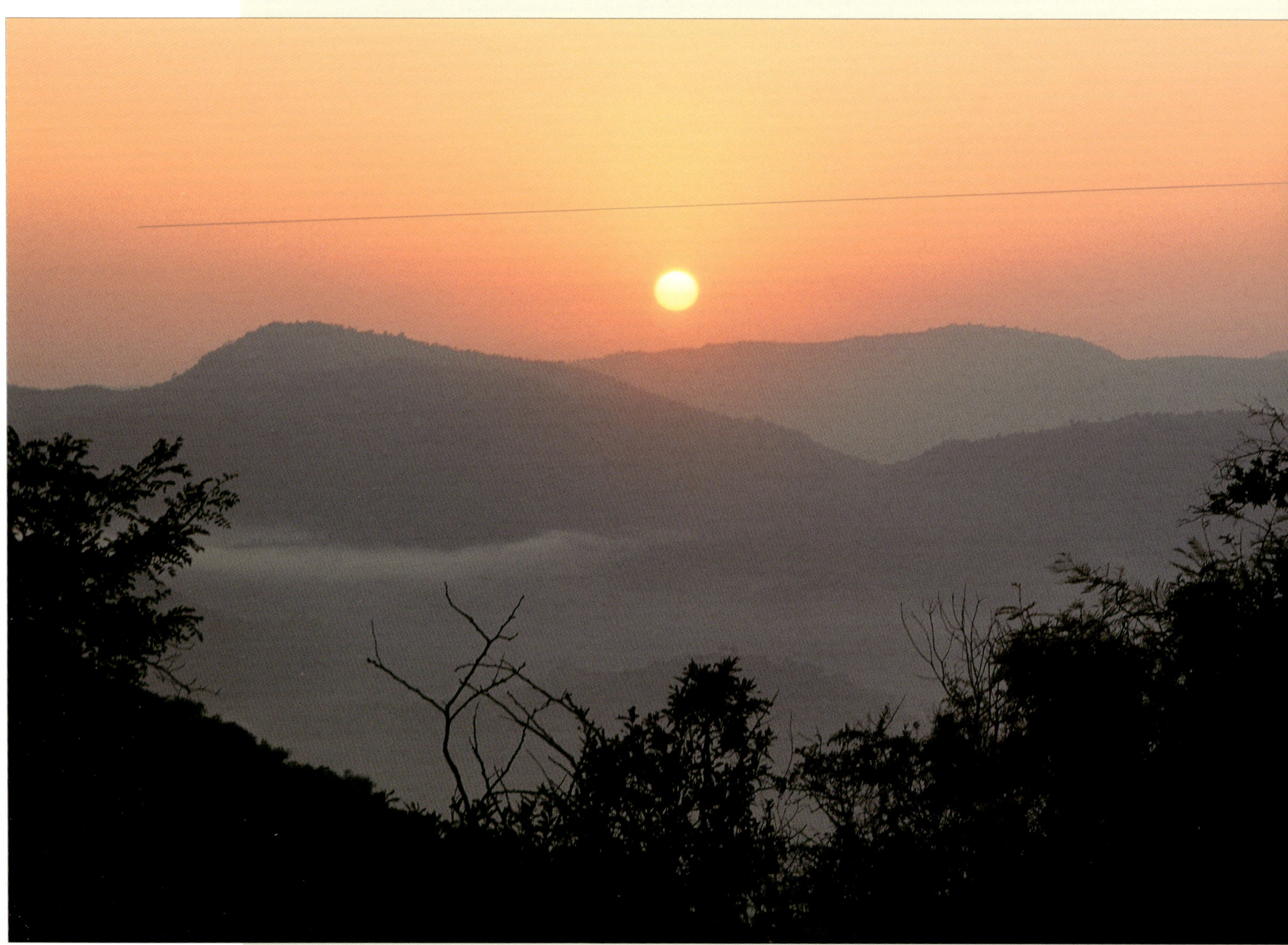

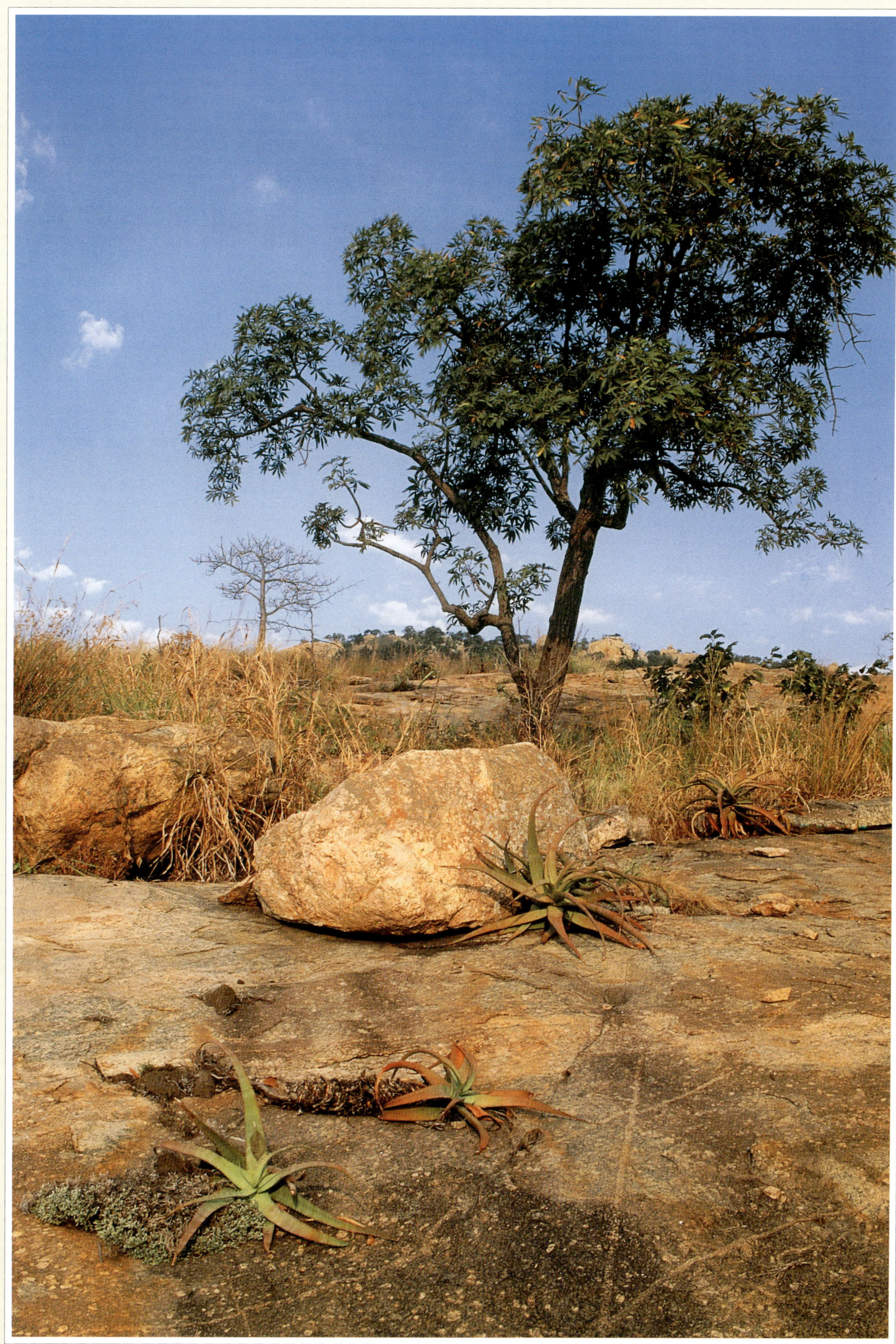

Bongani South Africa

RIGHT: Broad-leaved Coral Tree
(*Erythrina latissima*). These
trees are very sensitive to
damage by fire.

OPPOSITE: Broad-leaved Coral
Tree (*Erythrina latissima*).

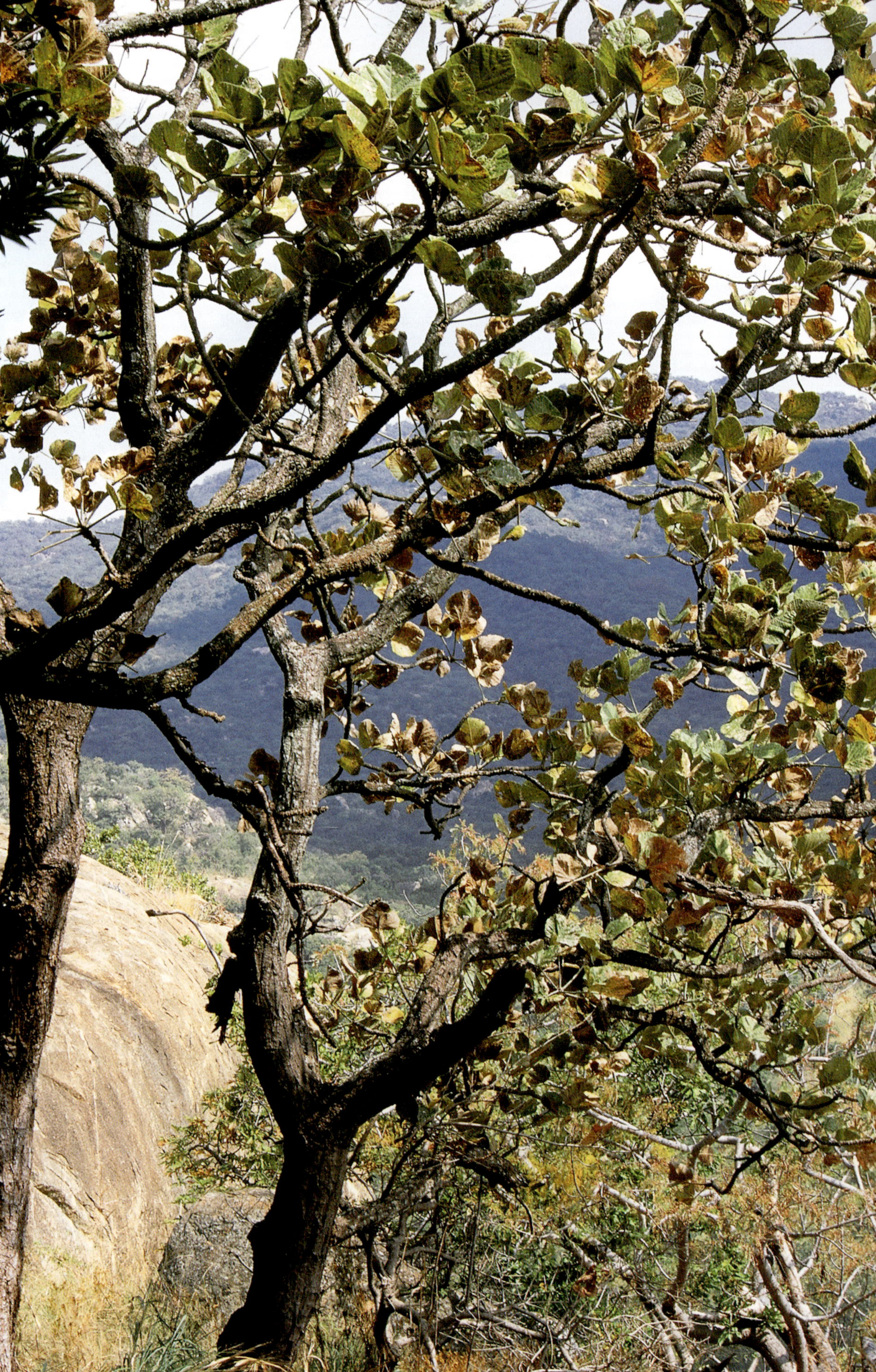

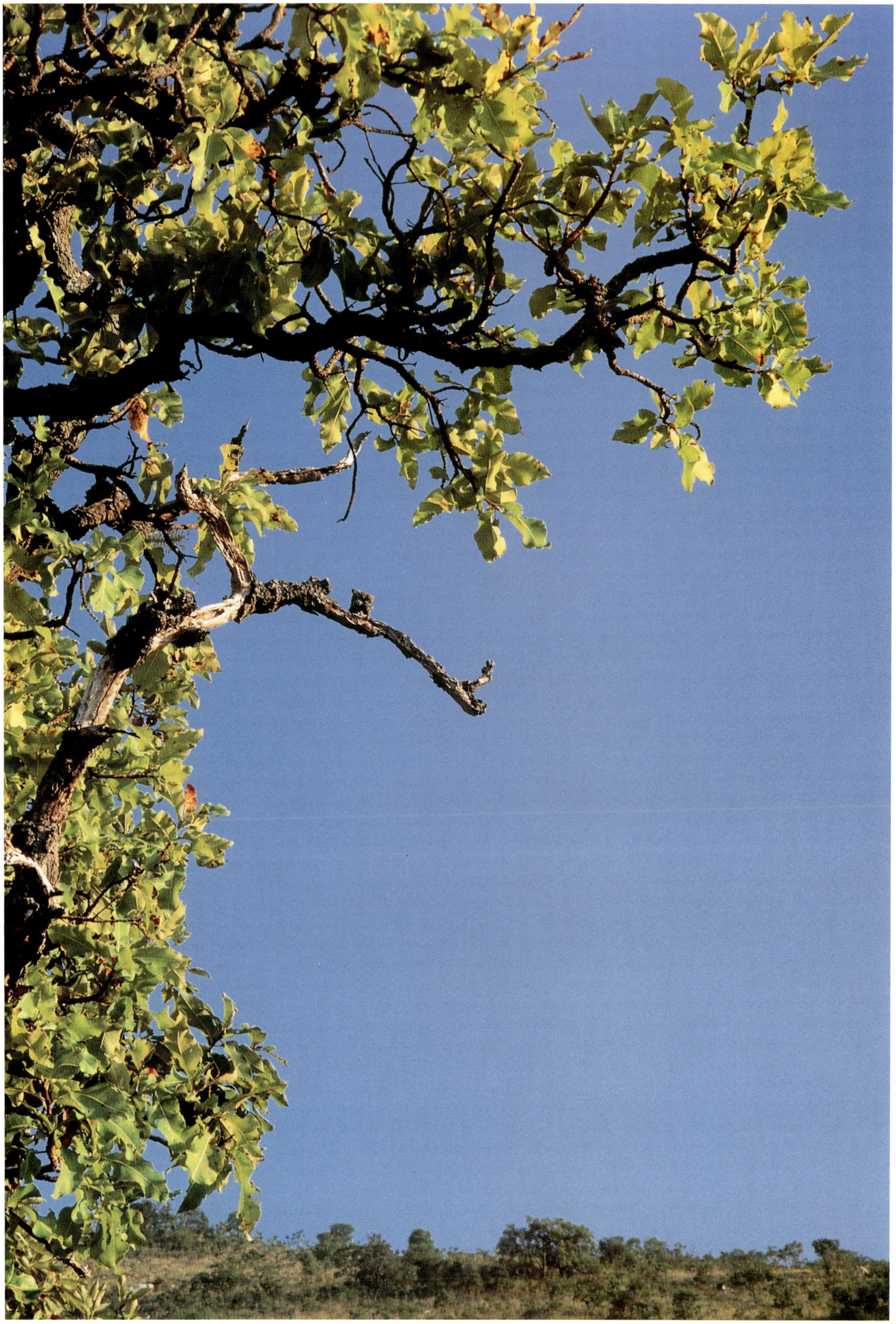

Bongani South Africa

BELOW: Broad-leaved Coral Tree (*Erythrina latissima*). Traditionally, the bark is burnt, powdered and used to dress sores. Common to all erythrinas are enormous crimson-to-brown hairy flowers that fall to the ground and are devoured by warthog.

OPPOSITE: Traveller's Joy (*Clematis brachiata*) is a perennial scrambler that displays its showy flowers and seeds during late summer and autumn.

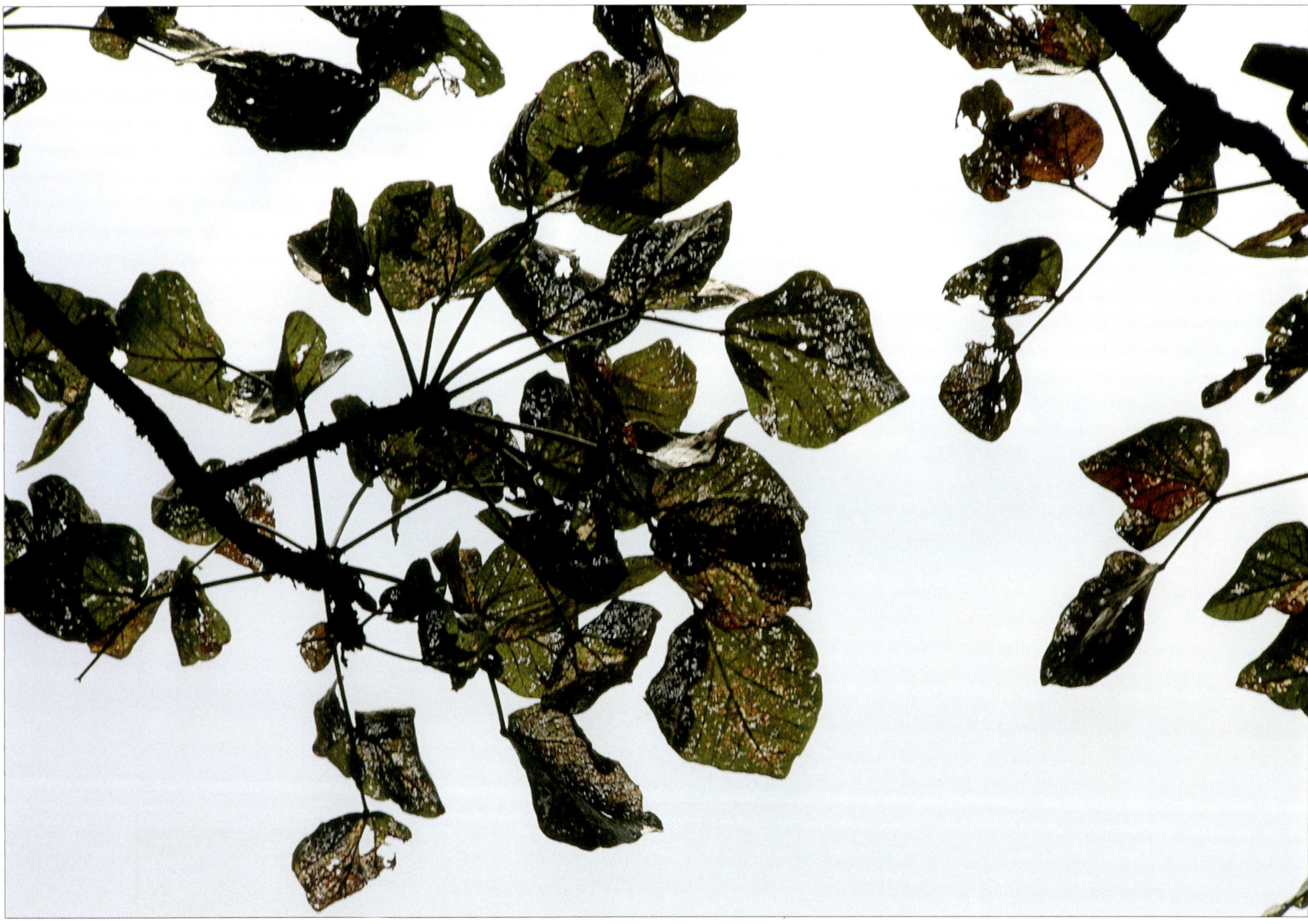

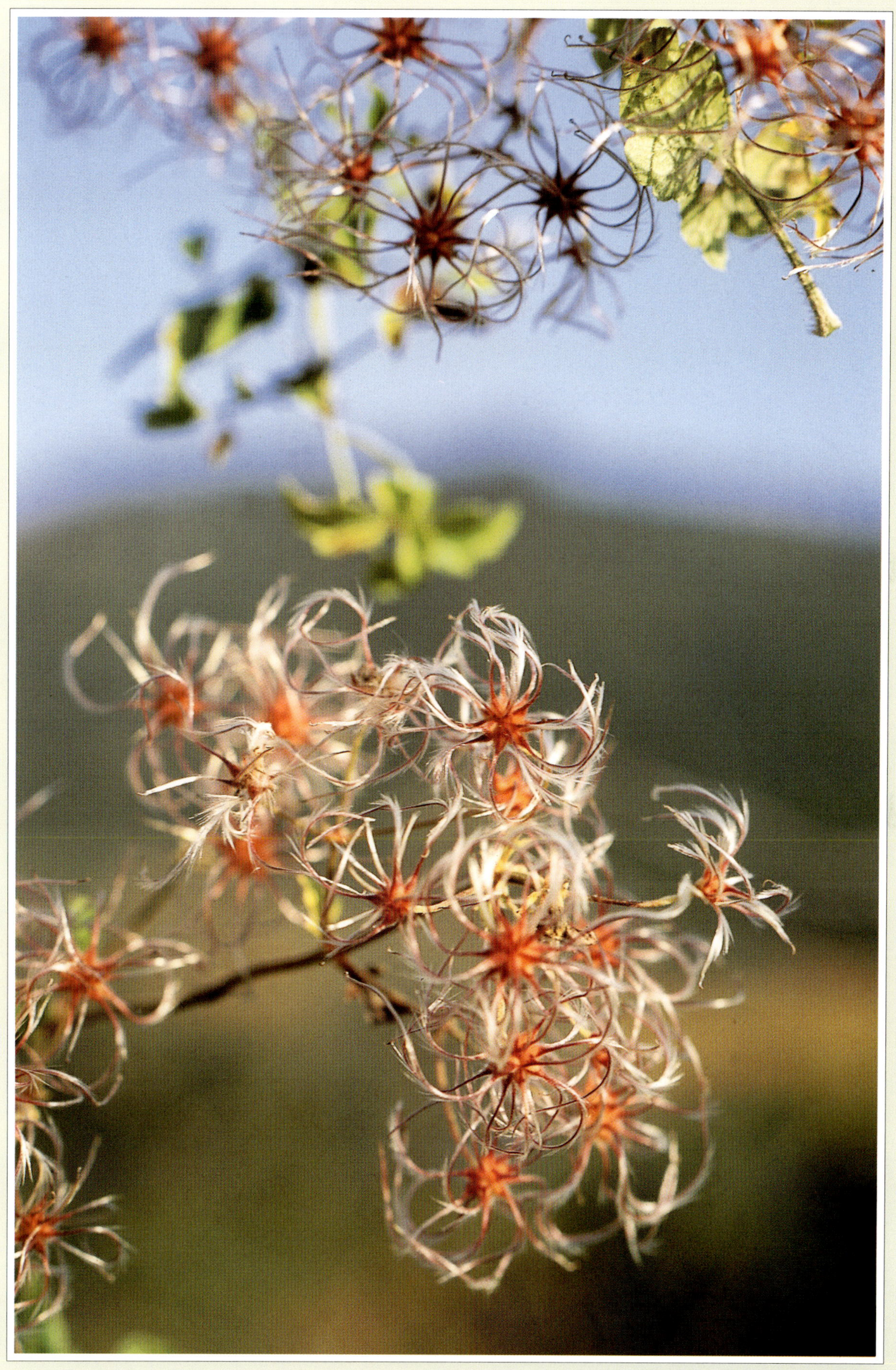

Bongani | South Africa

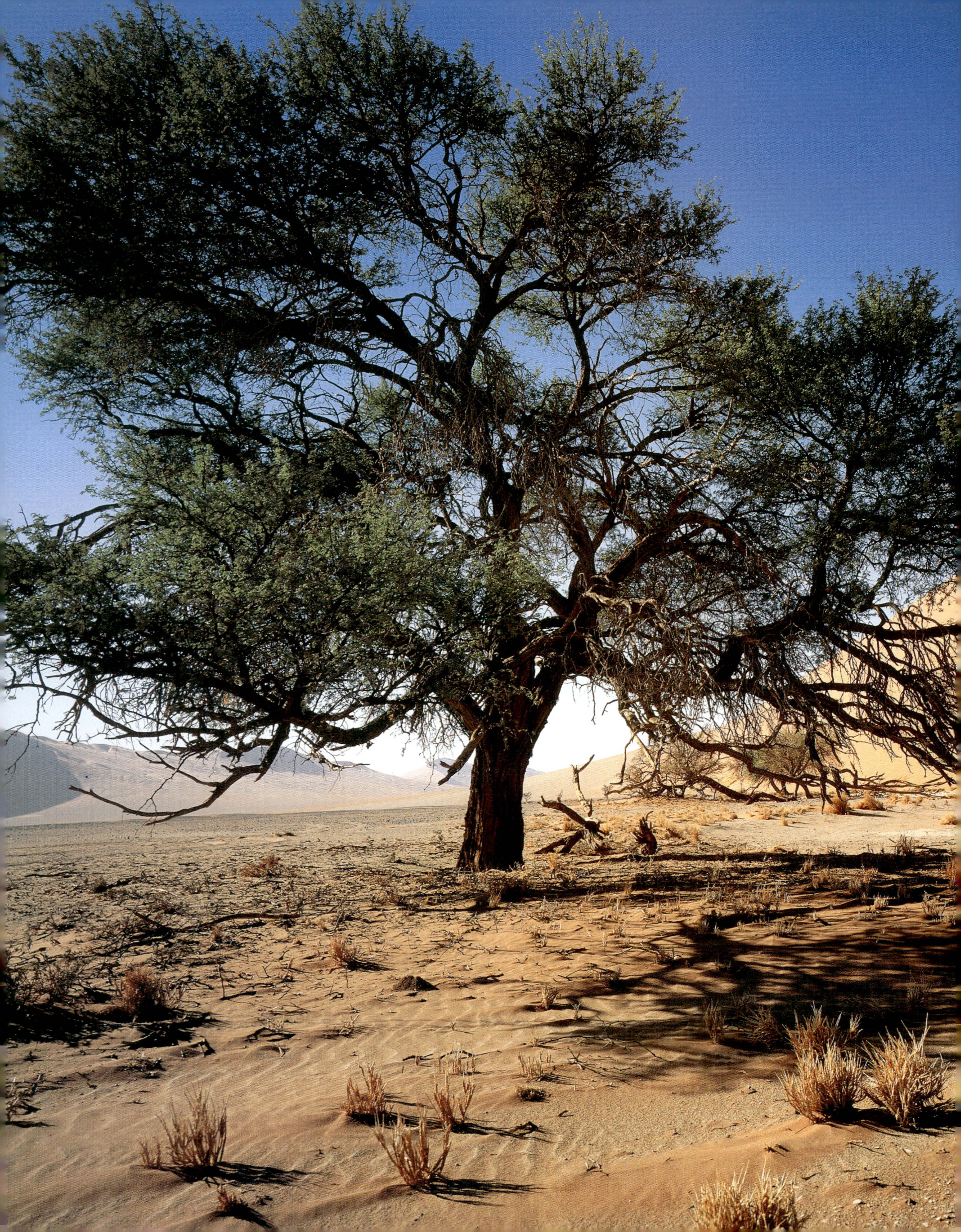

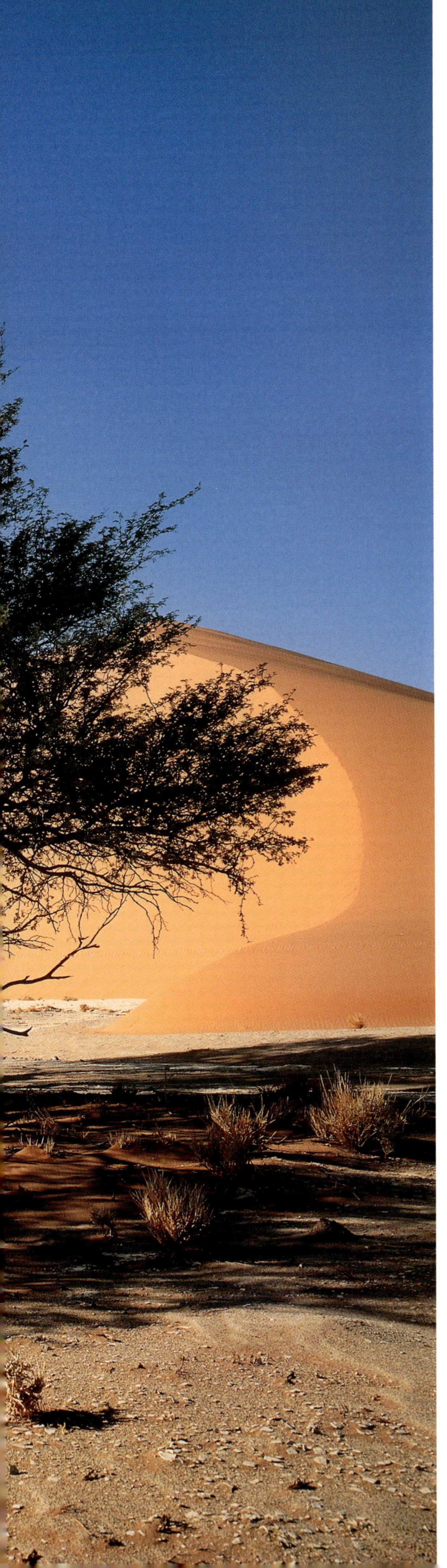

THE LIVING SAND

Covering almost 50 000 square kilometres, the Namib-Naukluft National Park is one of the largest national parks in Africa and protects one of the oldest deserts on Earth. Sossusvlei lies in the midst of a desert sea formed around five million years ago. At this age, in the sand that seems so lifeless, many endemic species have evolved to bring life to a seemingly waterless habitat. These life forms have adapted ingeniously to harness moisture from the coastal fog belt some 50 kilometres away. Looking beyond the dramatic colour, height and angles of the dunes, one finds beetles, fishmoths (silverfish), spiders, geckos, chameleons, golden moles, and birds that move in and out of the dunes in search of water.

LEFT: A deep-rooted Camel Thorn (*Acacia erioloba*) taps into underground moisture at Sossusvlei.

Sossusvlei Mountain Lodge
Namibia

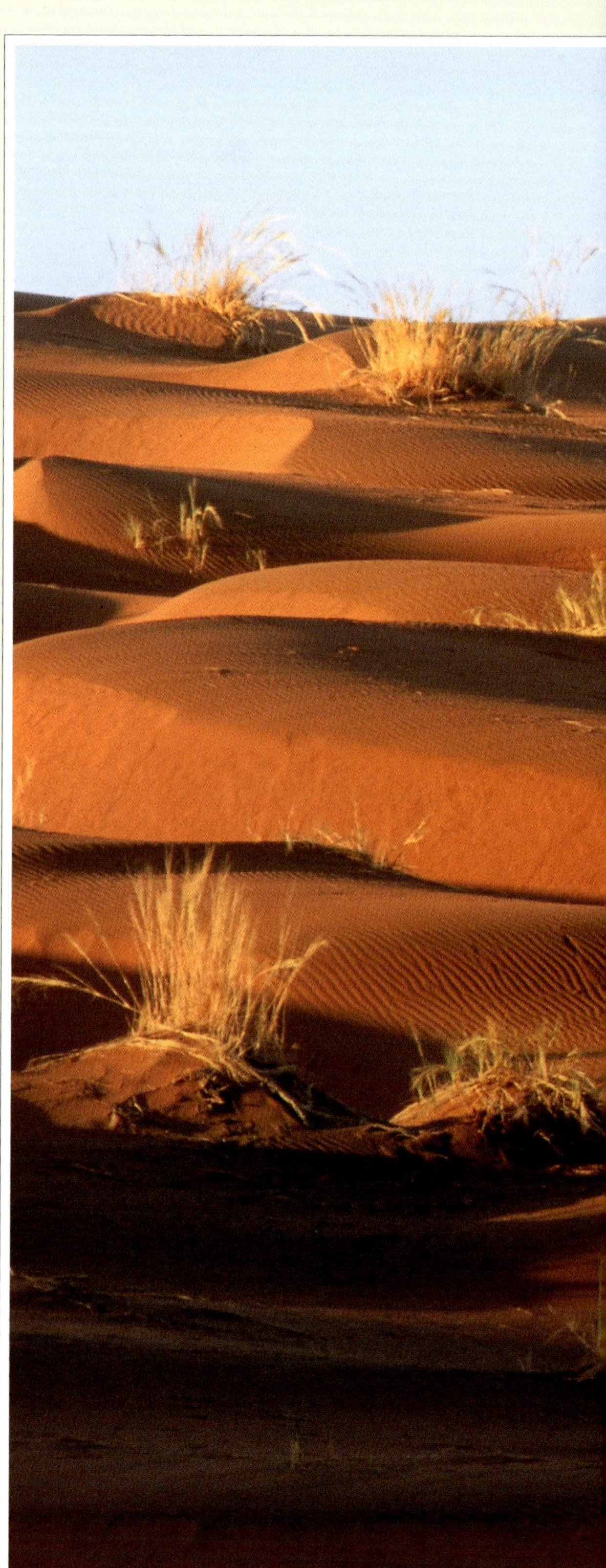

eaving Windhoek in a Cessna, we encountered only slight turbulence as we flew in a southwesterly direction towards Sossusvlei. Far below, splattered with silver reflections of water in the unusually green Namib countryside, the orange-and-yellow desert was soon glimpsed. The baking airstrip rose to welcome our landing and the silence began.

From the lodge, the view is best appreciated through a fish-eye lens. A half-crater shape of black mountains surrounds the lodge, with orange dunes bordering the one flank, desert in the middle, and green plains stretching into the distance. The colours provide a majestic contrast, drawing the viewer into a world of art far removed from everyday life. Yellows, blacks, greens and ochres, topped by brilliant blue sky, set a gentle background to a harsh environment where temperatures can reach 50 degrees Centigrade. In this majestic desert, the only sound seems to come from the heat above and the ground below.

And the trees? People laughed when we said we were taking photographs of trees in the desert. 'There are no trees,' they said – and, indeed, as we gazed into the distance, they are few and far between. We set off to prove them wrong. Our guide took us to one tree after the other. Camel Thorns (*Acacia erioloba*) feature in this part of the world.

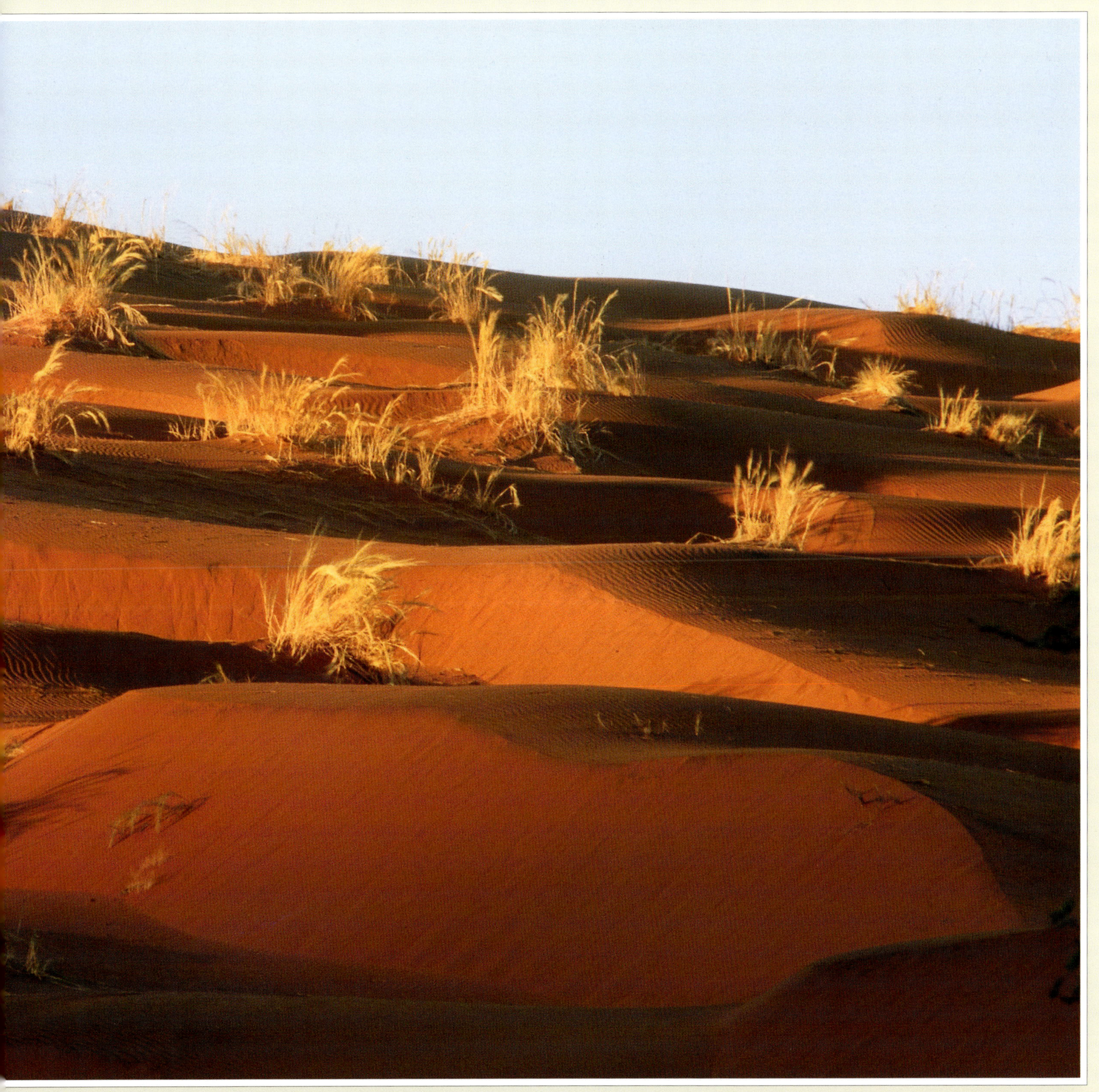

BELOW: The age of a dune can be determined by the colour of its sand; the lighter the colour, the older the dune.

Although they are not particularly magnificent on their own, their presence in this bone-dry climate seems like a miracle.

The Camel Thorns map the dry watercourses and runoff lines. Along the Arb and Tsuarag sand rivers, a long line of these tenacious trees trace the watercourses in their quest to reach Sossusvlei and beyond. The two rivers are like a desert fjord, wide apart at first and then narrowing to reach an apex at the vlei. Some 50 kilometres further lies the sea, but between the vlei and the Atlantic coast there is nothing but inhospitable orange sand dunes.

The dunes formed some five million years ago and miraculously left this fjord untouched. It is a wonder they don't blow their fine sand over the area and cover all forms of tree life. They are called star dunes. Winds blow in both directions, keeping the position of the dune relatively stable. It seems almost impossible that, two or three metres from the base of a dune, a proud Camel Thorn has stood for countless years.

Whereas Camel Thorn and Boscia (*Boscia coriacea*) are fairly easy to locate, other trees are not. Phantom Trees (*Moringa ovalifolia*) grow on mountain slopes sandwiched

RIGHT: Camel Thorn (*Acacia erioloba*) shadows.

OPPOSITE: Camel Thorn (*Acacia erioloba*). These lone landmark trees are photographed by thousands of tourists every year.

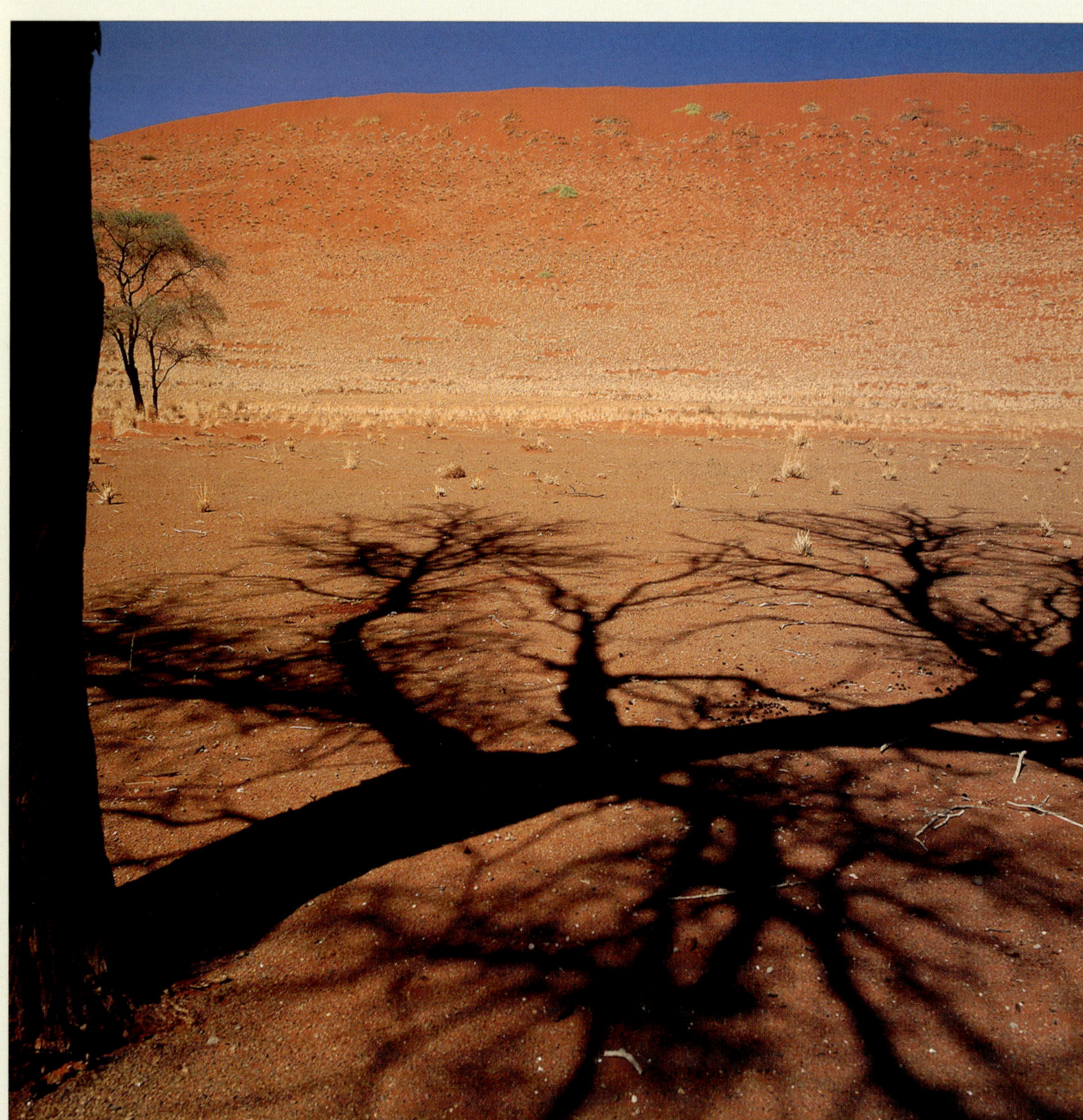

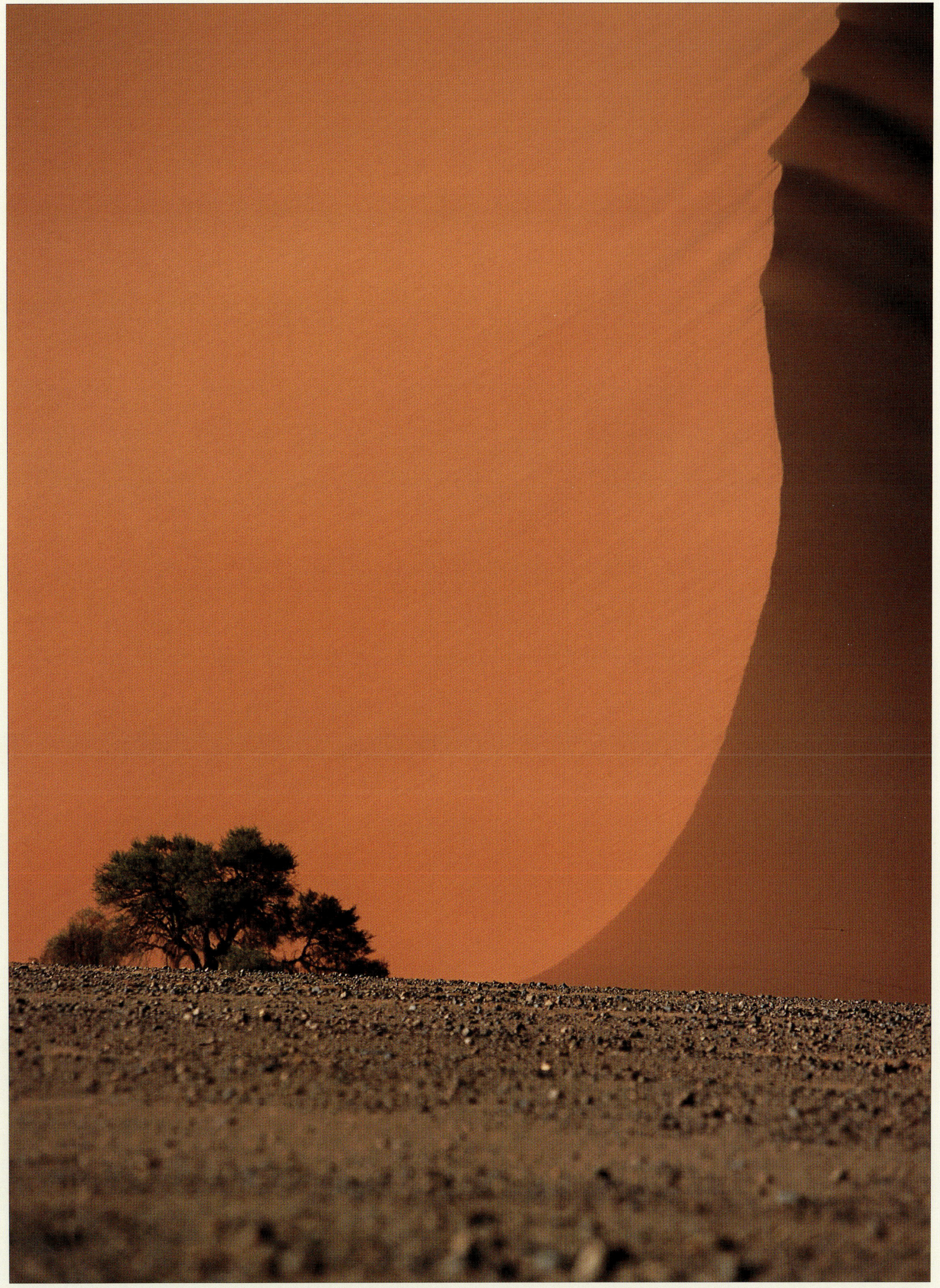

Sossusvlei Namibia

between chunks of rock. Their leaves are grass green mid-afternoon, but as the sun sets, the bulbous trunk lights up with reflections off the rocks and glows a burnt orange colour in the desert dusk.

Finding Quiver Trees (*Aloe dichotoma*) proved more of a challenge, being higher up, and when we finally reached them they were darkened by long shadows. Although we lost these shots, the image of the odd Quiver Tree bathed in sunlight against the black mountain rocks will remain a lasting memory.

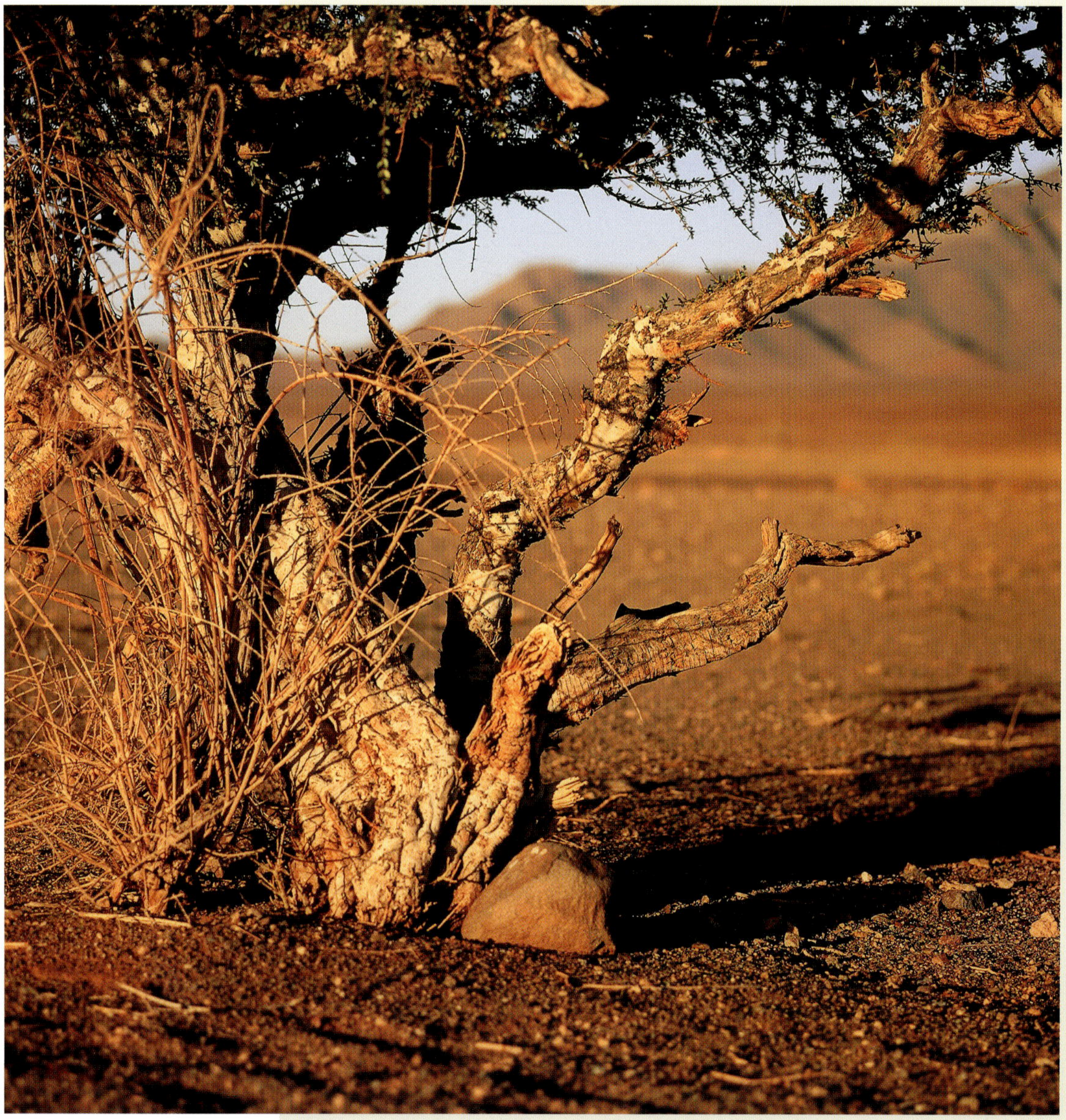

While the trees of the desert are usually overlooked, their scarcity makes them so much more important than they are given credit as sources of shade and shelter for animals such as the oryx. Aesthetically, their scarcity gives them the relative significance of a forest, with their green colour complementing the black stone, the red dunes and the yellow desert sands.

OPPOSITE: Shepherds Tree (*Boscia albitrunca*). The leaves are edible and sometimes pounded to make porridge, and the berries are stewed with meat to give it a nutty flavour. Flowers are pickled in vinegar and used as a substitute for capers. The Shepherds Tree is one of the most common trees found in southern Africa. Its thick fleshy roots are dried in the sun, then chopped and burnt over a fire to make a coffee substitute for those with an acquired taste.

BELOW: Camel Thorn (*Acacia erioloba*). The rough, deeply fissured bark is home to skinks, geckos and other creatures, including scorpions.

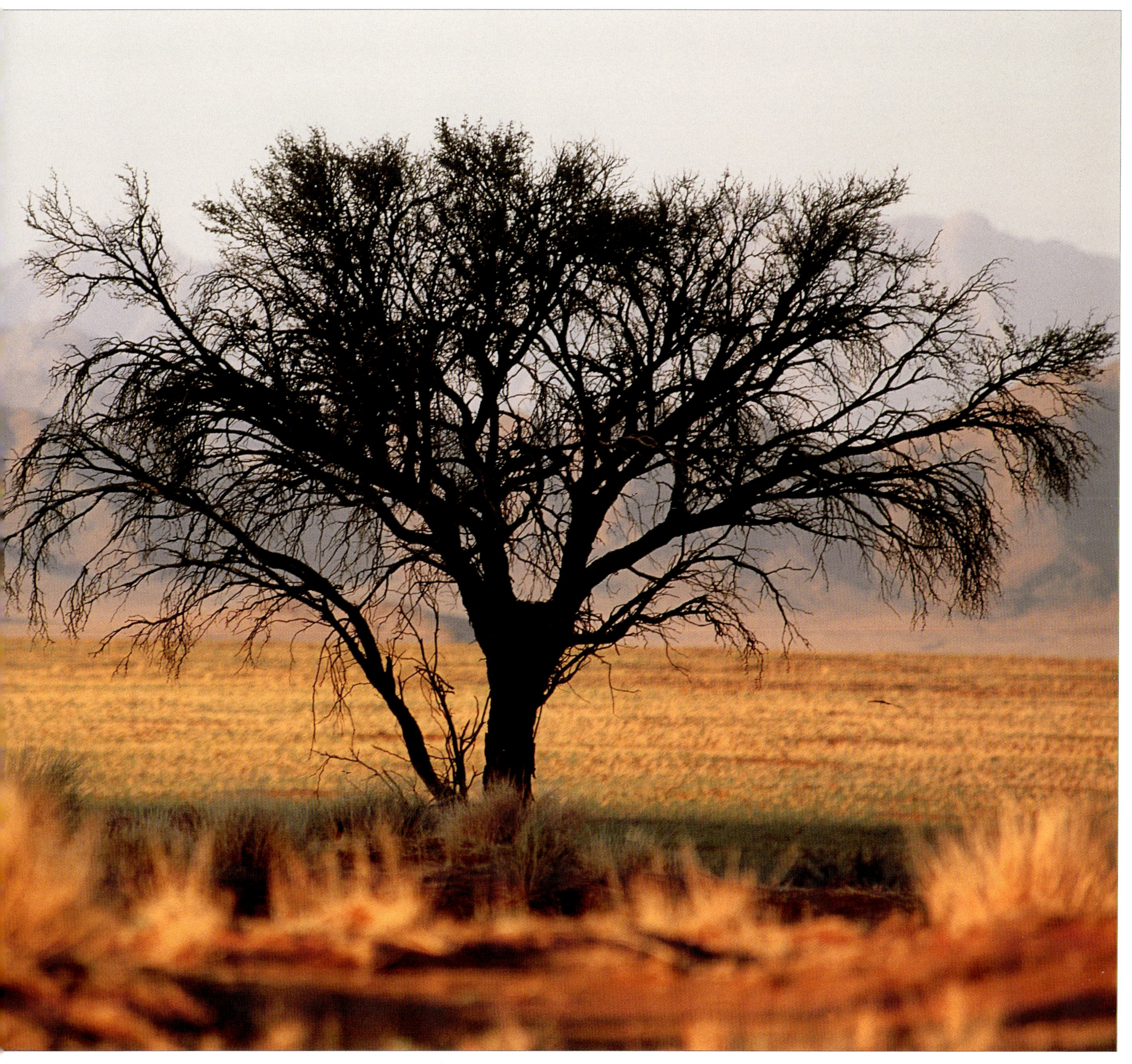

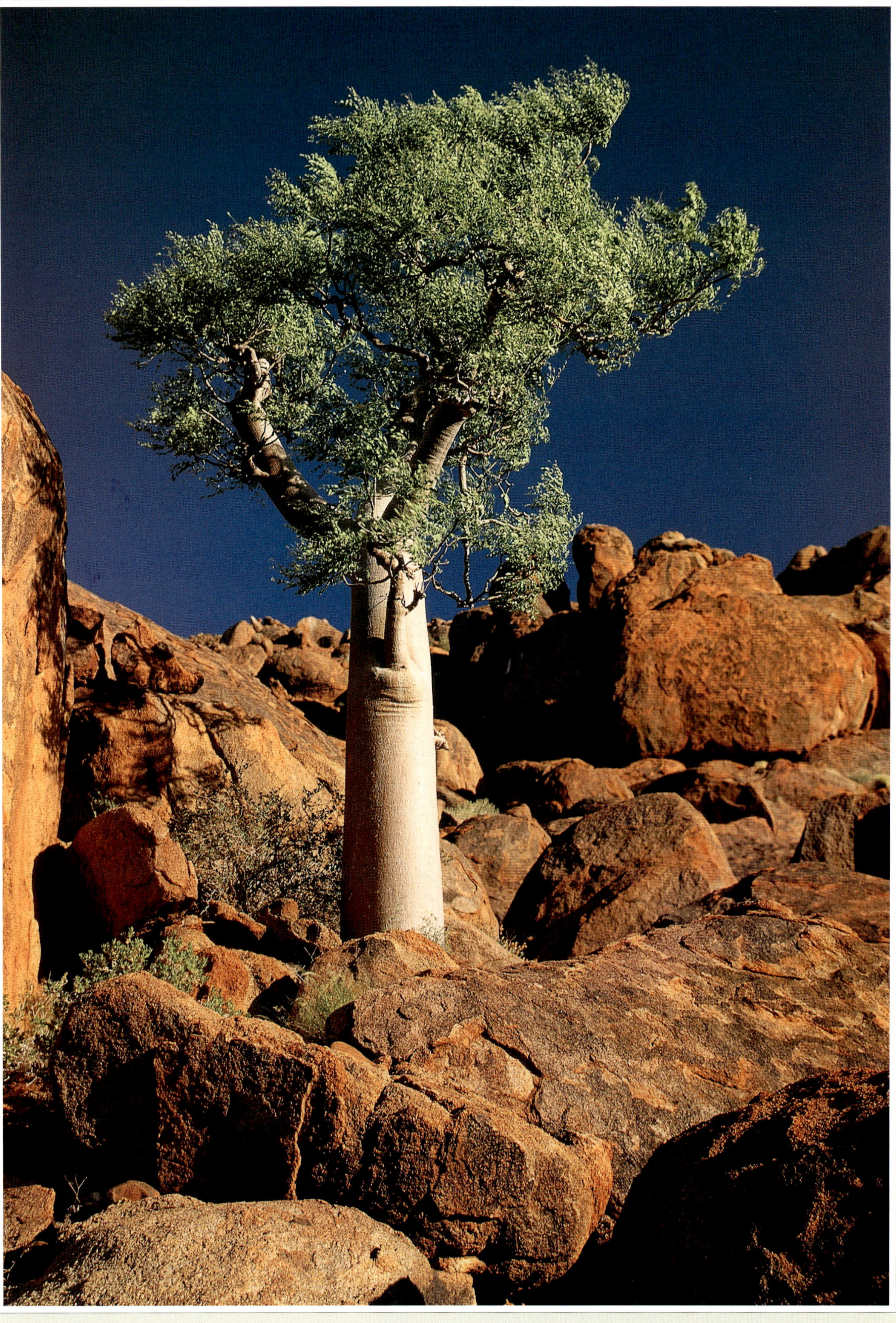

Sossusvlei Namibia

OPPOSITE: Phantom Tree
(*Moringa ovalifolia*).
The bark and roots of this
beautifully odd tree are
eaten by porcupine and
klipspringer, while giraffe
browse on the pale yellow
flowers. Elephants enjoy
rubbing themselves against
its smooth bark.

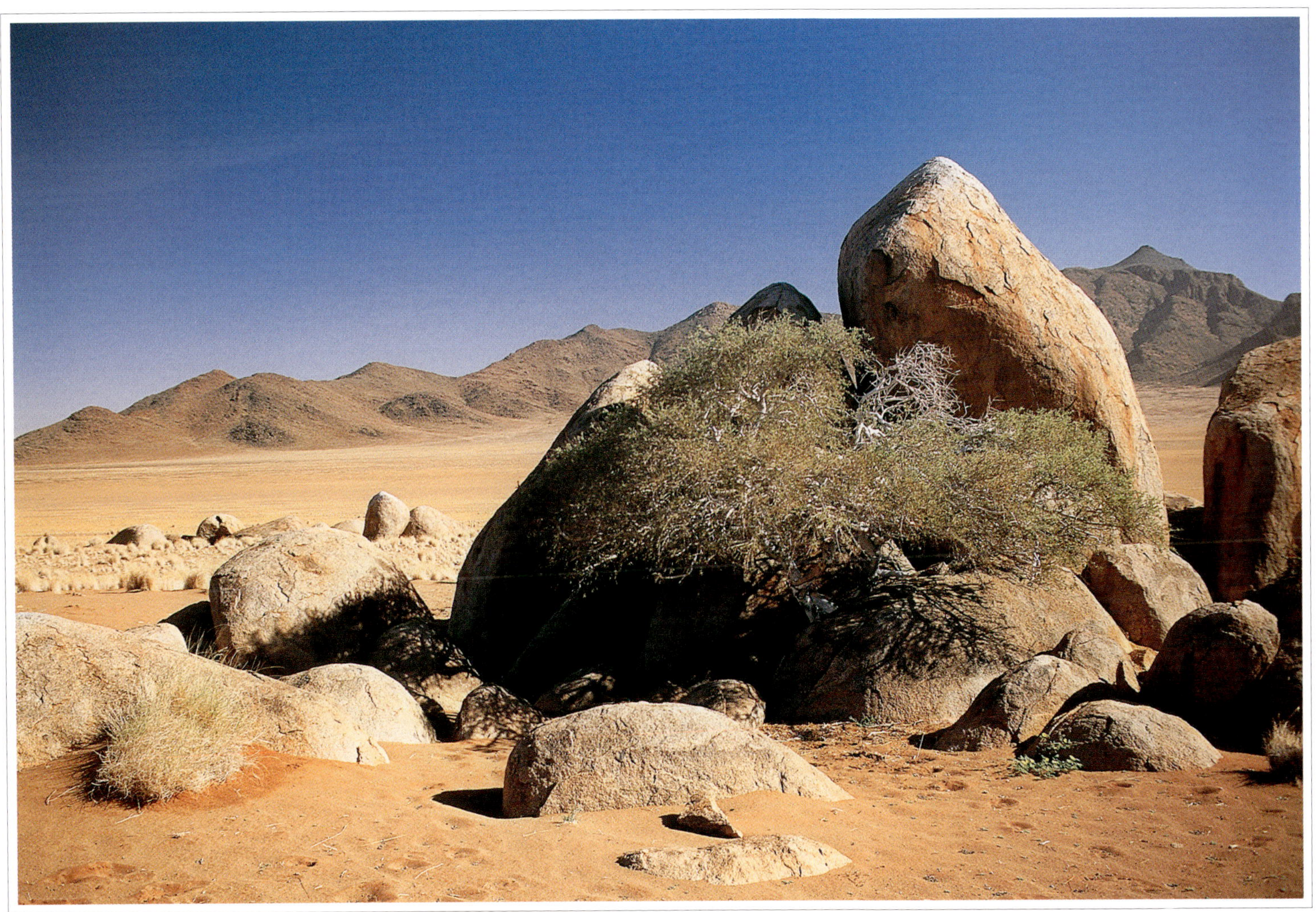

ABOVE: Stink Shepherds Tree
(*Boscia foetida*). The common
name comes from the flowers
and cut wood that have a
pungent and very unpleasant
smell.

BELOW: After the rains, the usually barren desert comes alive with an unexpected flush of green.

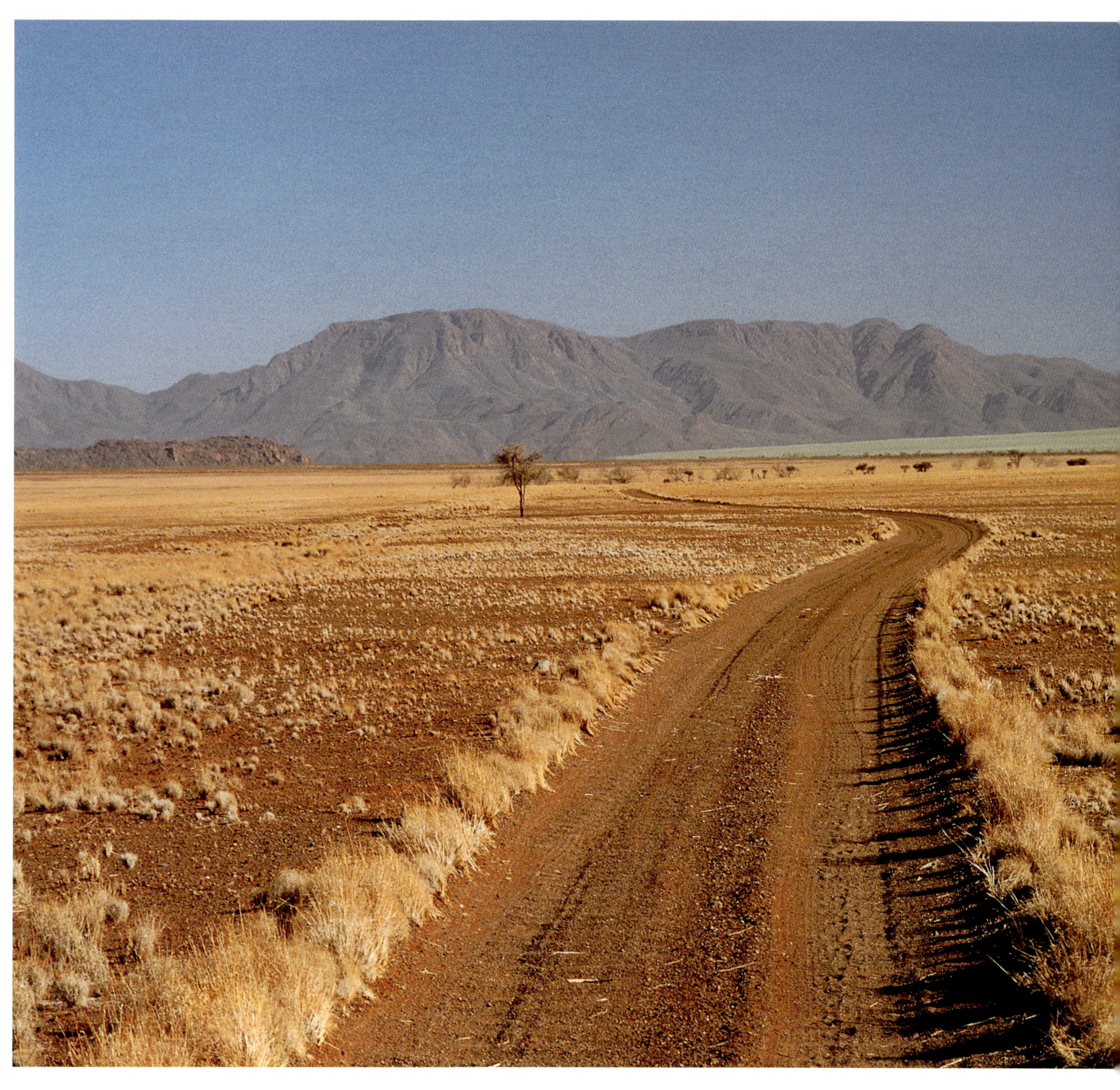

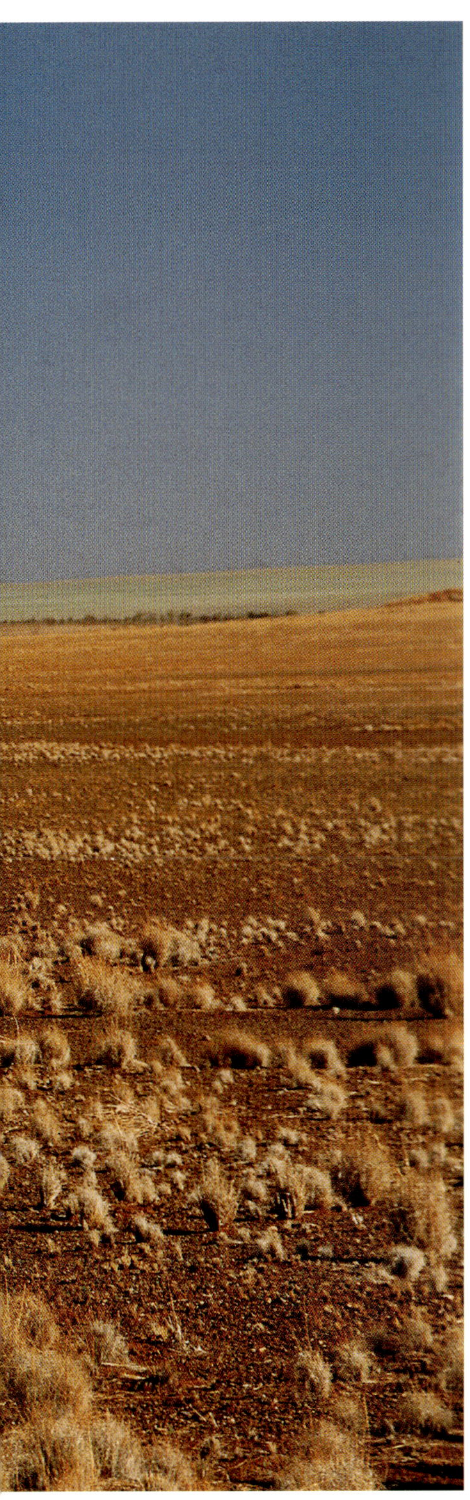

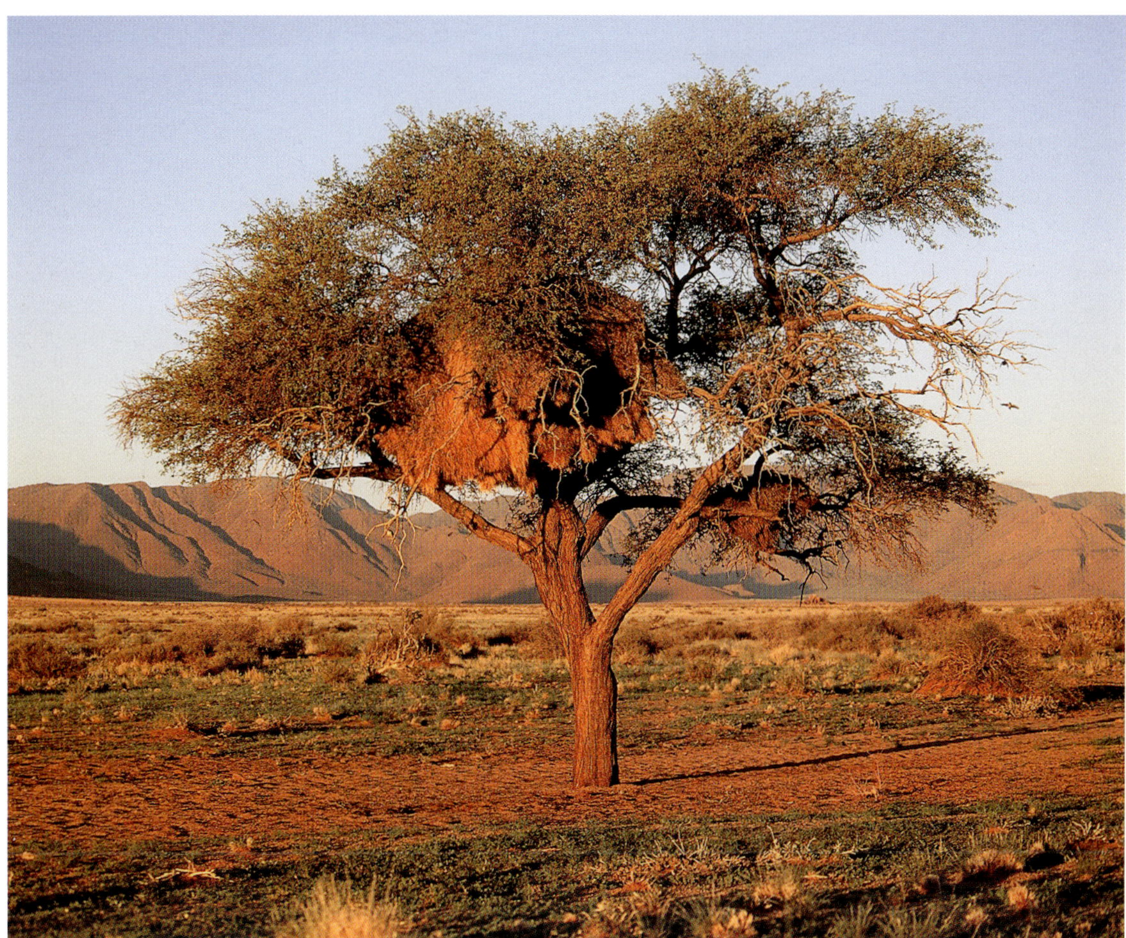

ABOVE: Camel Thorn (*Acacia erioloba*). Colonies of sociable weavers build their huge communal thatched nests in Camel Thorns, which are usually strong enough to support the structures. These busy little birds use grass to build their nests, with each pair occupying a particular chamber. Many other desert creatures covet weavers' nests, which provide wonderful insulation against both heat and cold. The diminutive pygmy falcon breeds only in the sociable weaver's nest, while giant eagle owls may lay their eggs on top of the structure.

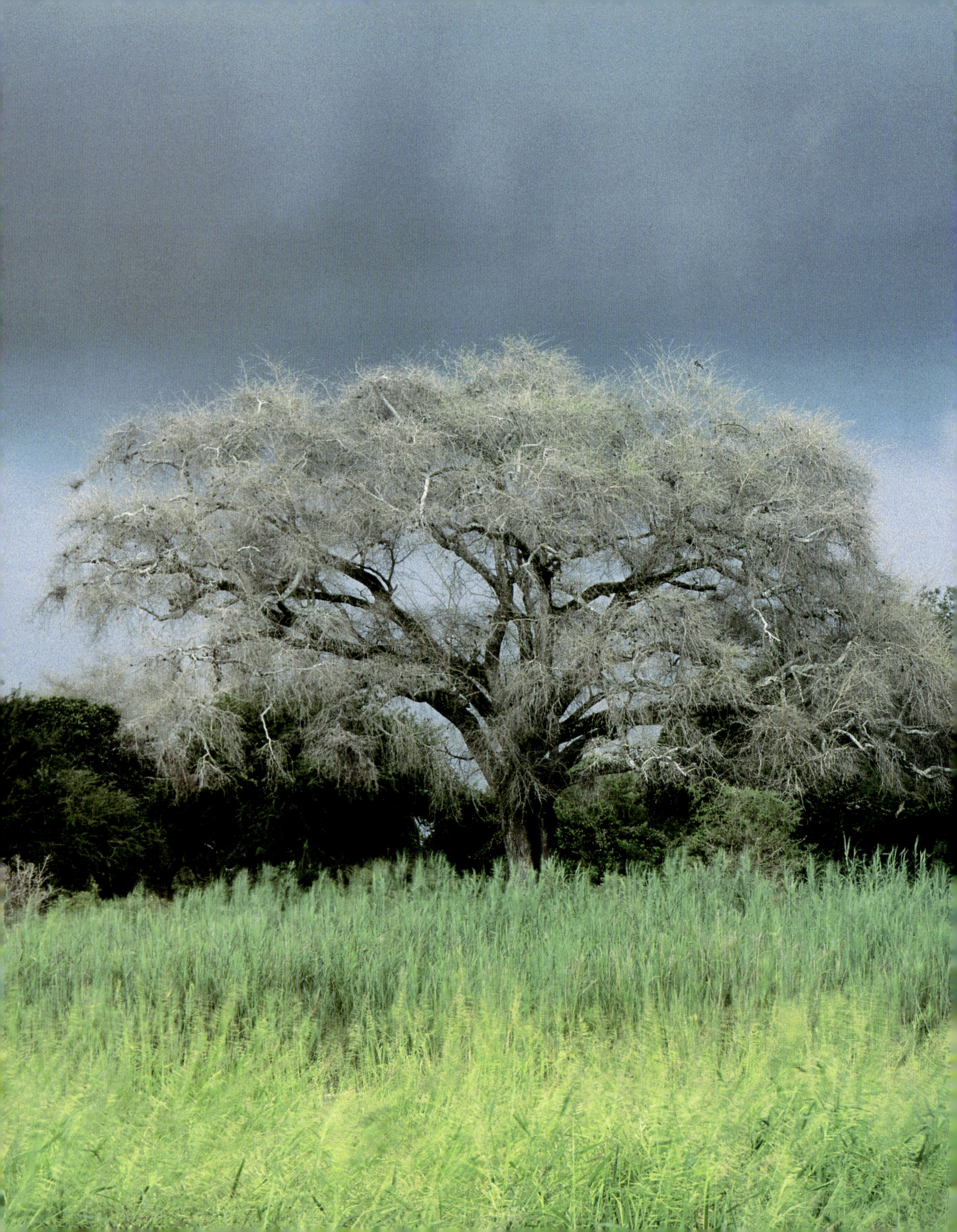

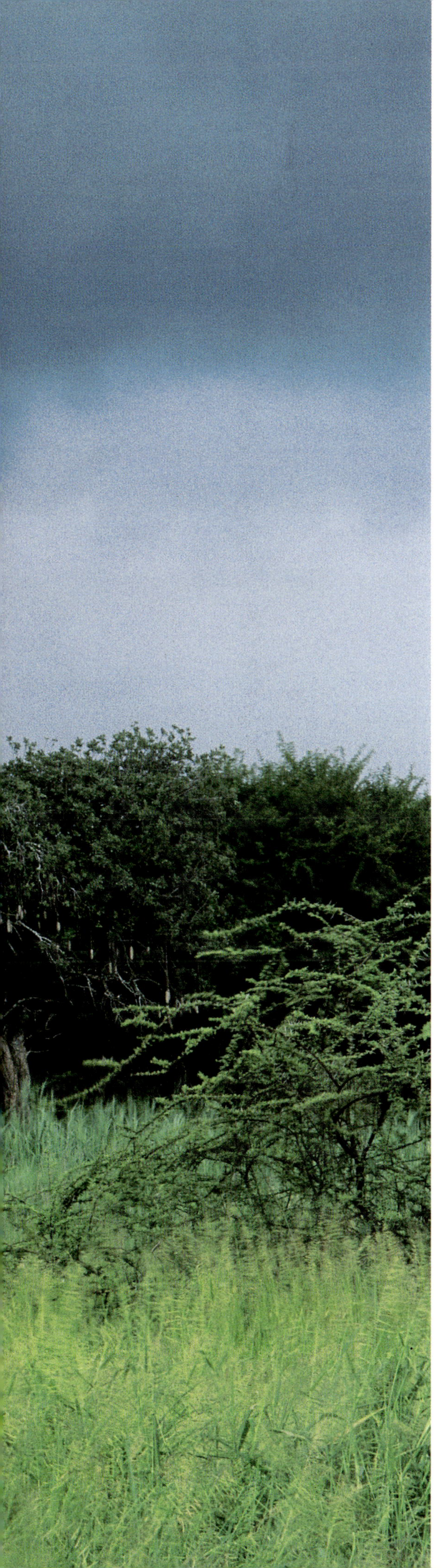

UNDISCOVERED, UNDISTURBED

Whereas land and frenzied tourist invasions became characteristic of most countries in Africa, time stood still in southern Tanzania. This time warp of underdevelopment has enabled the country today to boast about its immense, remote and wild places, which are among the last remaining in the world.

More than a million animals live in the Selous Game Reserve and the Ruaha National Park, through which the Great Ruaha River runs to join the Rufiji River before spilling out into the warm Indian Ocean. The southern circuit's slow start allowed it to learn from conservation errors. For the sake of the long-term survival of the World Heritage Site of Selous, the least visited national park in Africa, we need to take things slowly.

LEFT: Ana Tree (*Faidherbia albida*). Dugout canoes are made from the wood of larger specimens of this tree, which was once considered an acacia. They are important in the Ruaha ecosystem for the deep shade they offer during the hottest months of the year.
The seedpods are highly nutritious and much favoured by browsing antelope and especially elephant during the dry season. The great pachyderms often rise up on their hind legs to pull down bunches of these seedpods.

Jongomero
Ruaha National Park Tanzania

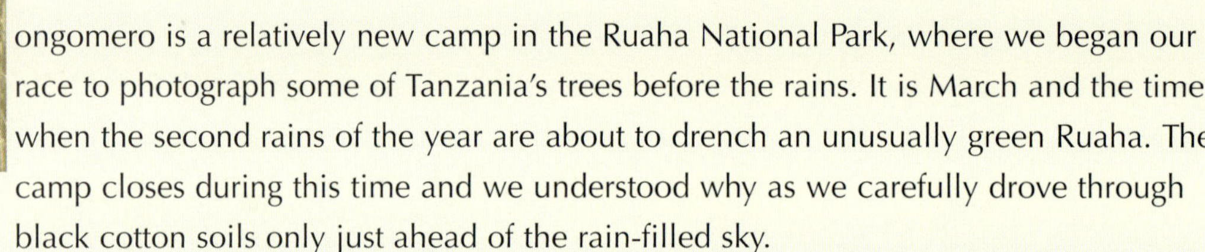

Jongomero is a relatively new camp in the Ruaha National Park, where we began our race to photograph some of Tanzania's trees before the rains. It is March and the time when the second rains of the year are about to drench an unusually green Ruaha. The camp closes during this time and we understood why as we carefully drove through black cotton soils only just ahead of the rain-filled sky.

Knowing we needed good light conditions, our ever-optimistic guide Emiel gallantly headed the vehicle to clearer patches of sky. But the weather won, leaving us no option but to photograph the incredible lushness of this beautiful area surrounded by grey sky.

Ruaha is wild and therein lies its beauty. It is relatively inaccessible, situated within and along the Rift Valley near the colourful town of Iringa. The Great Ruaha River flows along the southeastern border of the park to eventually join up with the Rufiji River. It is a majestic river, often in the shade of riverine woodland of albidas, figs, tamarind trees and palms.

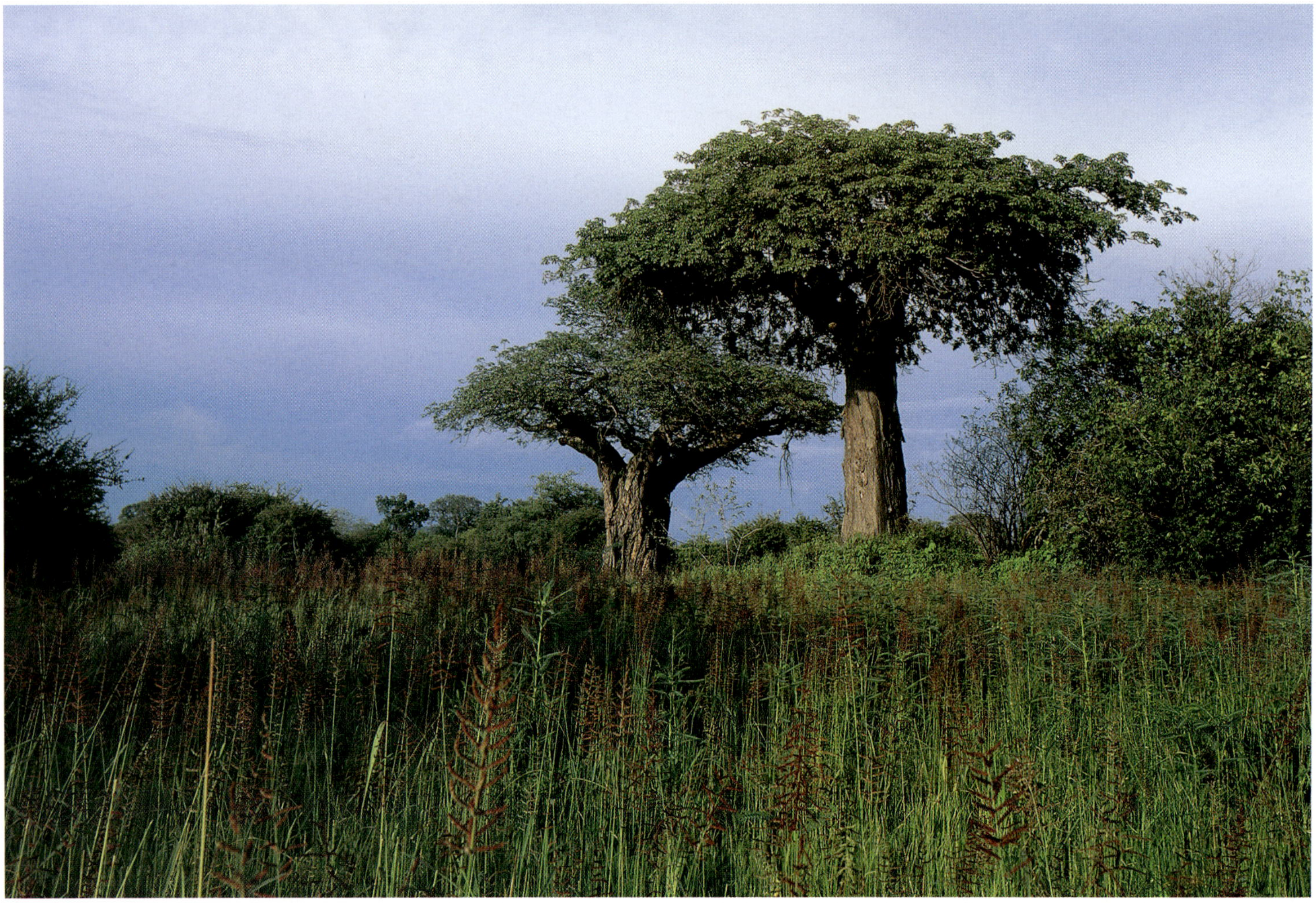

OPPOSITE AND BELOW: Baobab (*Adansonia digitata*). Baobab are known in Swahili as *mbuya*, meaning 'of' or 'at', and many villages are called Mbuyini. The Swahili people believe that a strong drink made from soaked Baobab leaves protects humans against crocodile attacks. Older specimens frequently have large cavities in which birds such as the barn owl, ground hornbill and Böhm's spinetail nest. Snakes such as the black mamba also favour these large holes. The striking white flowers last just a single night before turning creamy yellow and falling to the ground; fruit bats pollinate them. In the photograph below, the bark has been stripped to elephant height.

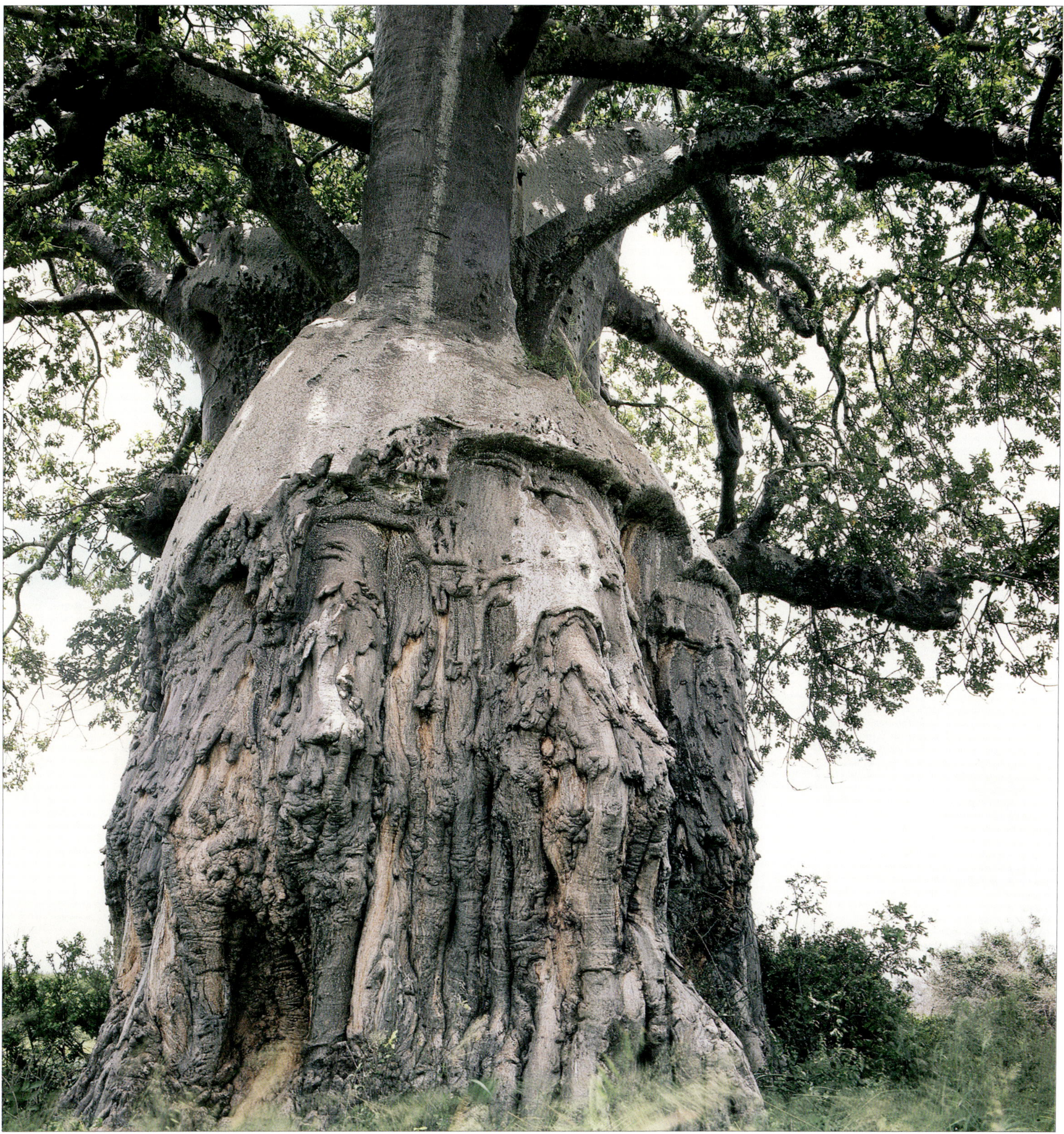

BELOW: Tamarind (*Tamarindus indica*).

OPPOSITE: Pod Mahogany (*Afzelia quanzensis*). The large woody pods contain shiny black and red seeds that are frequently used as ornaments or lucky charms. Dugout canoes are made from the close-grained wood and the demand for housing timber has led to the removal of many fine specimens beyond the protected areas.

The main road upstream runs from the entrance gate parallel to the river through combretums, baobabs and acacias. Many types of combretums are found here, but the Toothbrush Bush (*Combretum purpurifolia*) stands out before the rains, with its scarlet and pink flowers. Some 20 per cent of the park lies along the Great Ruaha River and most visitors stay within this area due to the nature of the roads.

Nearer Jongomero, commiphoras with their flaking yellow-green bark, acacias with their flat-topped signatures and Sausage Trees (*Kigelia africana*) with their bulbous pods dominate the southern corner of the park. These pods can grow up to a metre in length and are used to ferment beer. And everywhere, set back from the river, are the landmark Baobabs (*Adansonia digitata*) – not only the old, somewhat grotesque ancients, but also groves of young, growing healthily in stands. Many of the older Baobabs are devoid of bark for about five metres up their trunks thanks to the destructive chewing habits of elephants.

Commonly known as Ana Tree, Winter Thorn or Apple-ring tree, the *Faidherbia albida* are more impressive than usual because it is March and their leaves have fallen;

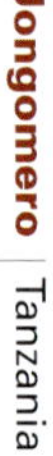

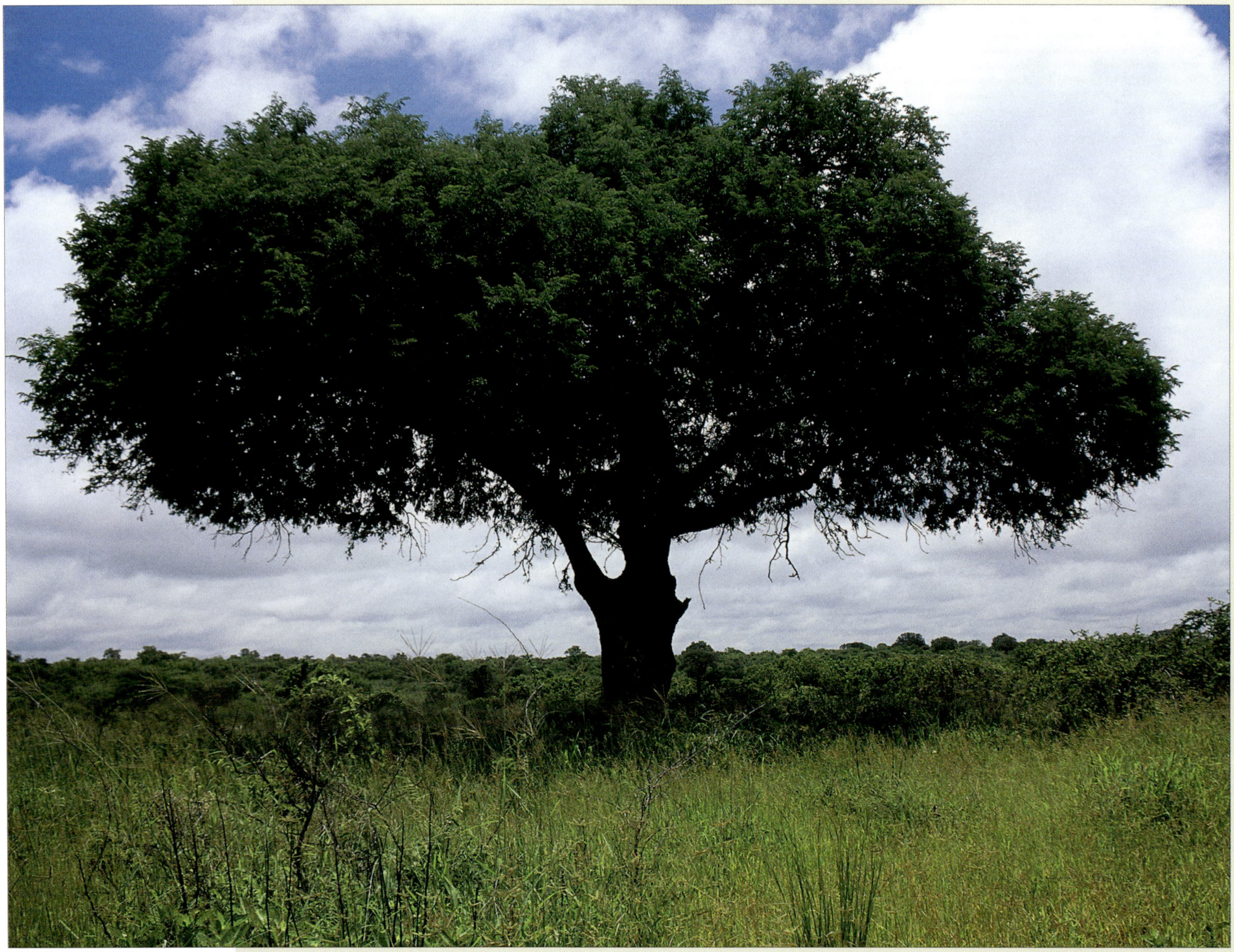

a contrast of grey against their green neighbours. These trees provide deep shade close to the river at the hottest time of the year and their roots bind the riverbanks, reducing erosion. Elephant are attracted to the Ana Tree, causing destruction, which has led to the shrinking of the groves. Its dense rounded crown, sometimes reaching 30 metres in height, makes it one of the dominant trees of the Jongomero area.

The Jongomero River usually flows into the Great Ruaha River, but it was almost dry at midday on our arrival at the camp. However, following a downpour during the afternoon, all the sandbanks were soon flooded. The views from the camp that evening were more spectacular than ever, with the river a raging torrent.

Very little has changed in the past ten years, which makes this reserve a gem in the southern Tanzanian circuit. It is an area to which one wants to return in different seasons, to see the effect of the rains and climate on the pods, seeds, fruits and flowers.

We left by bus from Iringa en route to Dar es Salaam, during which time we got to know Tanzania from the perspectives of our fellow travellers. It was an experience, not a journey, and one not to be missed.

FOLLOWING PAGES: Sausage Tree (*Kigelia africana*). The extravagant crimson flowers have a pungent scent and are pollinated by fruit bats. They are rich in nectar and visited by sunbirds during the day. Baboons feed upon the extraordinary fruits from which the tree takes its name. Leopard often rest during the hot daylight hours on the tree's broad-spreading branches.

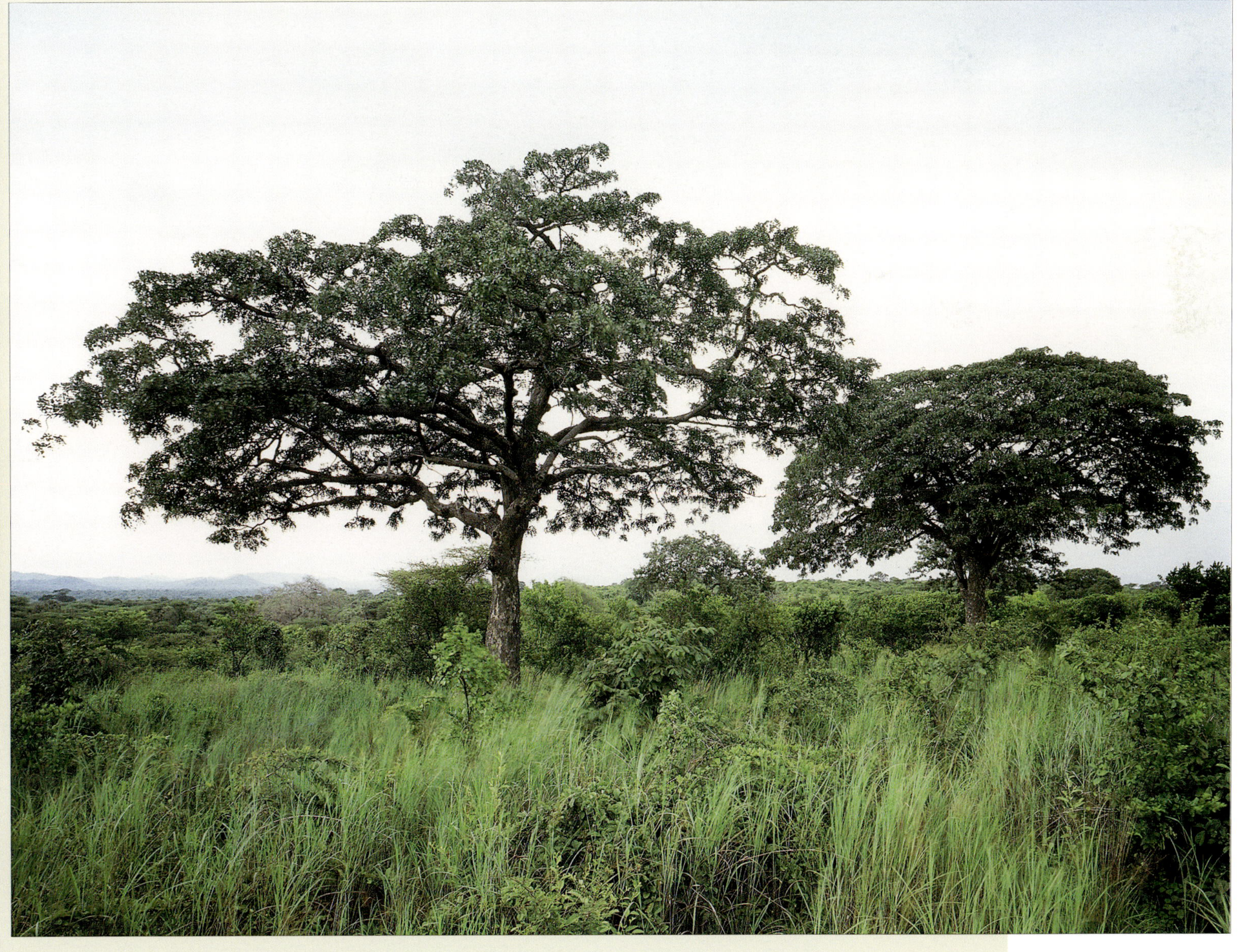

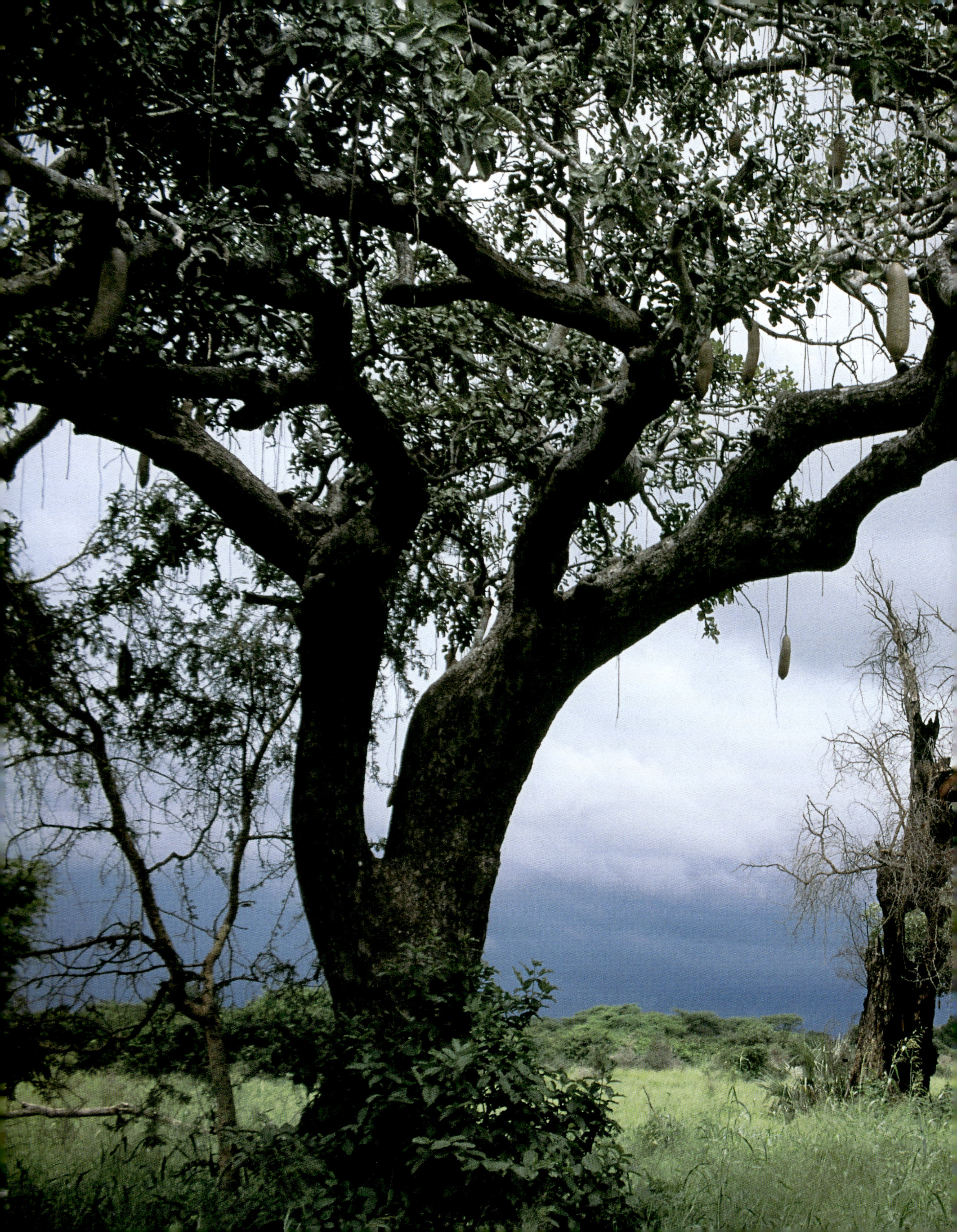

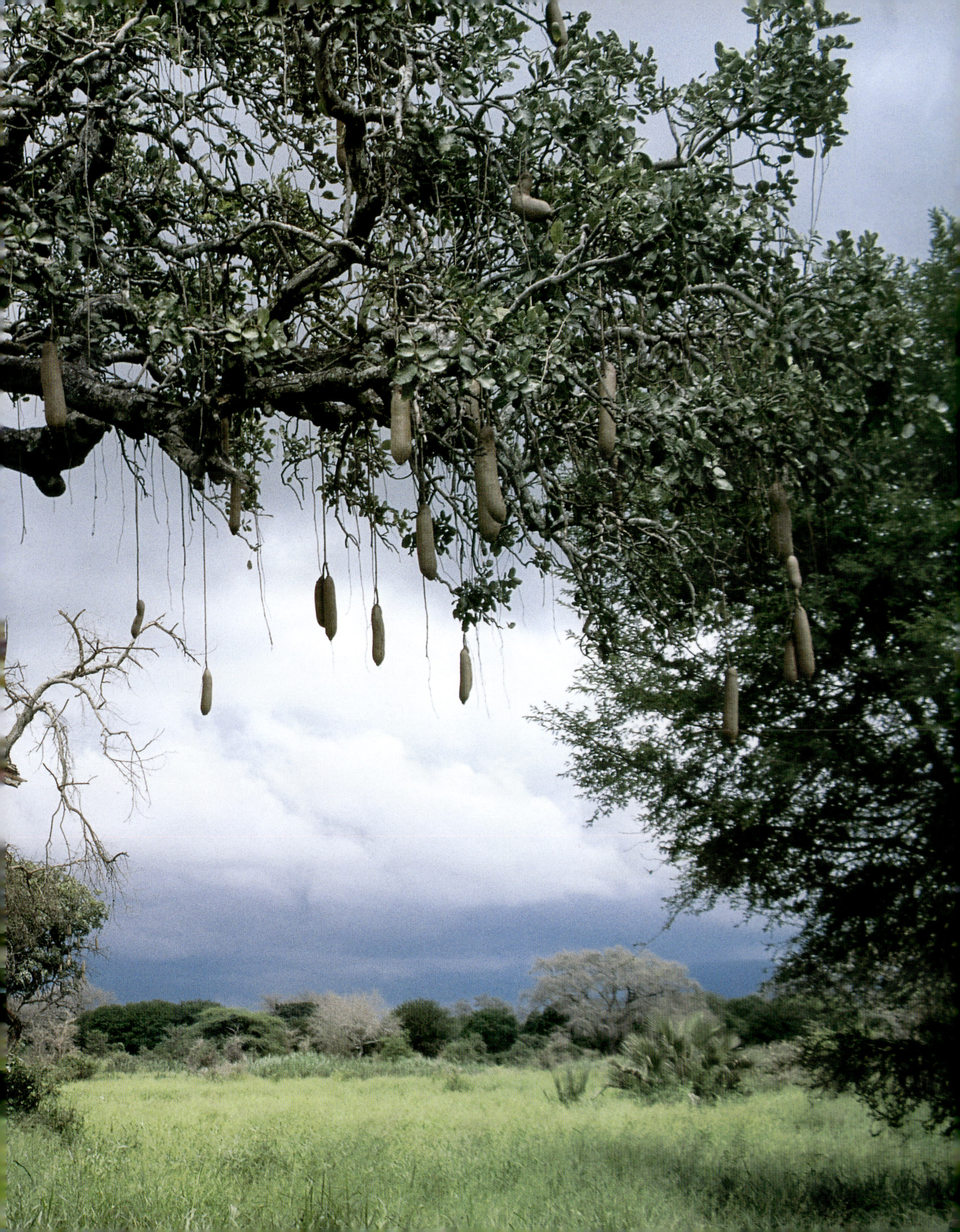

BELOW: Commiphora trees with their
luminous, flaky, peeling bark.

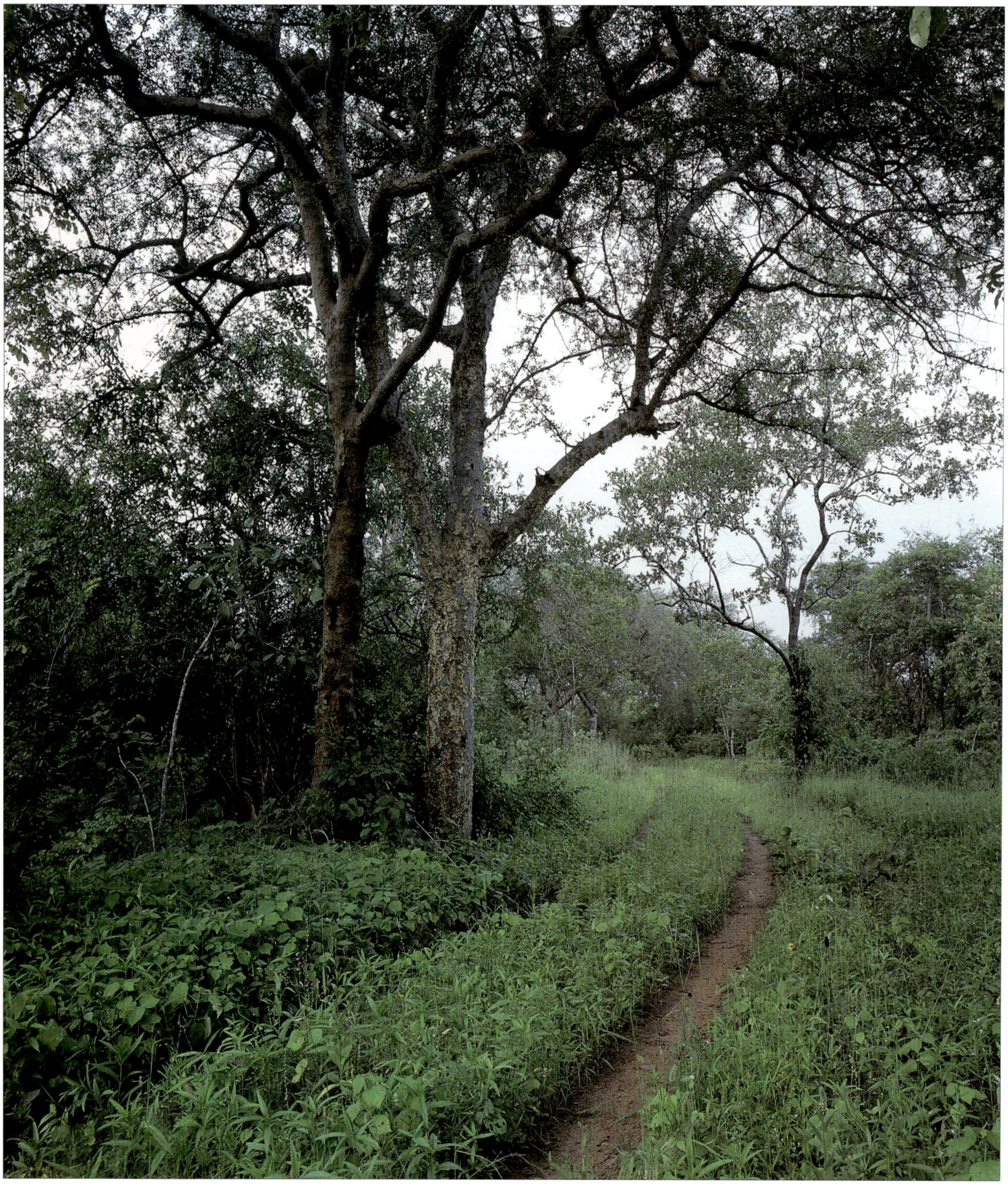

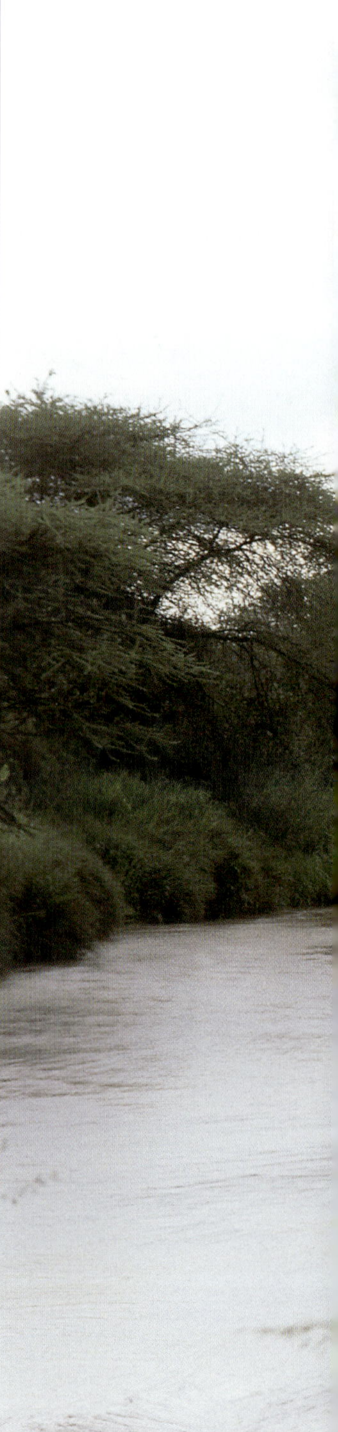

BELOW: A usually dry meandering Jongomero
River shortly after a midday downpour.

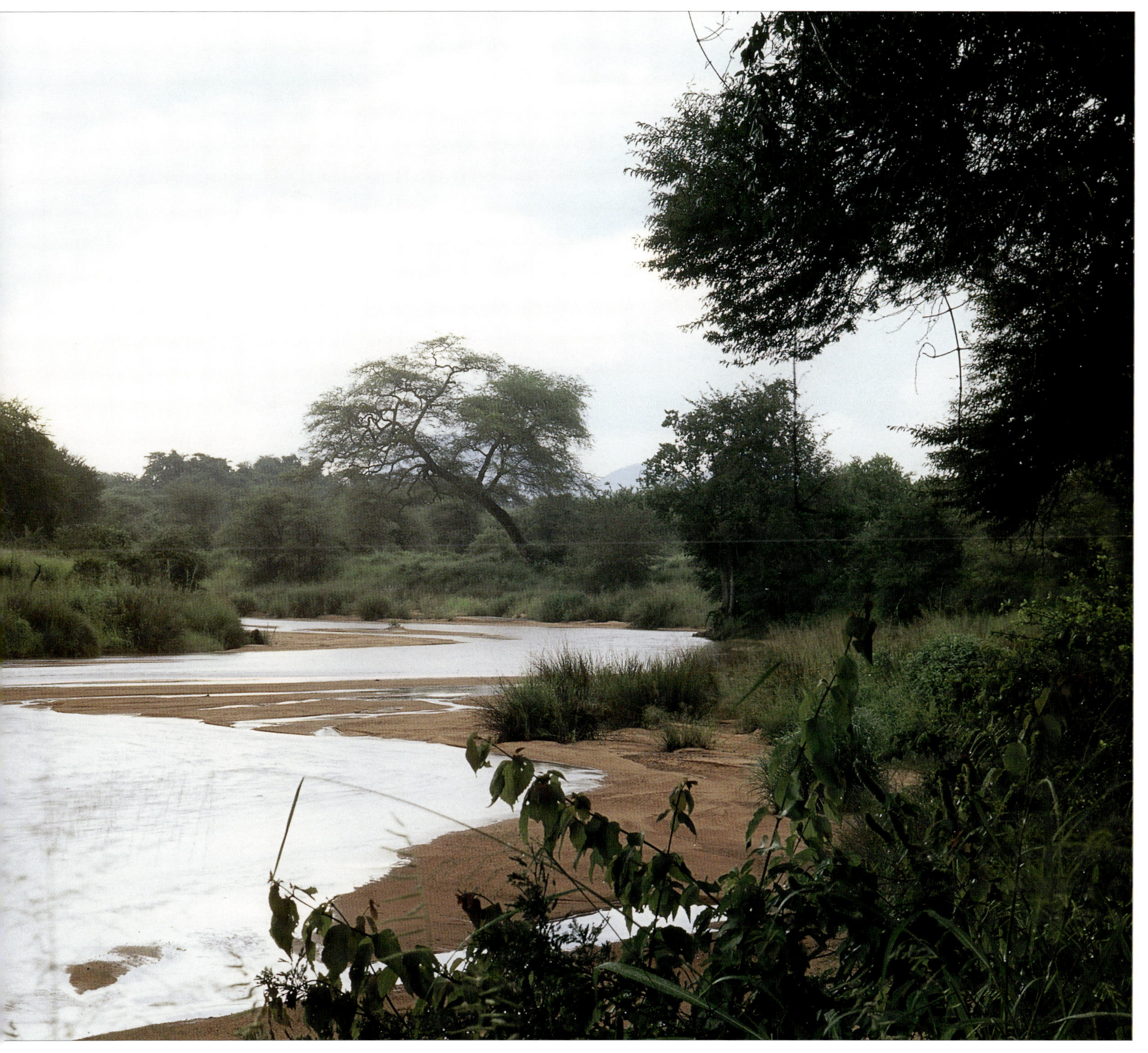

Ras Kutani
Tanzania

After the ferry crossing at Dar es Salaam, the tar road gives way to dirt heading south along the coast. Urban Dar es Salaam thins out dramatically over a short trip of 30 kilometres. At night, the road is a flicker of candlelight and cooking fires as we pass roadside stalls and occasional bars and restaurants. By the time we arrived at Ras Kutani we felt we were in darkest Africa. The 'Ras' of Ras Kutani refers to a bay and we immediately felt and heard the presence of the Indian Ocean. Everything around us, save the lights of the lodge, was as black as the night and we eagerly awaited dawn.

Ras Kutani is situated in one of the few East African coastal forests, although only a small area of closed canopy forest remains. The tiny forest is a tribute to the conservation efforts of the Dobie family who prevented its destruction to meet the charcoal demand of Dar es Salaam. The demand for charcoal started to be felt in the Ras Kutani region in the late 1980s and, today, all the trees on the village land have been felled. Every day, an estimated 1 500 trees are needed to supply Dar es Salaam with charcoal as its primary cooking fuel. Conservation efforts are ongoing, with a forest programme to get villagers thinking about the value of trees and to encourage forest husbandry.

Although the dawn is cloudy, it lightens our surroundings of forest, lagoon, beach and ocean. The forest extends for about three kilometres along the Ngaramia River, which ends in a lagoon. The occasional wind-filled lateen sail of an Arab dhow on the horizon is the only indication of a past filled with pirates, explorers and slave traders. This forest

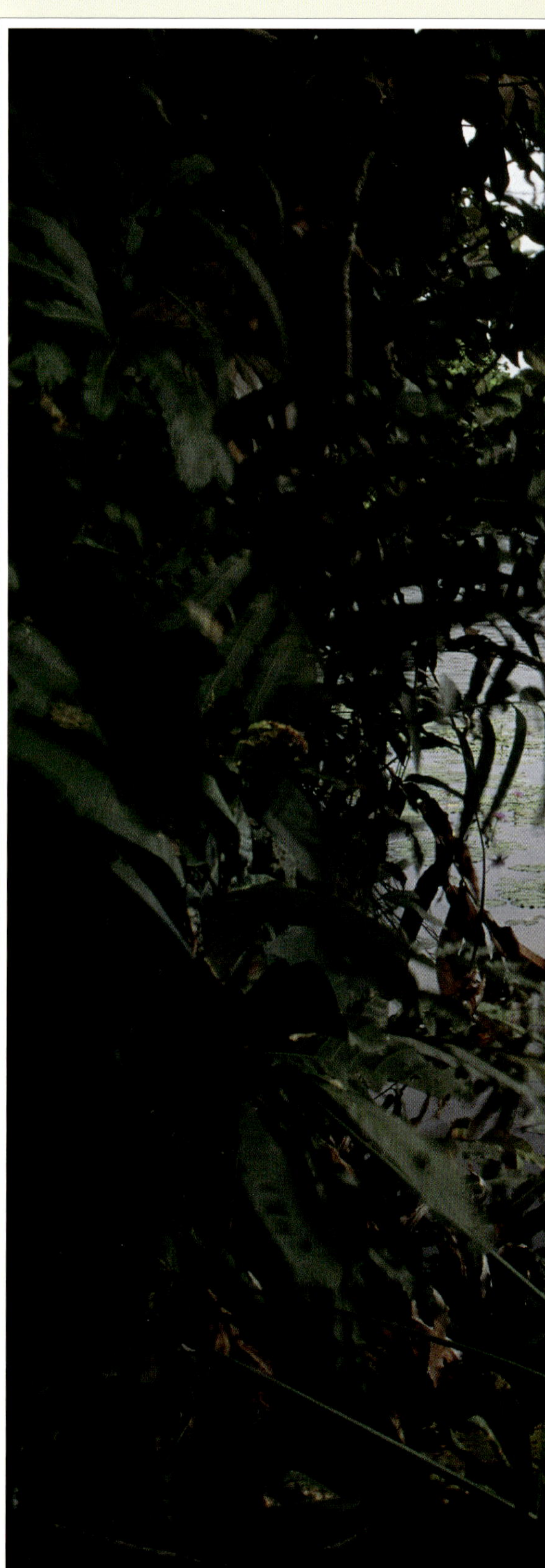

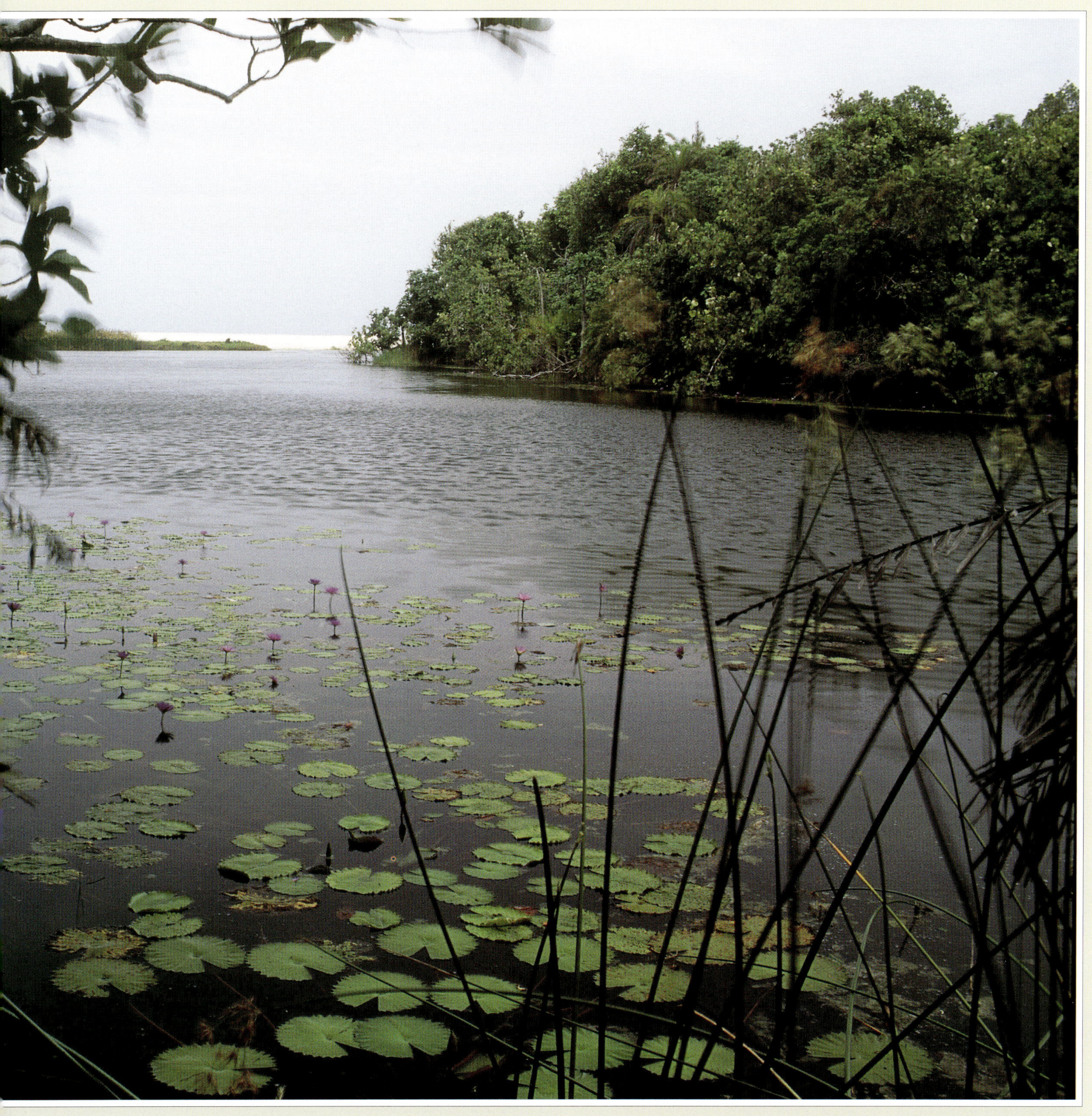

BELOW: Water lilies colour the Ngaramia lagoon, which is framed by the coastal forest and the sea.

has seen it all – the Gum Copal Tree (*Hymenaea verrucosa*), the Pod Mahogany (*Afzelia quanzensis*) and the Waterberry (*Syzygium cordatum*) among its witnesses.

The fringe of the coastal forest bearing the brunt of the onshore winds comprises, as usual, the Wild Date Palm (*Phoenix reclinata*) and the Doum Palm (*Hyphaene compressa*). Their orange-brown nuts shelter close to the trunk as the ever-flexing fronds gyrate to the tune of the wind.

We entered the forest on the north side of the lagoon and began a winding semi-circular route, crossing the river to eventually emerge on the south side of the lagoon and lodge. It is not a forest journey to hurry; its beauty is extreme – and extremely hot.

The cool coastal winds have little effect deeper in the forest. The closed canopy shields everything below and creates a microclimate of its own. The air is thick and

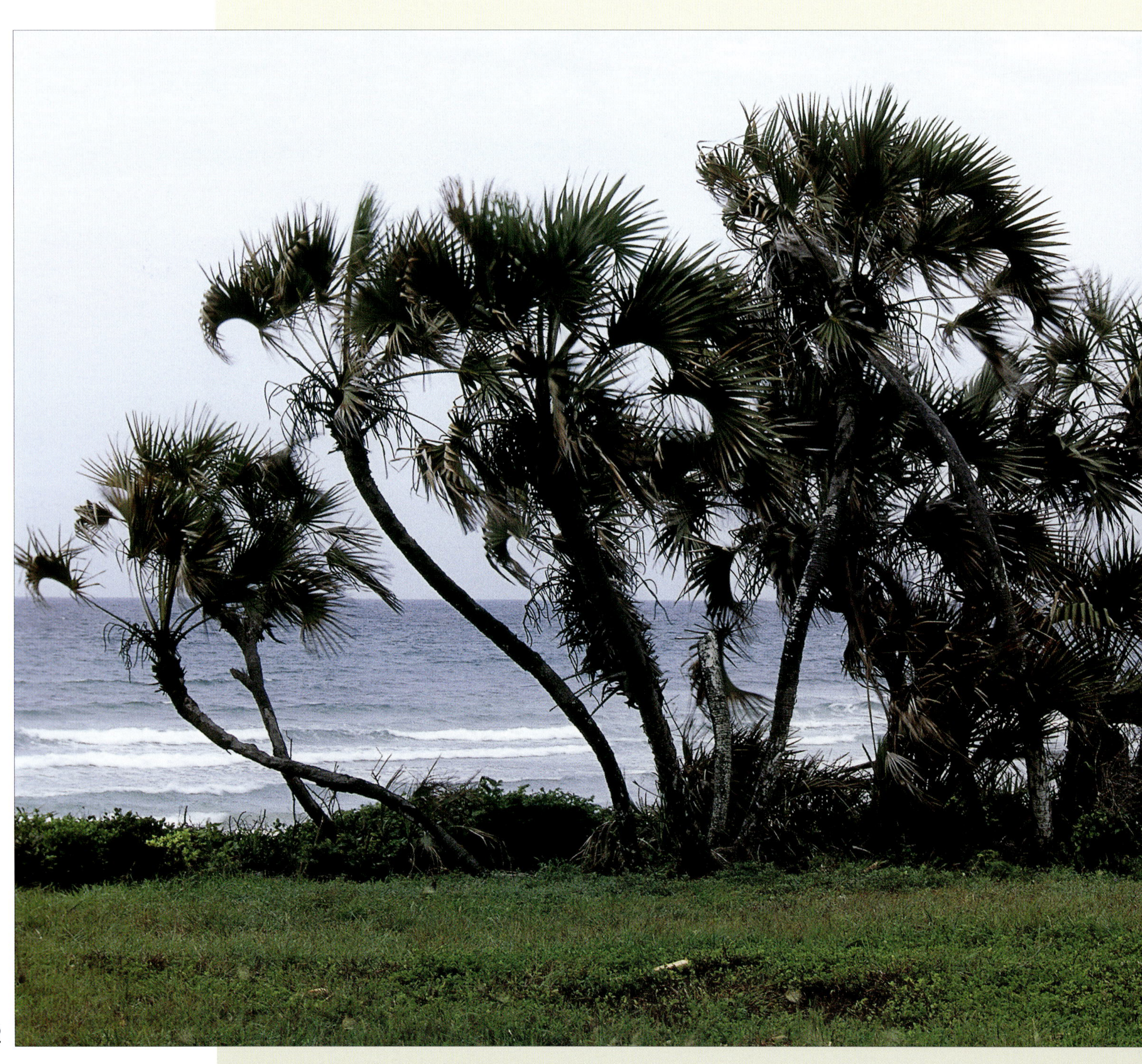

humid inside, protective and all-witnessing. Over 100 different species of tree, all competing for sunlight, share this climate with Angolan colobus, blue and vervet monkeys, as well as numerous shy forest bird species. The path and boardwalk undulate from riverbed to ridges close to canopy height. Among the beauty one realises the only threats to this forest are fire and human.

As we rehydrated in the coolness of the lodge, we watched a clawless otter breaching the sandbank from the ocean to the lagoon and pondered how easily this forest could have been lost to charcoal. Our return trip to Dar es Salaam took place in the early morning, when it was light enough to see the road that was previously shrouded in darkness. We passed the odd bicycle, each one heavily laden with a huge bag of charcoal.

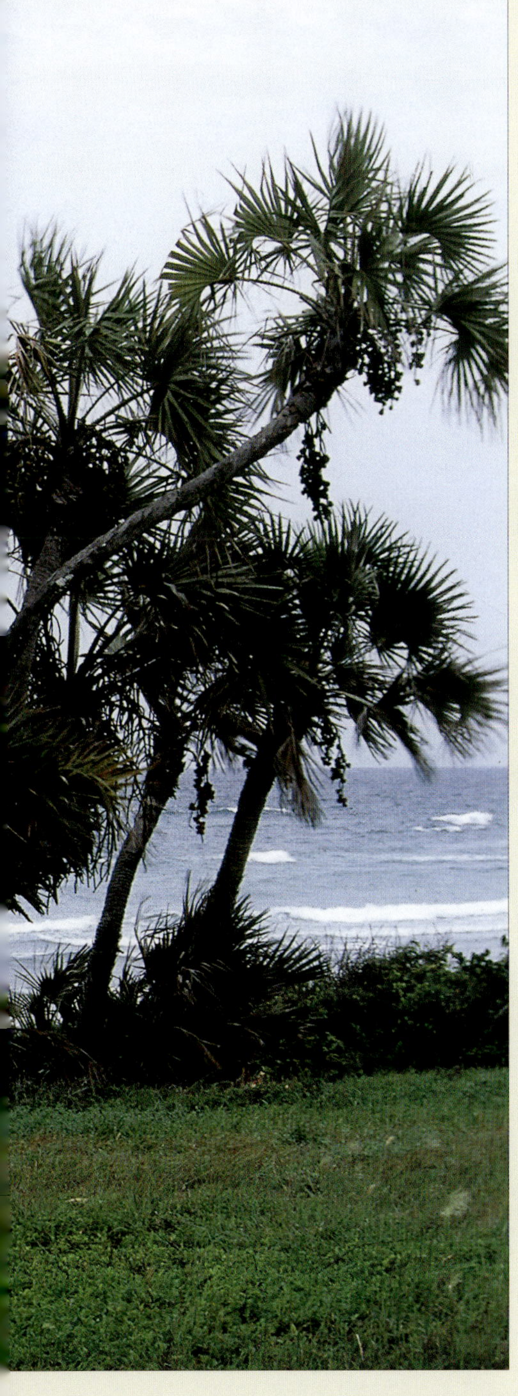

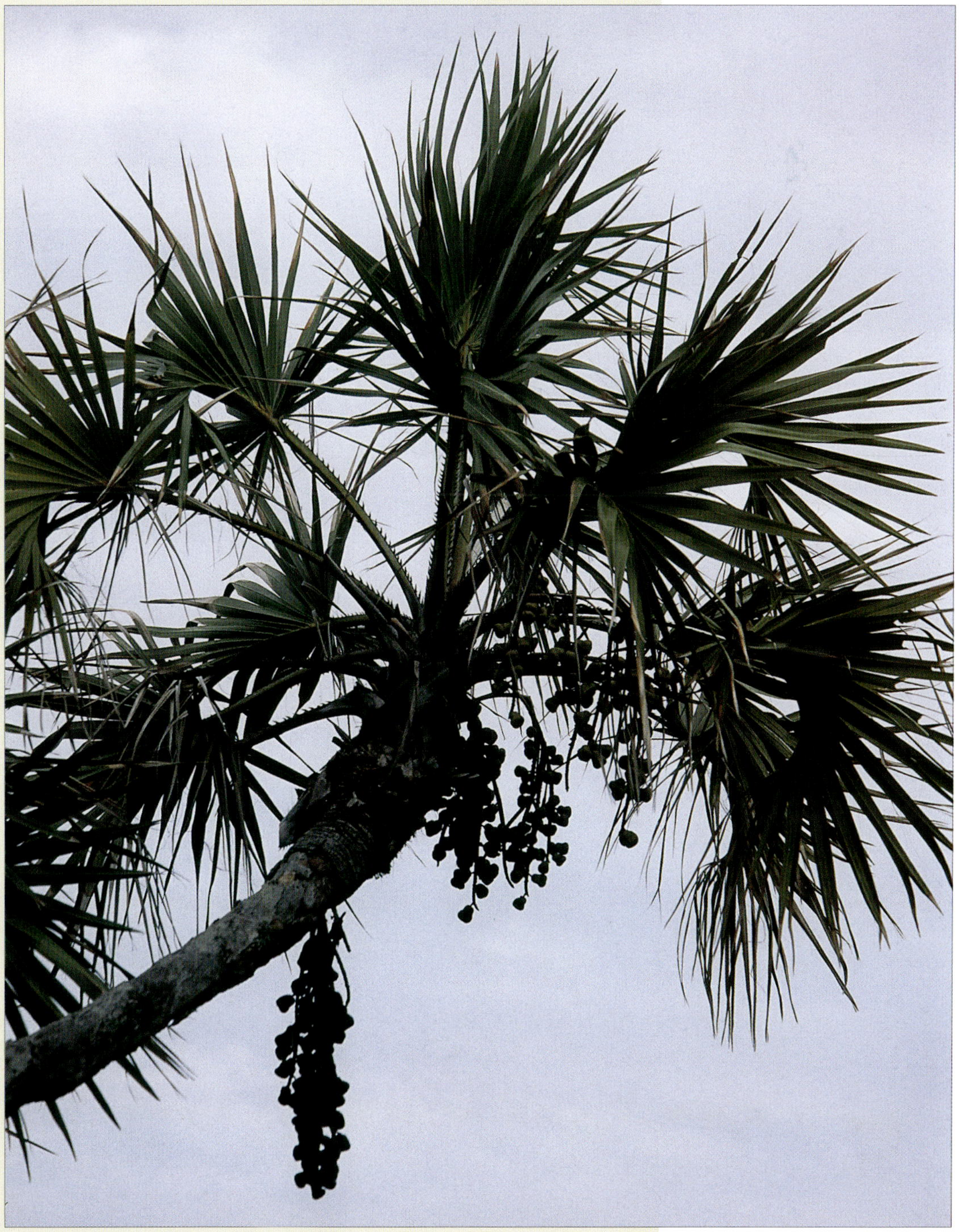

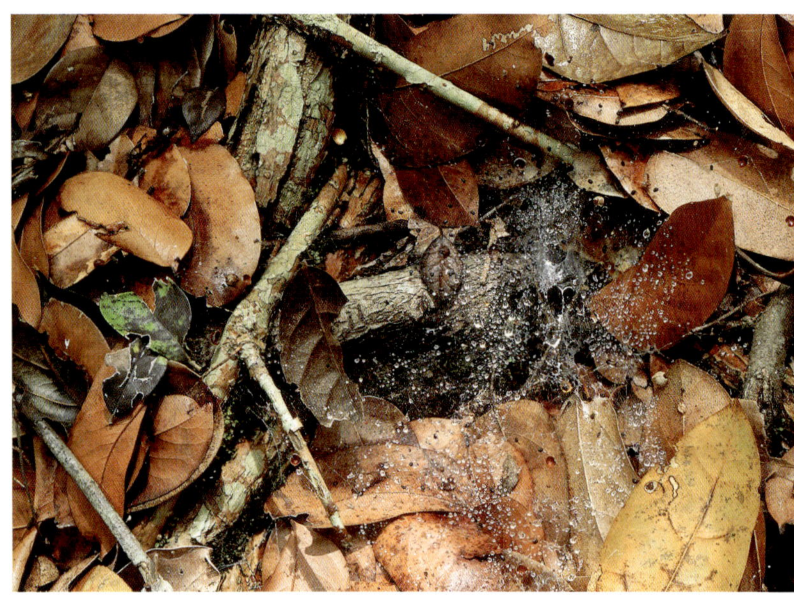

ABOVE: A moisture-laden
spider's web creates a platform
above the leafy floor.

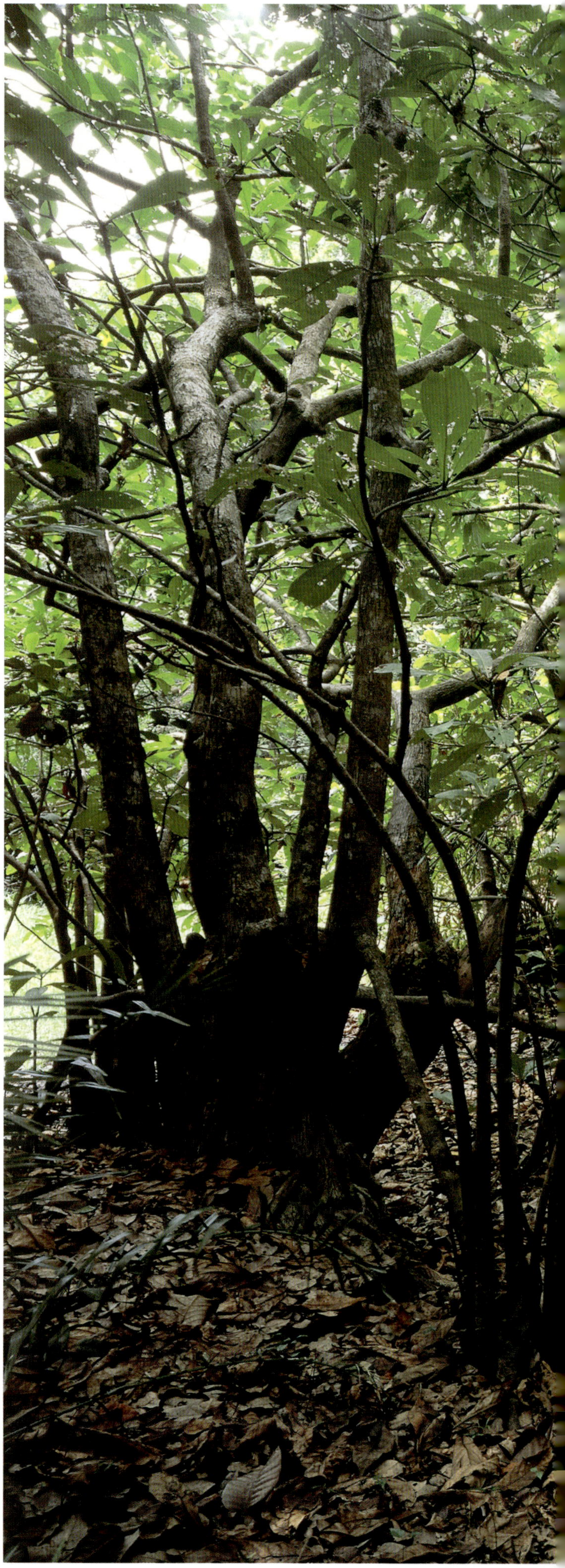

RIGHT: Groves of shiny-leaved Powder-puff
Trees (*Barringtonia racemosa*) crowd the
water's edge along the Ngaramia River.
Their stilt roots bear a superficial
resemblance to those of mangrove trees,
but, unlike the estuarine mangroves,
Powder-puff Trees thrive only in fresh
water. The tree's common name comes from
the clusters of showy white blossoms that
appear from November to March.

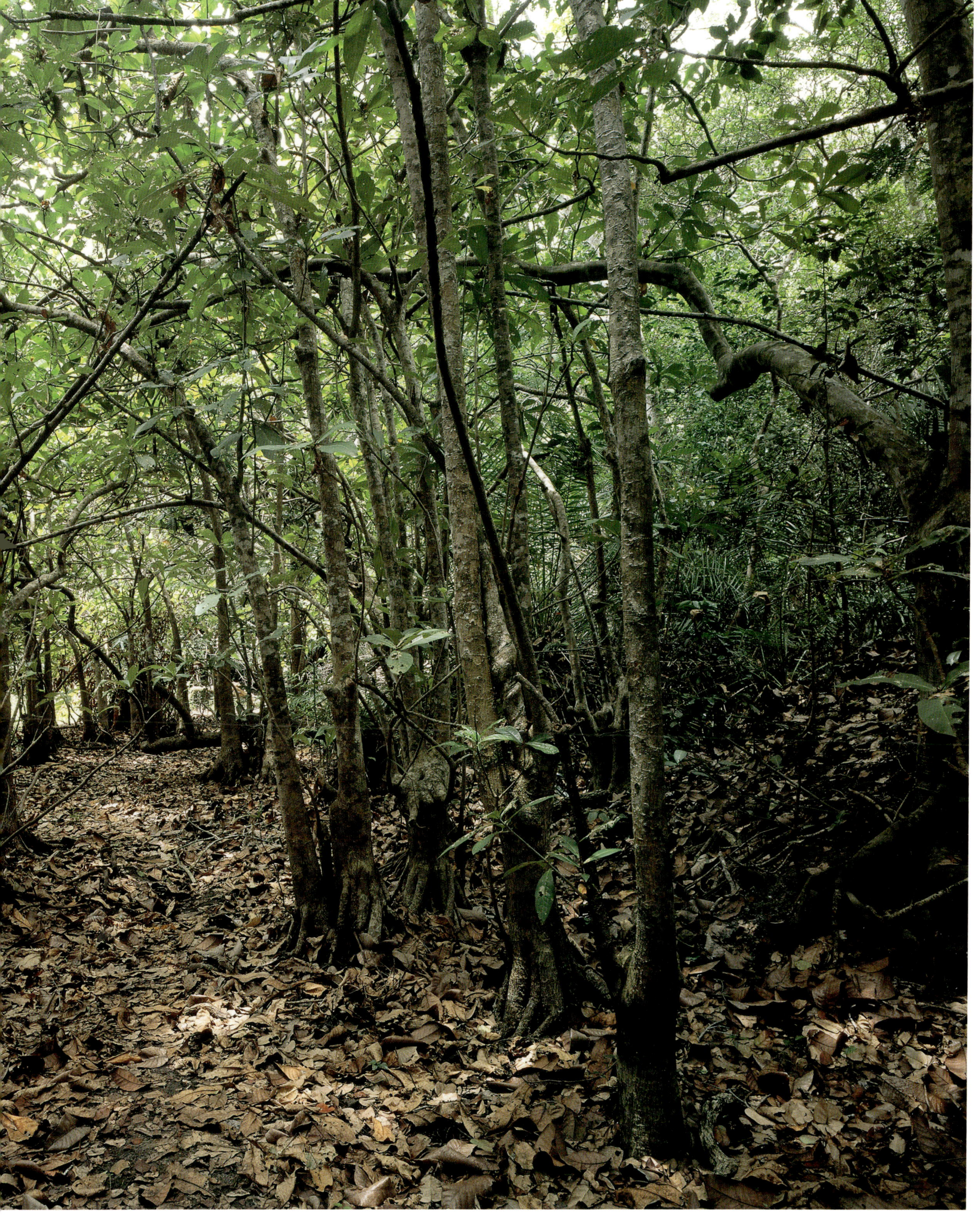

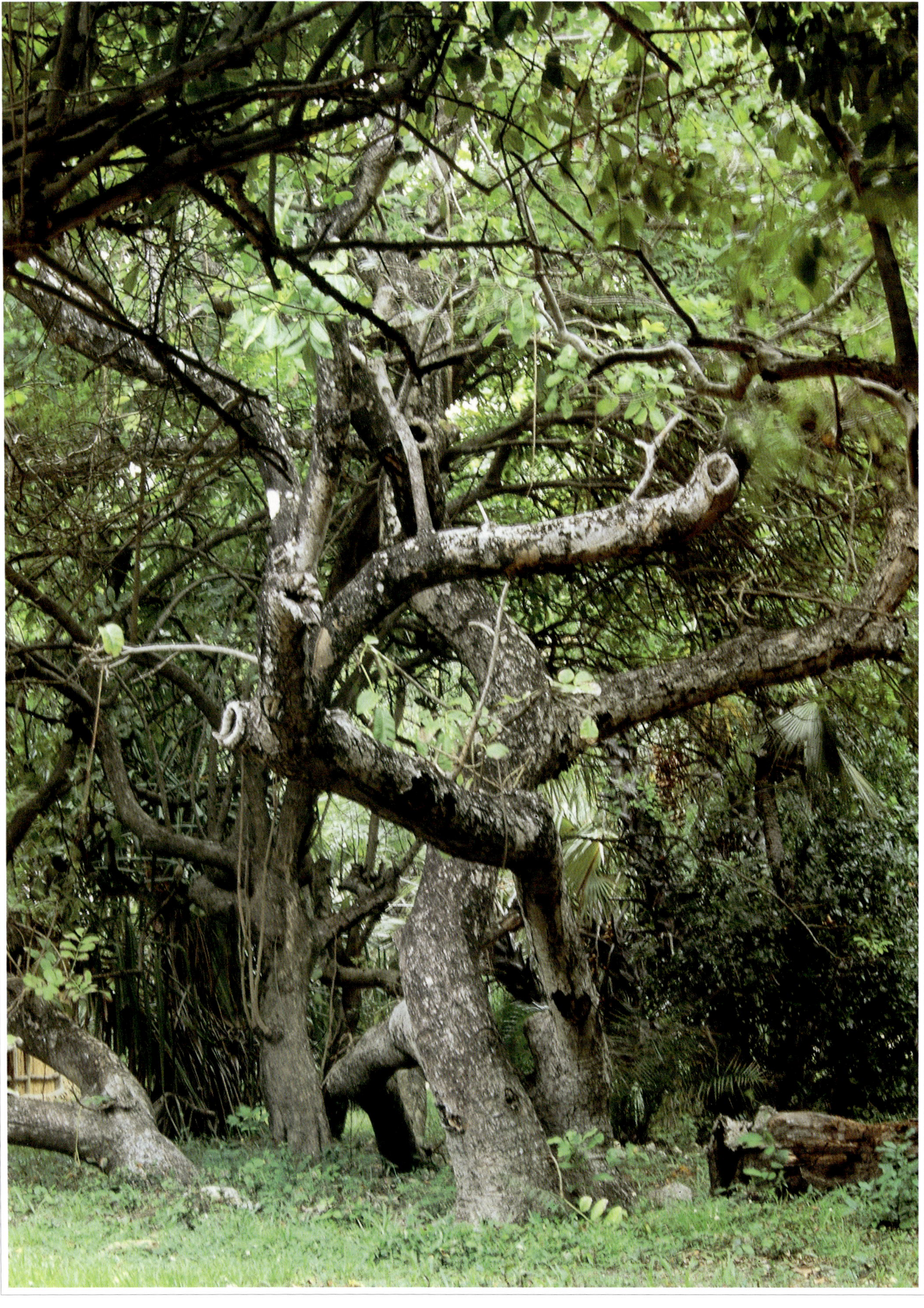

Ras Kutani Tanzania

BELOW: Doum Palm (*Hyphaene compressa*). Ancient Egyptians considered the Doum Palm sacred, and seeds from the doum nuts have been found in pharaohs' tombs. Also known as the Gingerbread Palm, it has red-orange, apple-sized fruit that tastes like gingerbread. The fruit's hard white nut is used to make buttons; nut rind is used to make a spice; and ground nuts are used to dress wounds. The palm's leaves are used to make mats and writing paper, and to bind parcels.

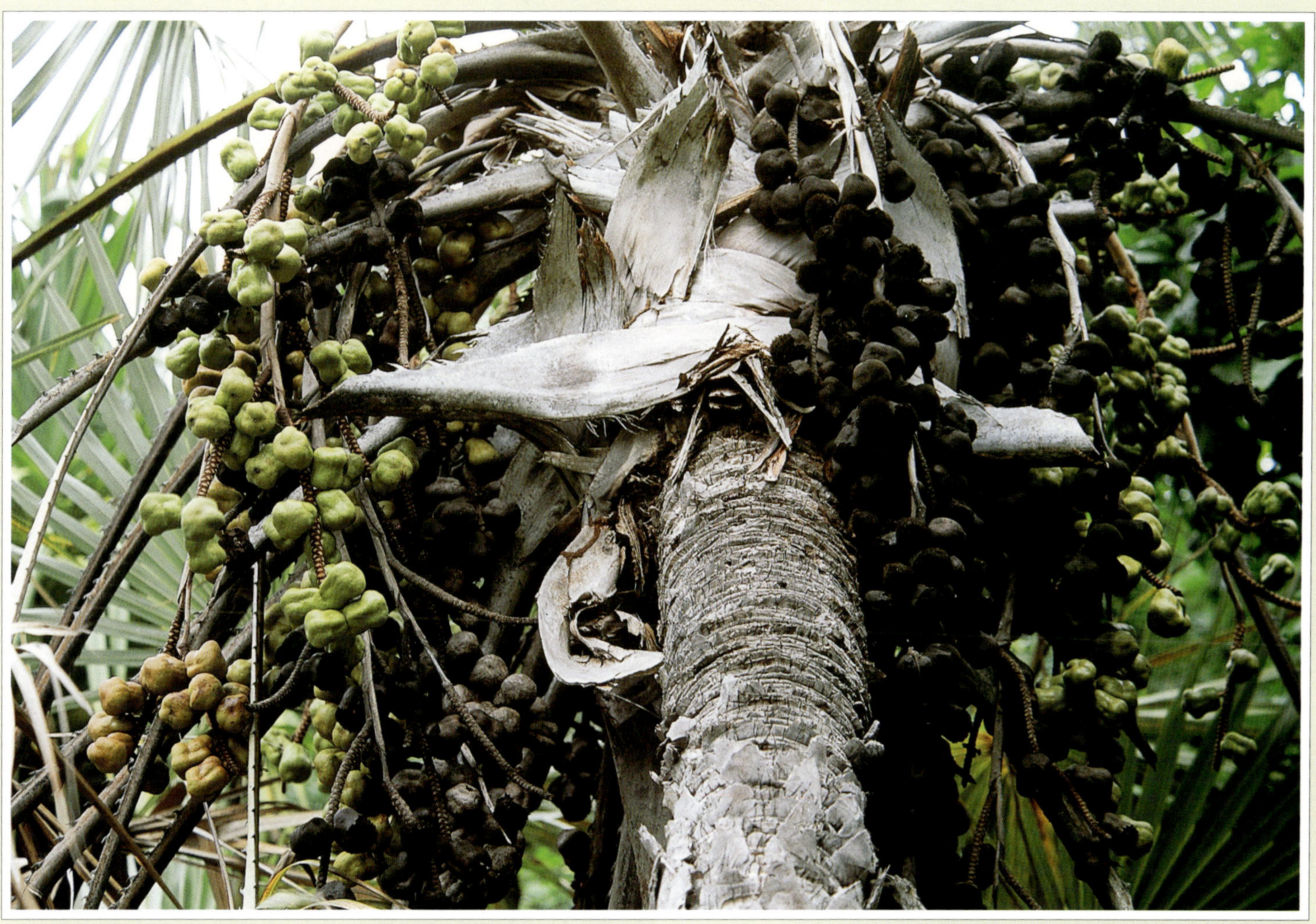

Ras Kutani Tanzania

Selous Safari Camp
Selous Game Reserve Tanzania

Selous. The word alone conjures up visions of adventure, inaccessibility and pristine East African wilderness. To be there, on the banks of the mighty Rufiji River, is proof indeed. The Selous Game Reserve, with its proximity to the coast and its low altitude, makes for a wildly different African bushveld experience. The heat at midday is so tremendous that even the reflections of Borassus Palms (*Borassus aethiopum*) rise off the muddy river like steam off a hot iron.

Selous is verdant in March, just before the second rains of the season. Soon all the safari camps will close for two months as life is restored in the compacted black cotton soil. As tyre ruts get deeper, even the tracks carved around old roads become too waterlogged to use. We were just about the last visitors to stay in the tented camp which would soon be left to the magnificent sound of riverine birds, the wood owl and buffalo in long grass.

Every reserve has its flat-topped speciality and here, as we approached the open woodland area of the camp, the Flat-crown Cluster-leaf

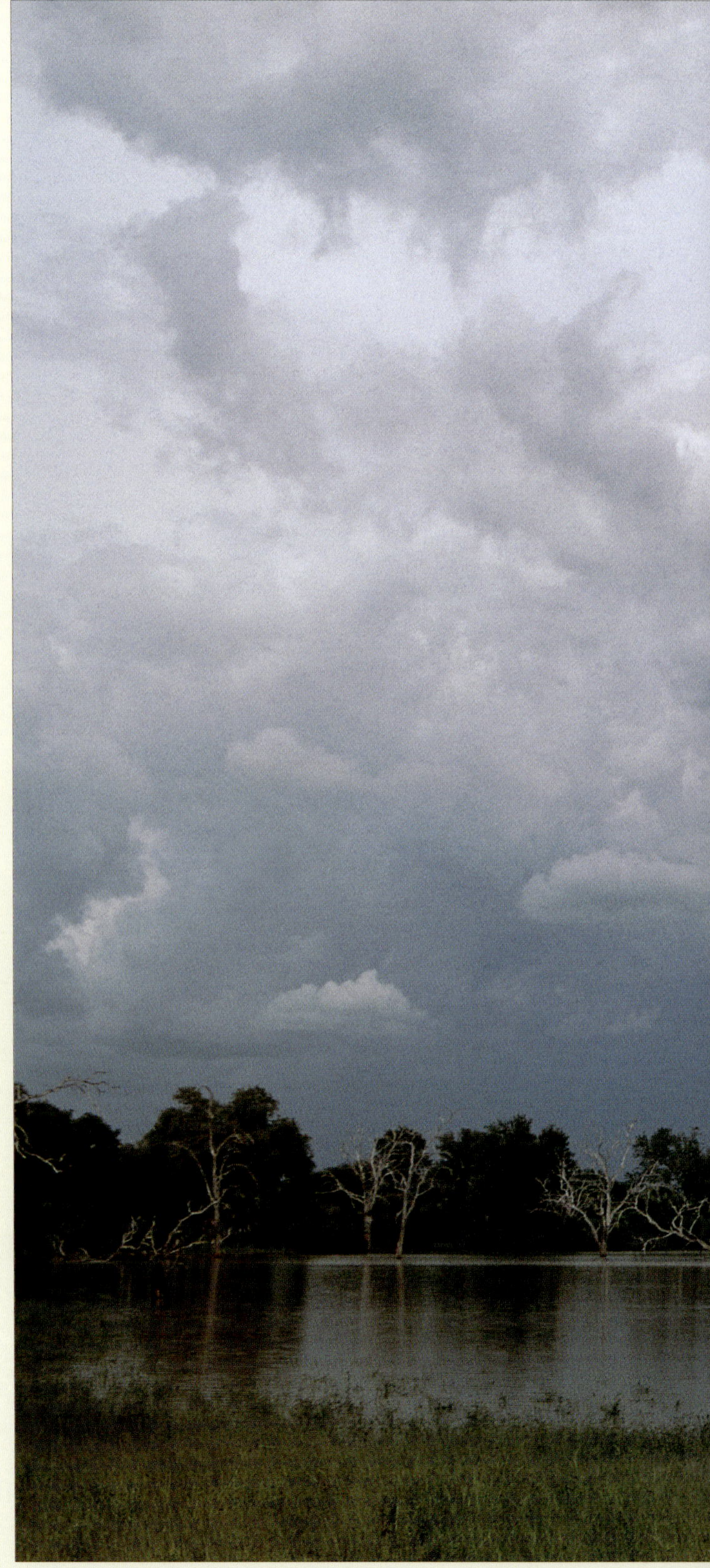

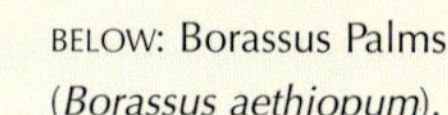

BELOW: Borassus Palms
(*Borassus aethiopum*).

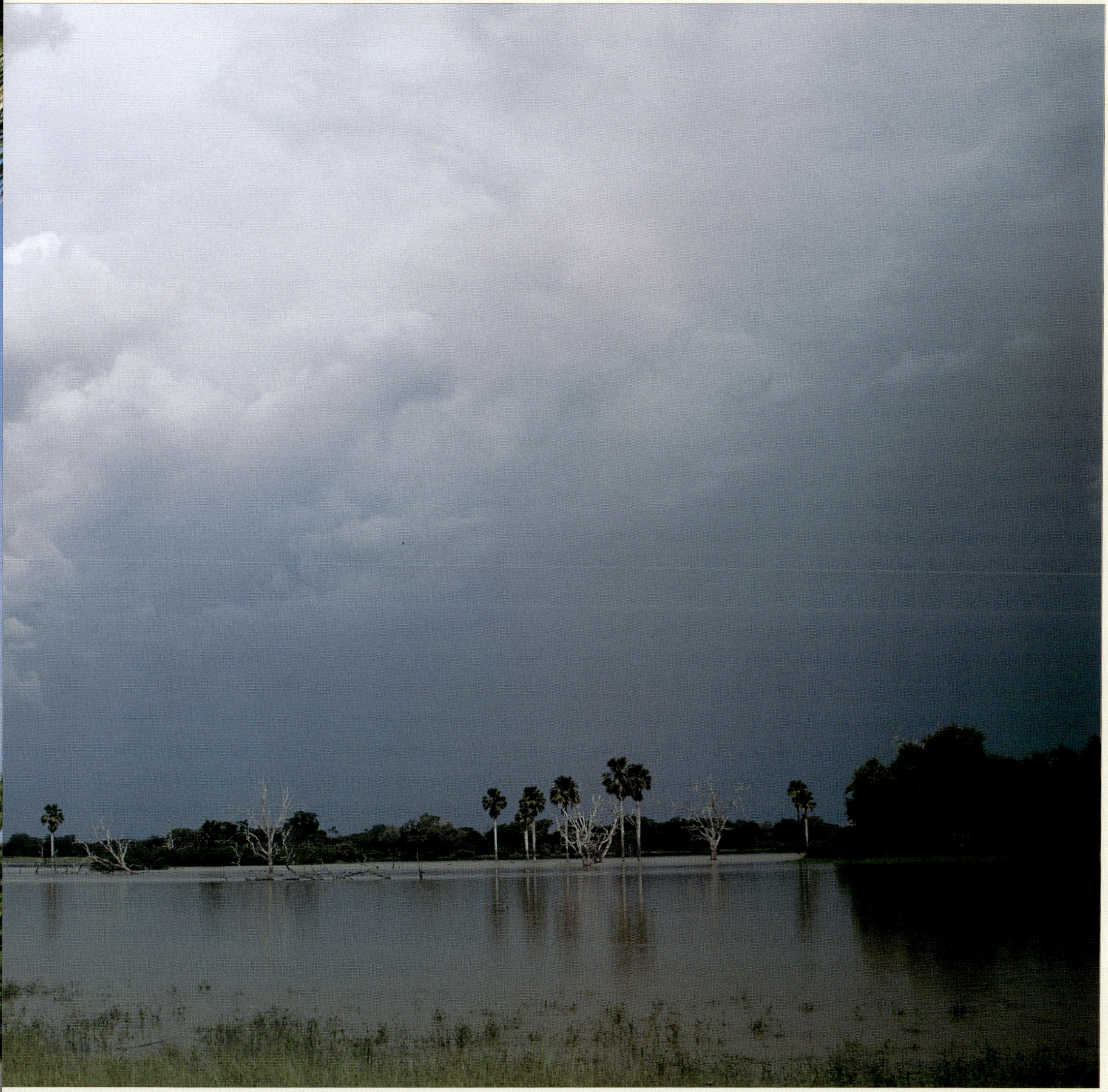

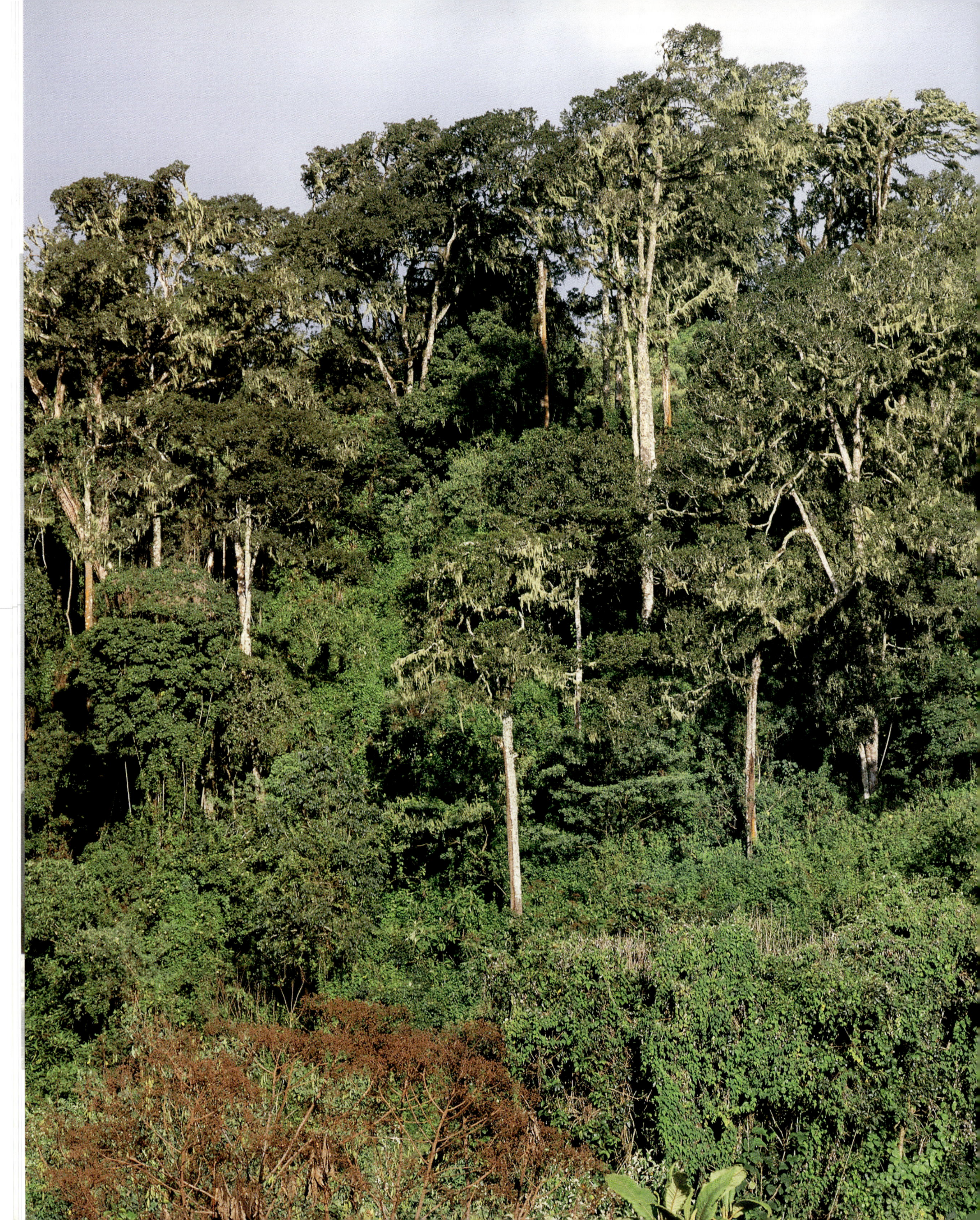

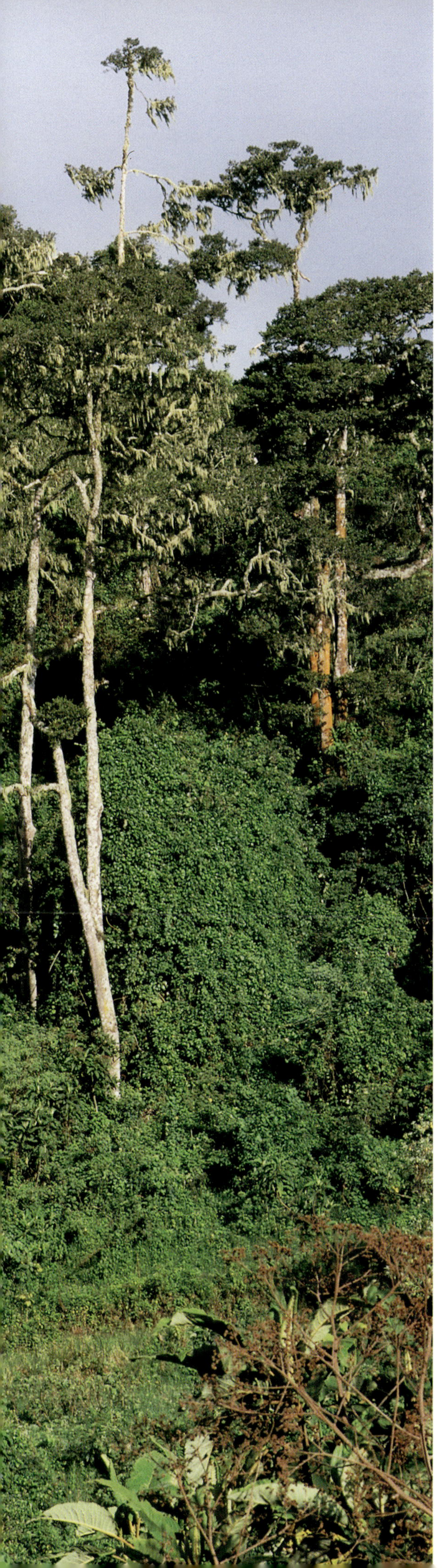

RIFTING LANDSCAPES

The Great Rift Valley is a 6 500 kilometre fissure in the Earth's crust, stretching from Lebanon in the north to the mouth of the Zambezi River in the south. Local people are quick to tell you that it is one of the few geological features that can be seen from the Moon. Lake Manyara and the Ngorongoro Crater are two of the wonders set in the Rift Valley. Separated by a magnificent escarpment and swirling mists near the rim of the crater, they are surprisingly close together, yet very different in character. The unpredictable future of the changing Rift Valley adds a special dimension to appreciating its diverse flora.

LEFT: Pillarwood (*Cassipourea malosana*). With its straight trunk, this spectacular tree stands tall among other giants of the cloud forest on Ngorongoro Crater's moist eastern slopes. It is a valuable timber tree and few sizeable specimens survive outside protected areas. Its alternative English name 'Onionwood' alludes to the distinct smell of the cut wood. Pigeons and turacos eat the small fruits.

Ngorongoro Crater Lodge
Tanzania

Along the well-used road from Manyara National Park, leading to the Ngorongoro Crater, then deep into the Serengeti, everything takes on the colour of the soil. Acacias, round huts, makeshift shopfronts with painted logos, and even goats and cows are caked in red ochre. This is the colour of the Maasai and the fertile farmlands that are the livelihood of rural Tanzanians living scattered amidst rolling hills and ploughed fields.

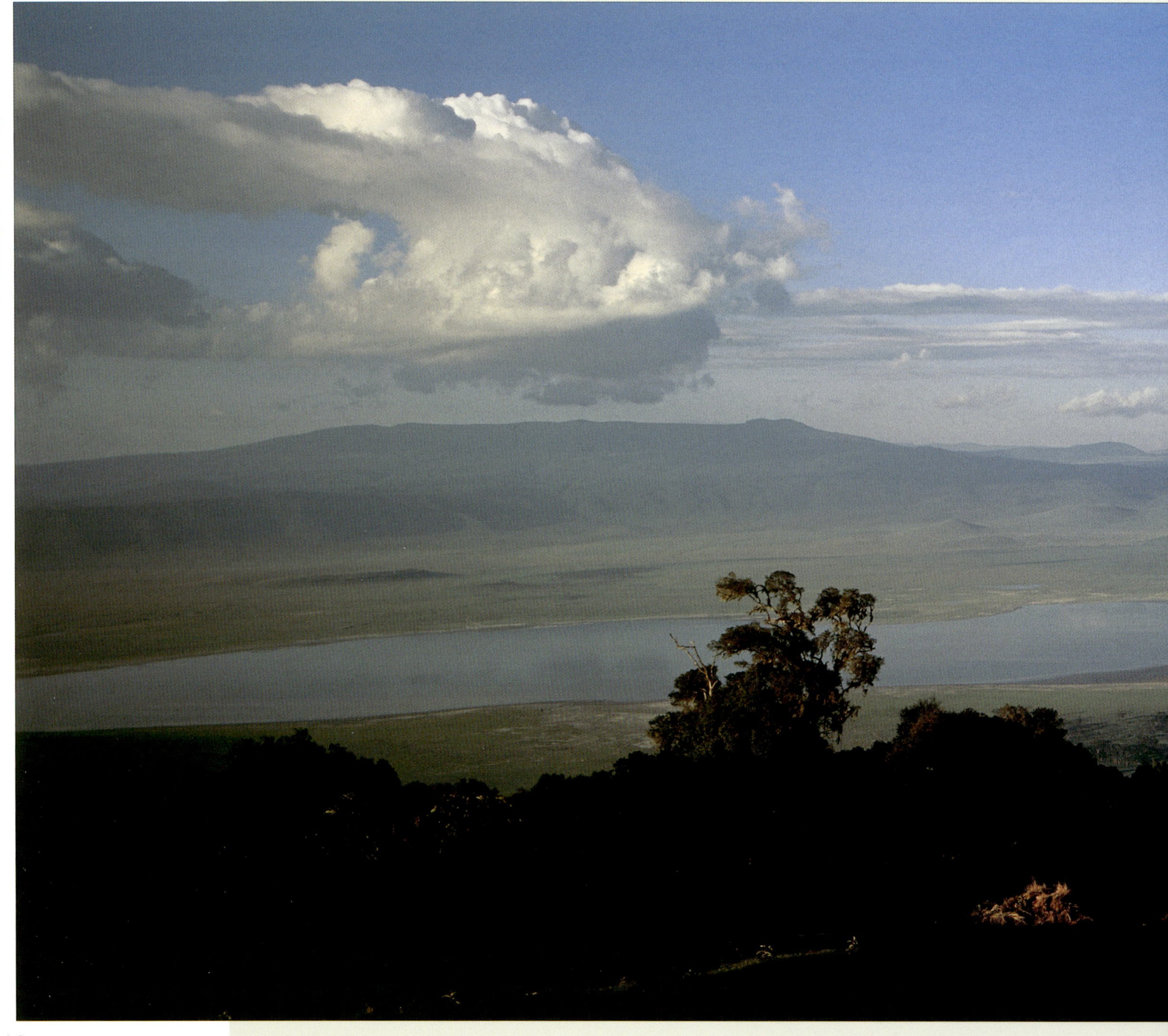

The hot burnt orange of the tilled and deforested earth ends abruptly, just short of the gate to Ngorongoro Conservation Area. It is replaced by a dense green tapestry of cool leaves and matted lichen hanging off soaring highland forest trees on the south-western outer rim of the crater. This impenetrable montane forest, which has remained intact for thousands of years, is a part of eternity. It represents solitude, timelessness and abundance.

Regular rain and a shroud of mist enhance the growth of Pillarwoods (*Cassipourea malosana*) with beautiful epiphytes. Forest Nuxia (*Nuxia floribunda*), with their fluted and often gnarled trunks, are the dominant trees in the forest, reaching towering heights, escaping the rampant creepers and characteristic old man's beard hanging off

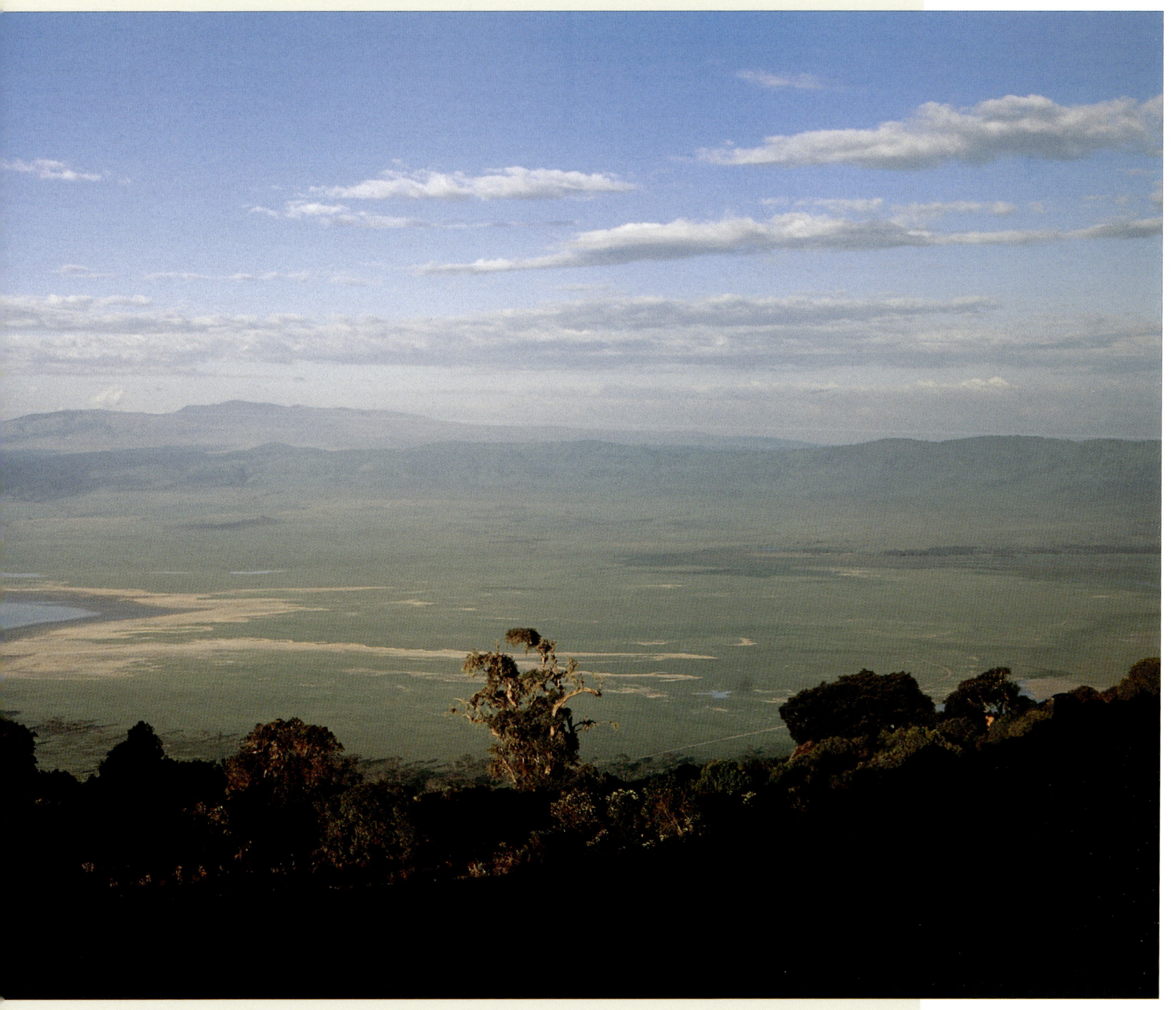

BELOW: The collapsed cone of the volcano forms the caldera with its flat base.

lower branches. The air is crisp and we breathe again after weeks in the low-lying clammy south. Even in midsummer, swirling mists keep the climate on the crater rim cool.

A visit to the largest unbroken and unflooded caldera in the world is a prerequisite for every traveller to Tanzania. The self-contained flatland scooped out of the remaining mountain has an almost ghostly appearance. Around three million years ago, in its place stood a volcanic mountain possibly higher than Mount Kilimanjaro. The soda lake, called the Magadi, mirrors the clouds that move across the sky while teeny dots of teeming animals, protected by their natural environment, graze in total silence.

The cluster of Fever Trees (*Acacia xanthoploea*) on the crater floor, named the Lerai forest by the Maasai, was our first planned photo point. As the sun rose, low warm rays reached randomly thickened trunks, turning them a glowing buttery yellow. These acacias grow dense bark around their trunks as protection against elephant. The forest depends on groundwater, which springs from the crater wall, but it is said to be very slowly moving from its present location, between Lake Magadi and the ascent road.

The smooth, flat crater floor is almost entirely grassland. There is little shelter for animals apart from the small Fever Tree forest and the vegetation along riverine streams,

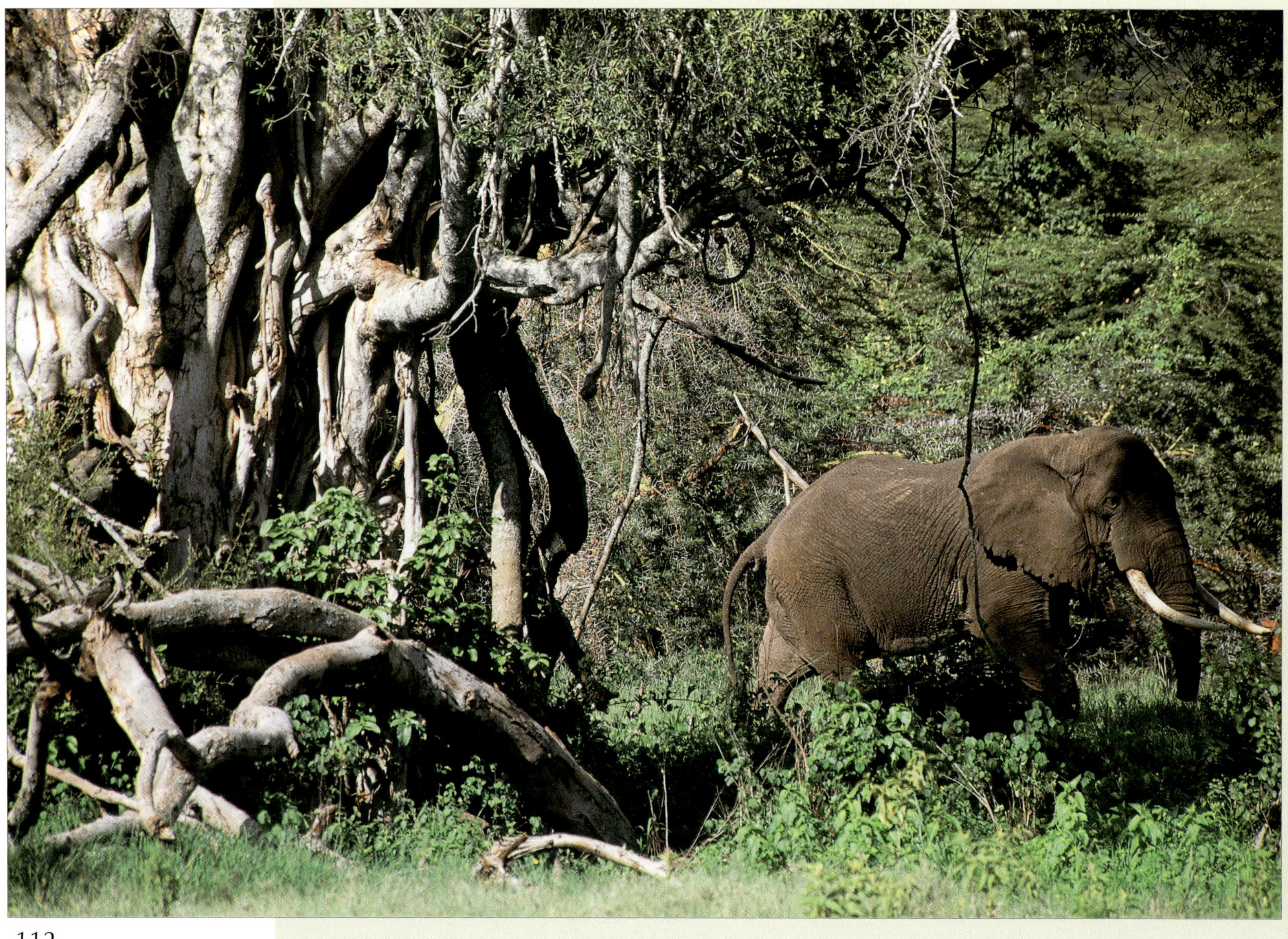

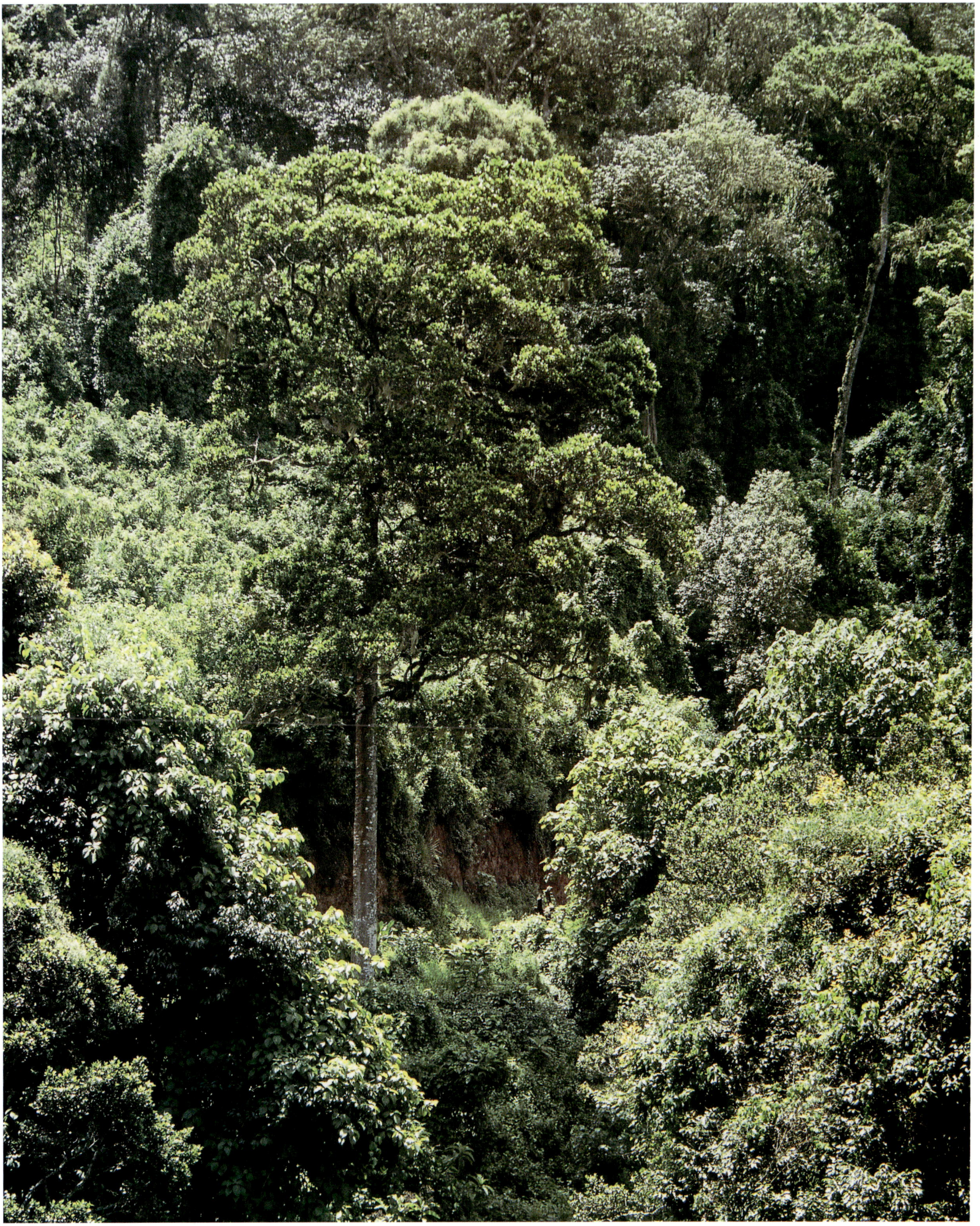

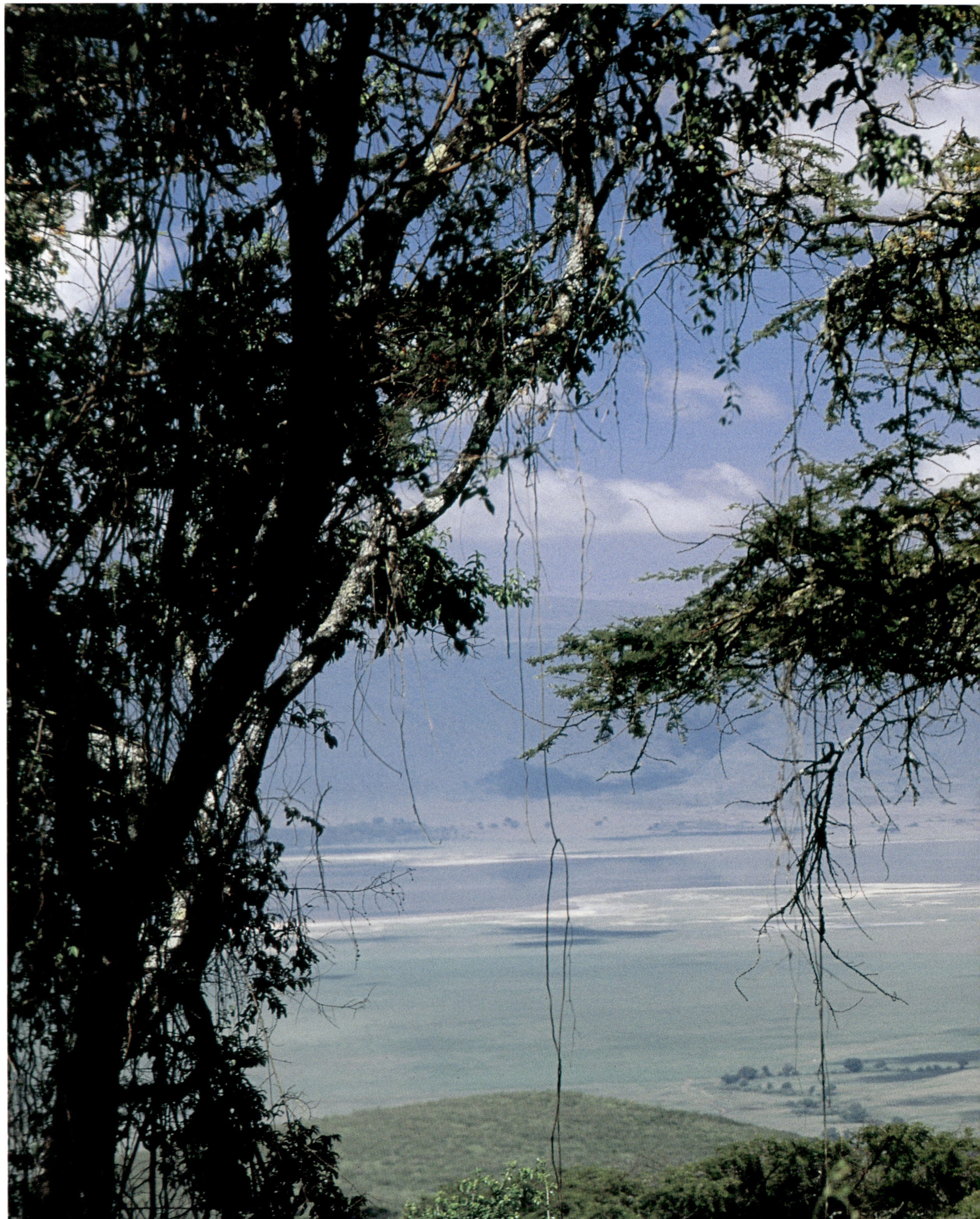

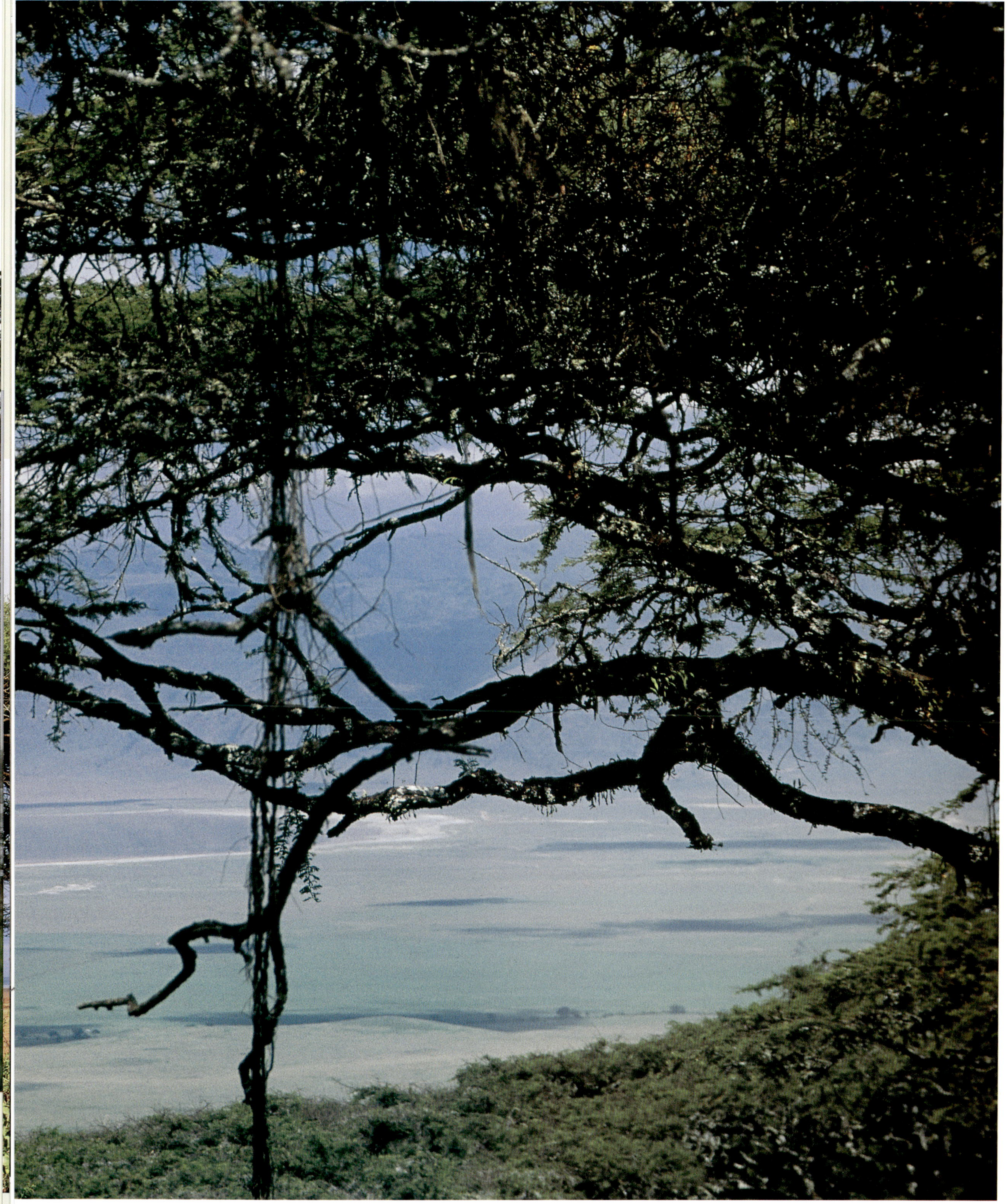

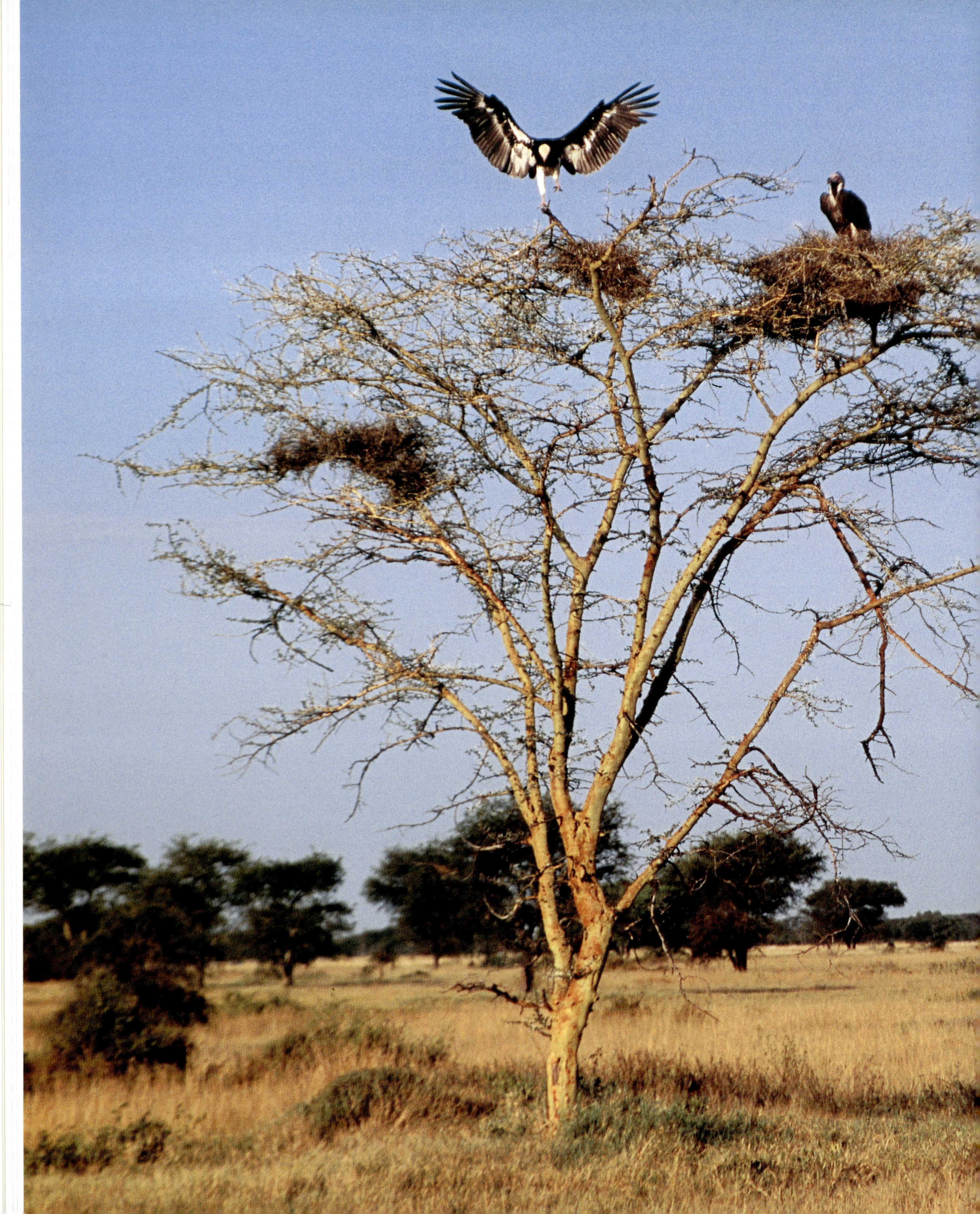

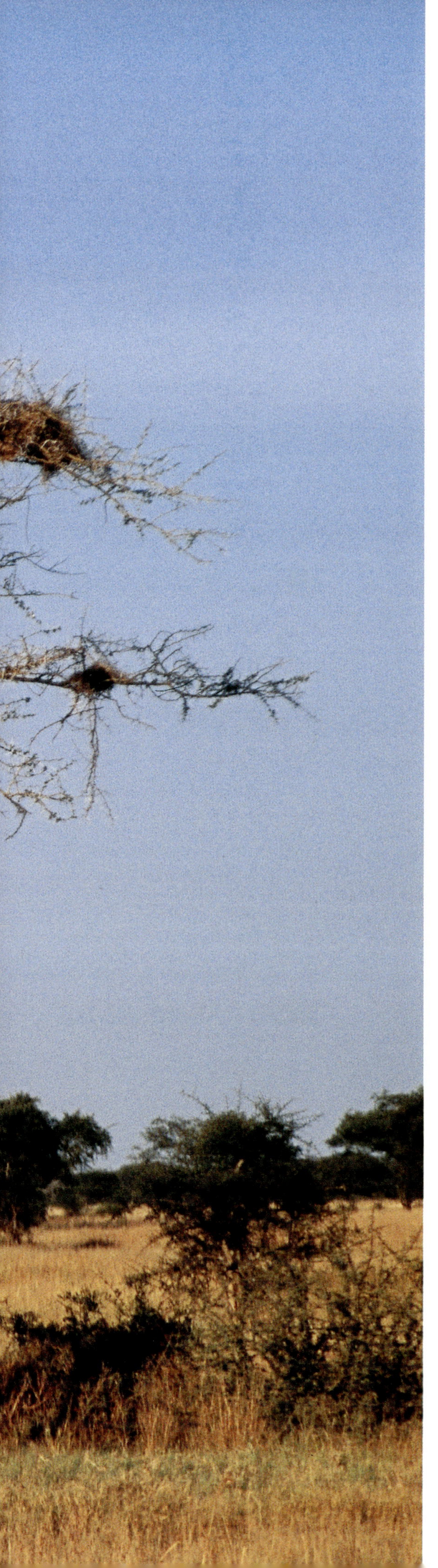

PERENNIAL THIRST

The Serengeti and Masai Mara are the stage for Africa's annual Great Migration. The romance and excitement of Africa exists for many as a vision of thousands of ungulates leaping into rivers to reach greener pastures. Predators lurk in the open plains, which are speckled with flat-topped trees. It is a mighty land spanning two countries, rich in wildlife and as interesting botanically. Our journey begins in the western corridor of the Grumeti River of the Serengeti and moves north, near the source of the same river, into the Masai Mara. As much as the spectacle of this land is one of nature's miracles, it is also a triumph for conservation, with communities and their cattle peacefully coexisting on the fringes of the reserves.

LEFT: Vultures build their stick nests in the canopies of flat-topped acacia trees. In some cases they may add to the bulky communal nests of buffalo weavers or wattled starlings.

Grumeti River Camp
Serengeti Tanzania

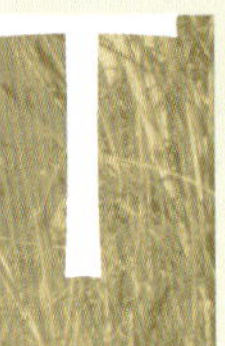

The sight of massive snorting hippopotami covered in water lettuce, as they burst out of an oxbow pan formed by an overflow of the Grumeti River, added to our sense of exhilaration on arriving in the Serengeti. Seeing the hippo, just metres away from us, was our first experience of the prolific game in the area. During the Great Migration, so many wildebeest and zebra congregate around the Grumeti airstrip that two Land Rovers are on permanent duty to ensure the safety of the aircraft. For the rest of the year in this remote western corridor of the Serengeti National Park, large herds of resident animals, amid scattered Thomson's gazelle, cheetah, elephant and lion, move around relatively undisturbed.

'Serengeti' in the Maasai language means 'endless plains'. Wasting no time, the camp manager, Peter, took us across the short grass where off-road driving is allowed for an overview of the Rift Valley Plateau from the top of the granite Kitunga Hills. The shores of Lake Victoria, some 50 kilometres away, can be seen on a clear day from this favourite viewpoint. Lone buffalo shade under Desert Date (*Balanites aegyptiaca*) and Boscia (*Boscia coriacea*) across flat grassy plains reaching the horizon, where sunsets and sunrises rival the best on Earth.

Whistling Thorns (*Acacia drepanolobium*) are among the most dominant of the acacias in this part of the Serengeti. They are well-known throughout East Africa and found in areas where there is black cotton soil. They are fascinating because of their relationship with cocktail ants that live in the swollen thorn bases, ready to attack any browsing antelope or beetle. In the rainy season, when their leaves are green and tasty, any disturbance on the tree will cause aggressive cocktail ants to rush out in its defence. A whistling sound can be heard when the wind blows over the hollow swellings at the base of its thorns.

The four different species of ant that colonise Whistling Thorns are intolerant of one another. Experiments done by tying together branches of neighbouring trees occupied by different ant species resulted in fighting until a whole colony of enemies was wiped out.

While marvelling at the aggressive nature of ants, we came across a bigger and meaner fighter with a gigantic appetite. On the banks of the Grumeti River, a stealthy Nile crocodile was fighting over a zebra kill with two protective lionesses and some cubs. The interplay between the mother of the cubs and the mighty crocodile confirmed who rules the Serengeti. We were told that many of the Nile crocodiles in the Grumeti River only eat opportunistically during the migration when wildebeest and zebra stumble into their territory.

The parts of the riverine forest along the Grumeti River that have not been disturbed by hippo are rich and imposing. While photographing a large Sycamore Fig (*Ficus*

BELOW: White Thorn (*Acacia polyacantha*).

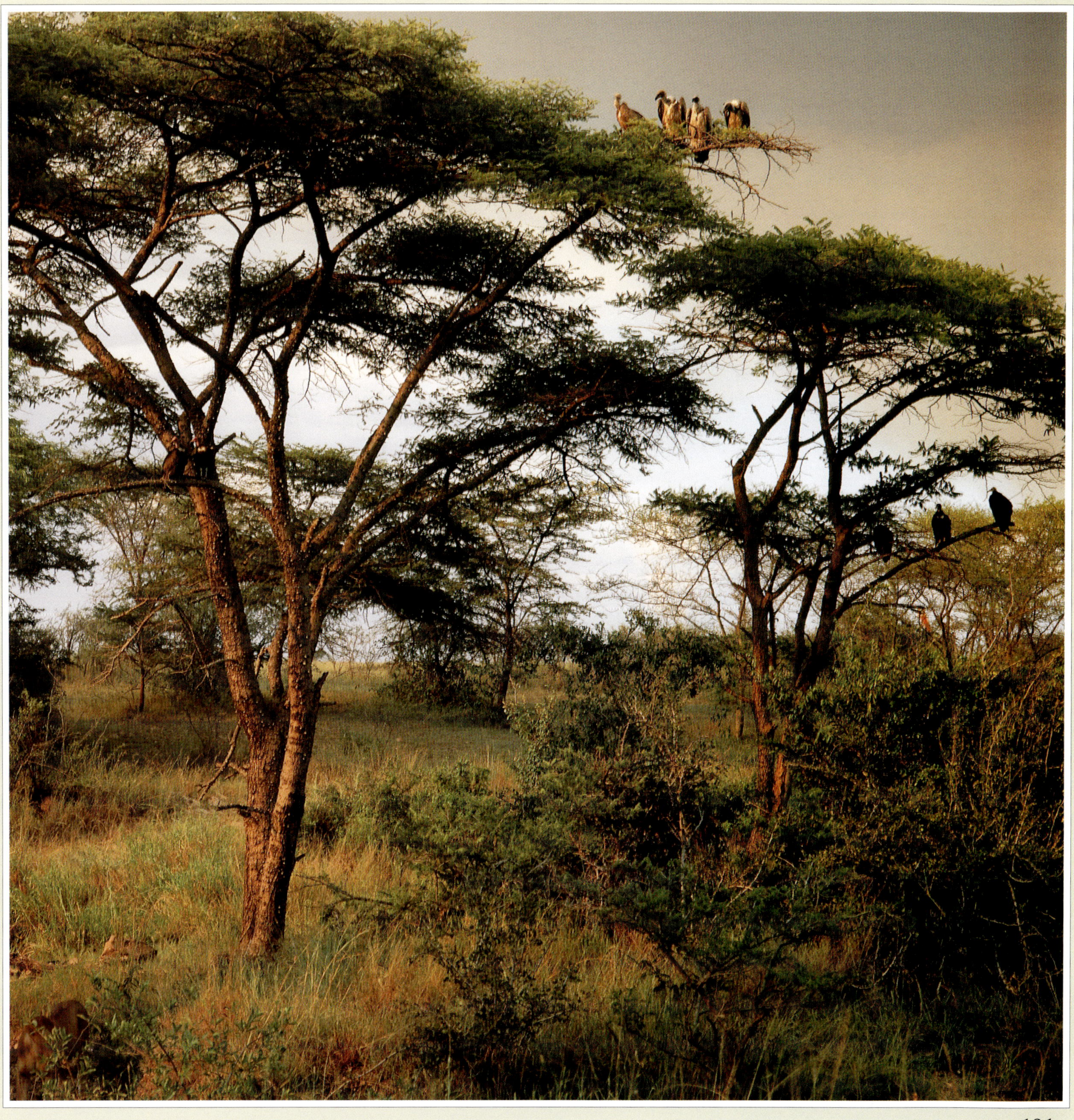

sycomorus), we were lucky to spot the black-and-white flash of a shy Colobus monkey high up in the branches of a Tamarind Tree (*Tamarindus indica*). The abundant game around the river often made it unsafe to get out of the vehicle to take pictures, but the sight of a convention of Maribou storks with their feet in the shallow river bed was irresistible. On the plains we had more time to focus on the Floodplain Acacia (*Acacia kirkii*) and the Slender Three-hook Acacia (*Acacia senegal*), so prolific in the grassland where they rapidly colonise disturbed or altered areas.

Storms brewed in the late afternoon, clouding out the long-awaited sunset over Lake Victoria. We heard that the migration was building up in the Ngorongoro conservation area around Ndutu. Hordes of tourists follow over two million herbivores, some 200 000 zebra, 18 000 eland, 50 000 Thomson's gazelle and one-and-a-half million wildebeest, yet only a few travel as far as Grumeti River Camp, which has remained a sanctuary in a secluded area of paradise.

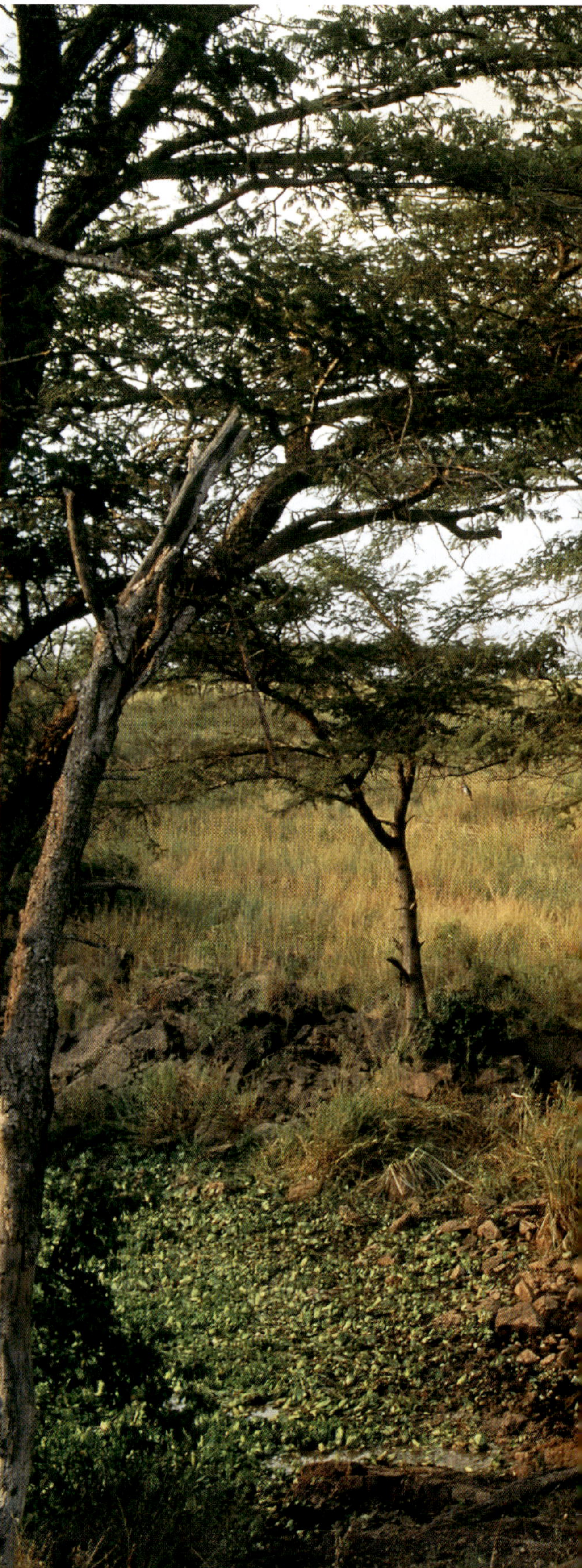

RIGHT: Lion kill on the banks of the Grumeti River with White Thorn (*Acacia polyacantha*) in the background.

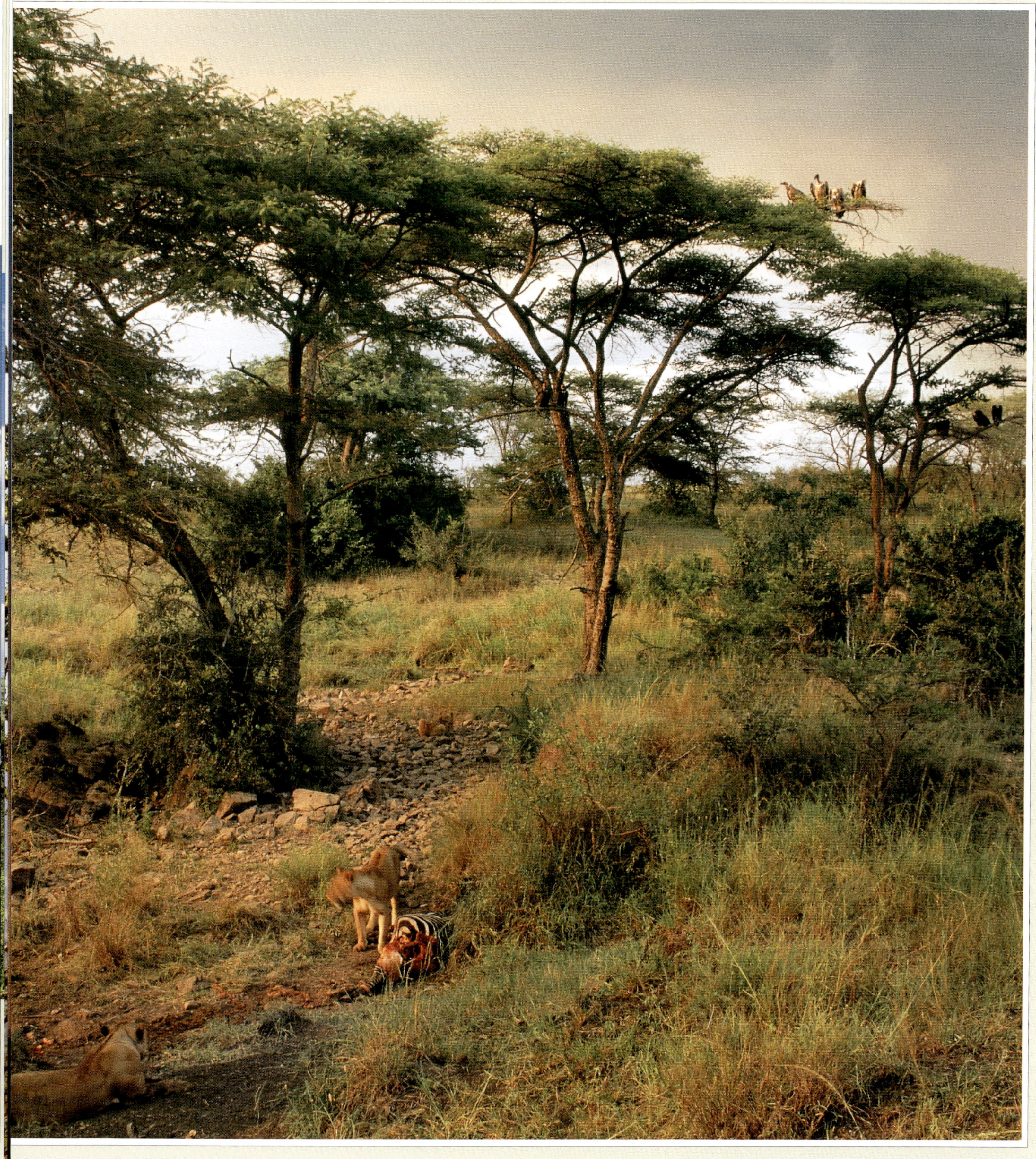

Grumeti | Tanzania

Kichwa Tembo
Masai Mara Kenya

BELOW: Haroni Fig (*Ficus vallis-choudae*). Several enormous specimens of this tree grow along the Sabaringo and Mara rivers, where their ripe fruit attracts hornbills and turacos. Like all members of the fig family, it has a specific fig wasp that performs the role of pollinator.

The flat, spotted landscape of the Masai Mara is one of the classic images of the African landscape. Lone, flat-topped trees dotted across runaway grassland as far as the eye can see, mark the place where millions of spontaneous, thirsty and unpredictable wildebeest complete their astounding migration. The dangerous crossing of the Mara River provides the drama of the migration, where luck determines which animals will drown or become a feast for crocodiles as large as barges on the Nile.

Being at Kichwa Tembo on the border of the Masai Mara in March, during the low season, when there is a sense of calm in the long grass, was a privilege. On the western

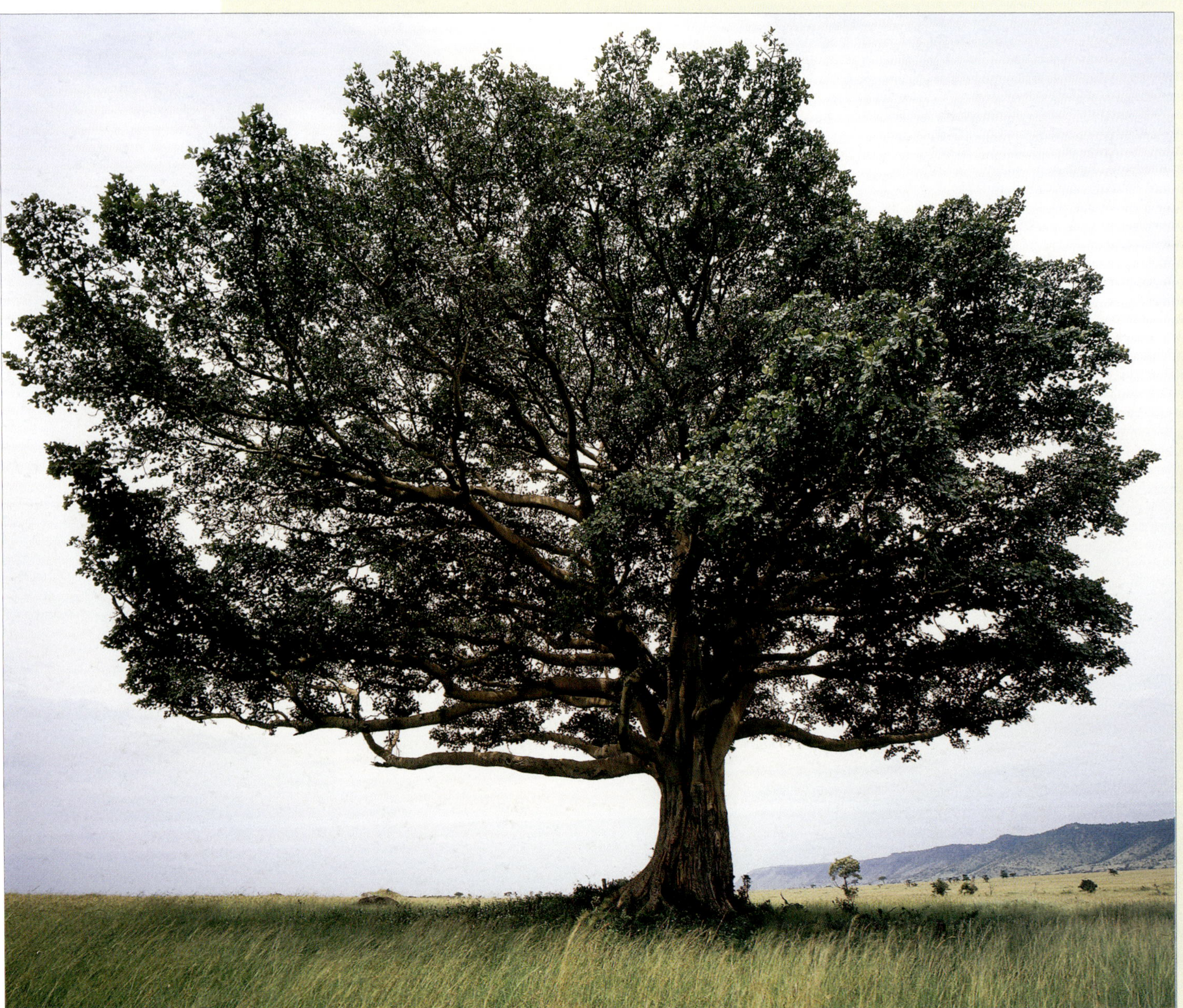

boundary of the reserve, marked by the Oloololo escarpment and the Sabaringo River, lazy buffalo, overfed lion and resident antelope hardly make a dent on the great food supply in store for millions of ungulates in the months to come. For now, lion in prides of up to 22 and cheetah relish an easy kill every day, surrounded by beady-eyed vultures and hyena.

Water-laden clouds hang heavily, shielding the Mara from the harsh sun. They are a welcome respite for all living beings except photographers and filmmakers.

The legendary animal interaction in the Masai Mara takes place amid lone Desert Dates (*Balanites aegyptiaca*) that are flattened out at the top by browsing giraffe to take on the shape of the great Umbrella Thorn (*Acacia tortilis*). They are tough trees that provide shade for buffalo and feeding felines. Even the occasional enormous, succulent Finger Euphorbia (*Euphorbia tirucalli*/Ol-oile) that stands alone in the golden grass has adopted an umbrella shape in the absence of competition. Unfortunately, due to

BELOW: Boscia (*Boscia coriacea*). The small waxy leaves are highly nutritious. Extreme browsing pressure prevents rapid growth and many ancient specimens in the Masai Mara have assumed bonsai proportions.

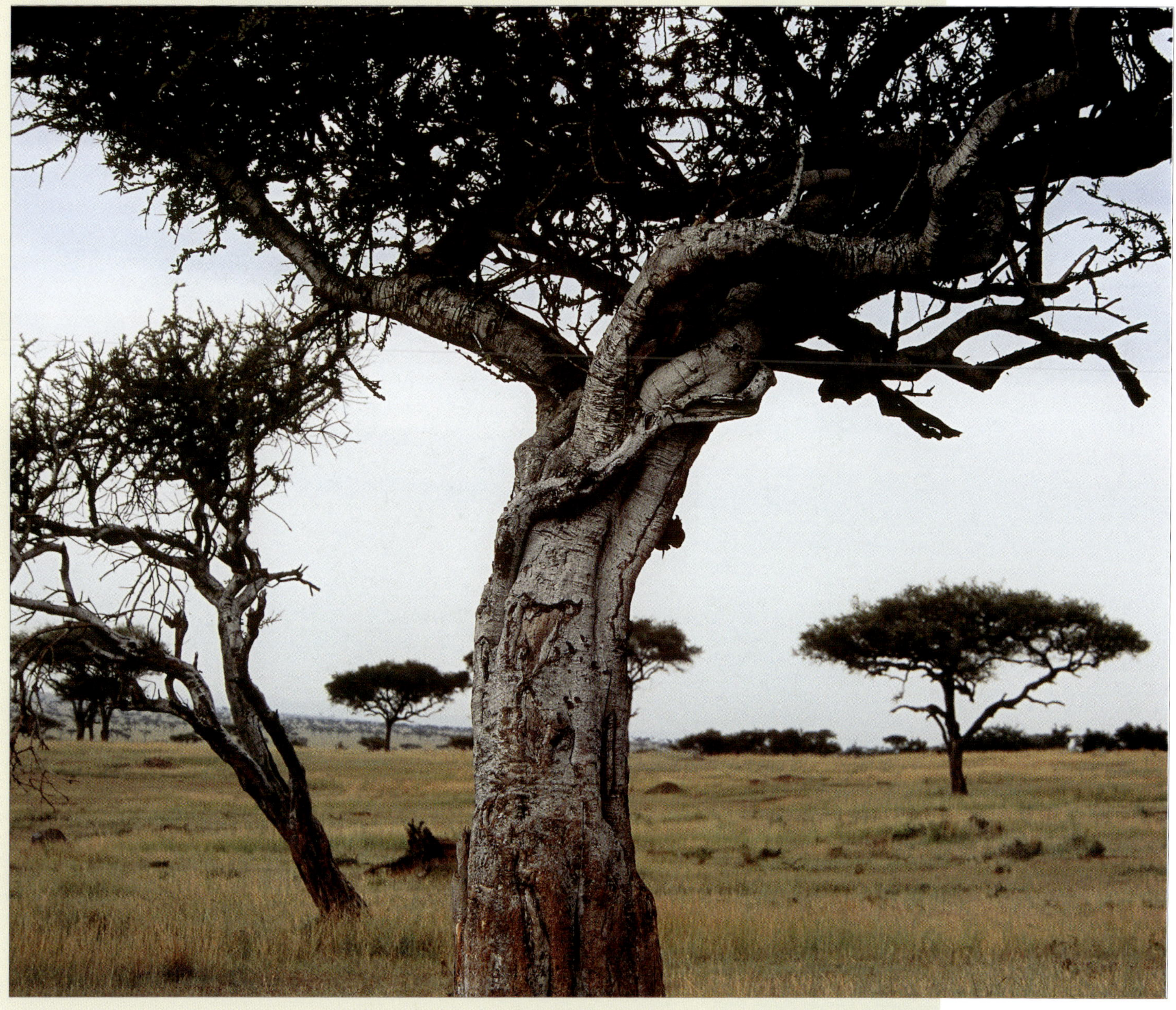

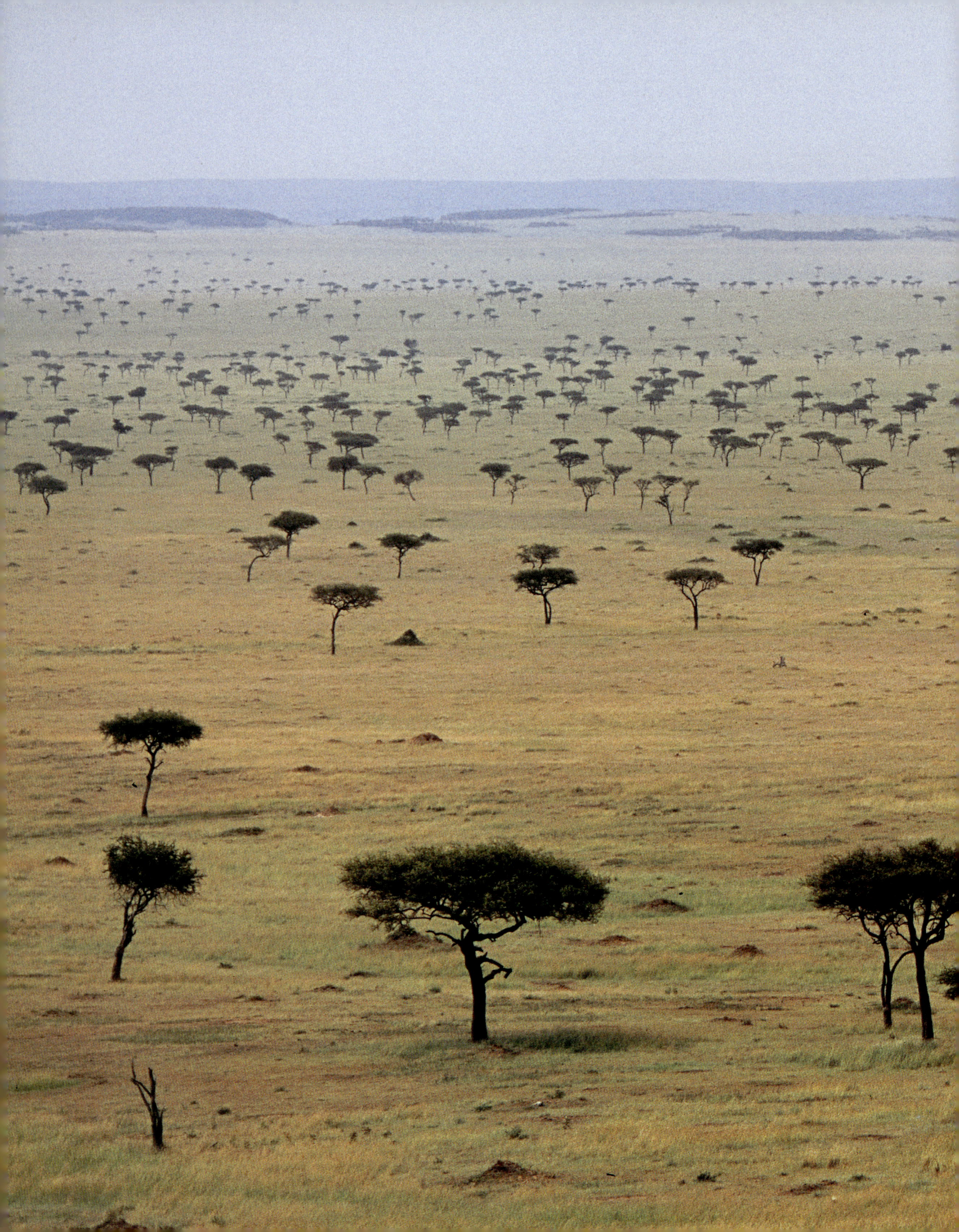

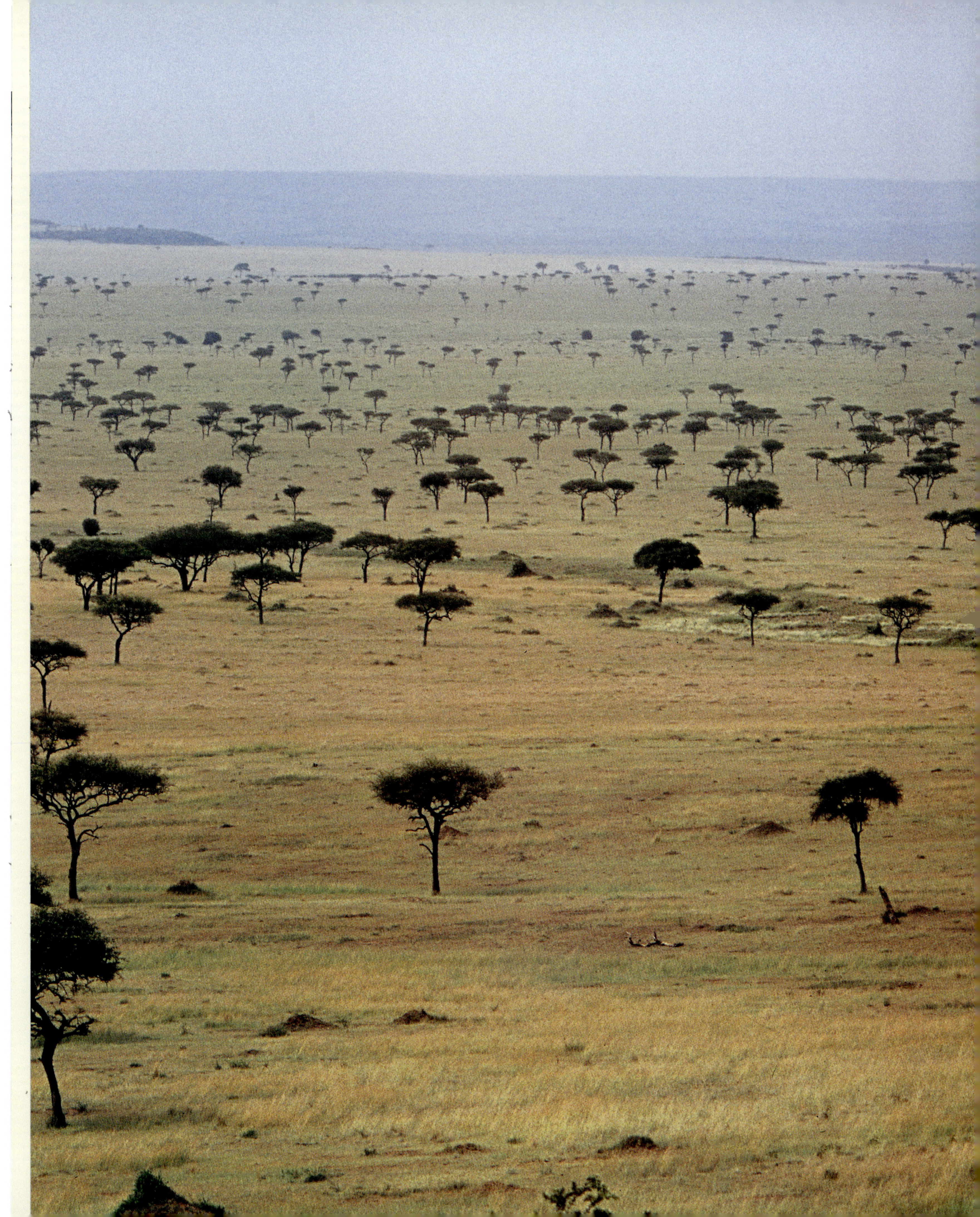

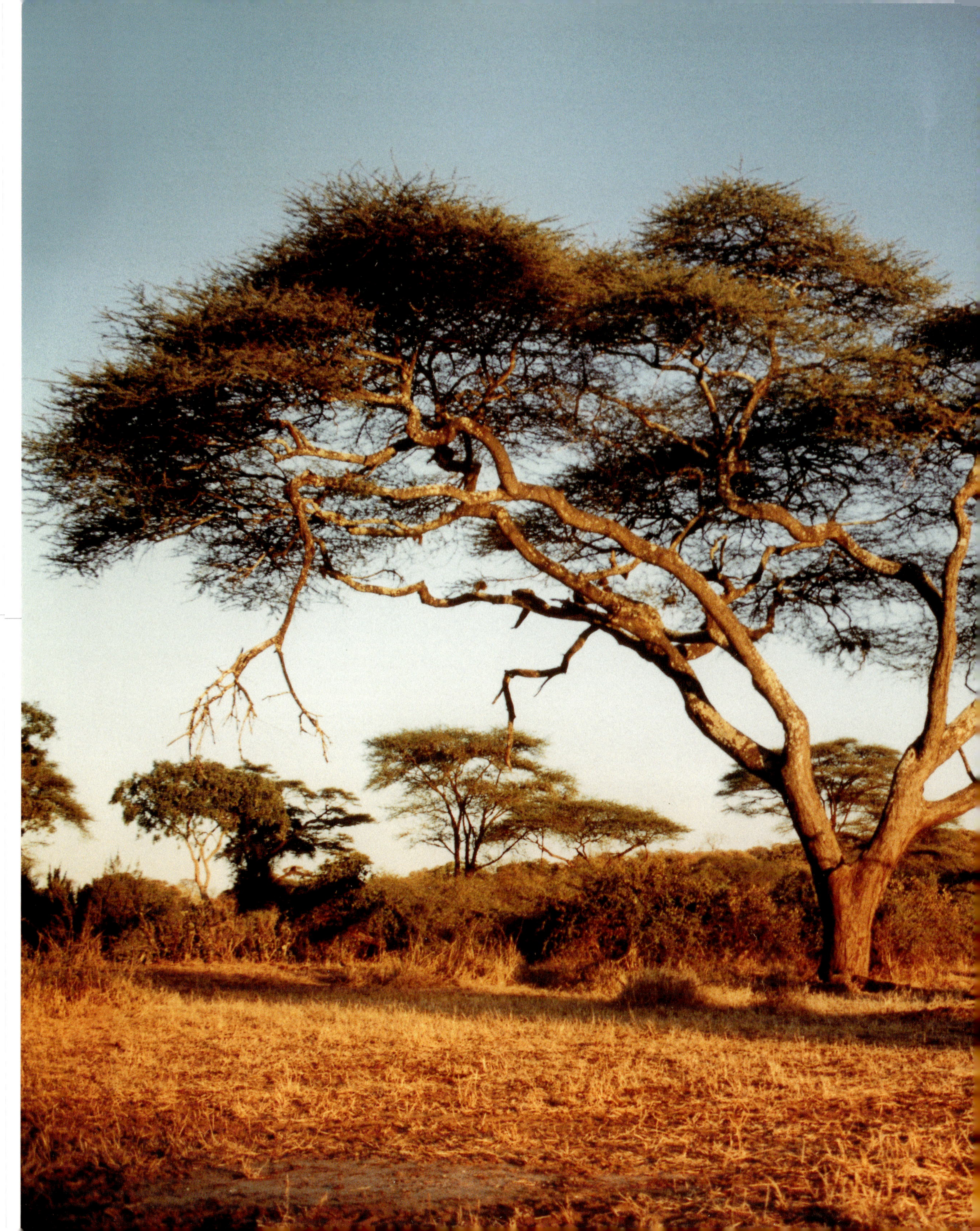

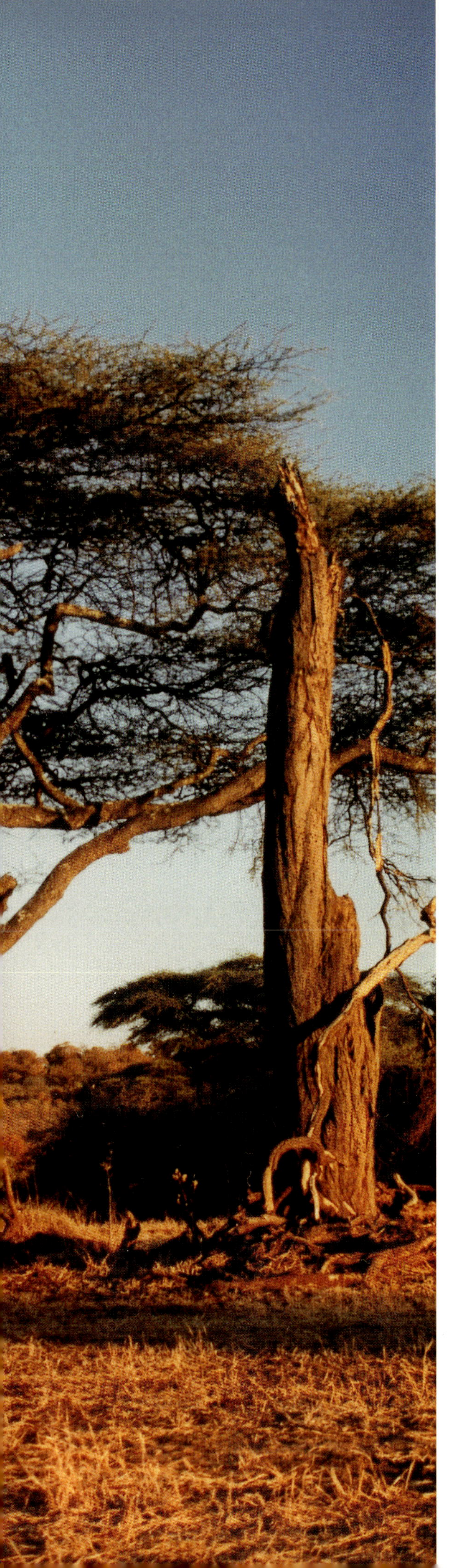

ANCIENT WATER SYSTEMS

The Okavango waters originate in the Angolan highlands and disappear into the Kalahari Desert, while the Zambezi River has its source in Zambia and ends in the Indian Ocean. Today these are different rivers, yet it is thought that, long ago, both flowed as one massive river across the Kalahari, filling the Great Makgadikgadi Lake and on to the Limpopo. This changed as the Zambezi was diverted by the Victoria Falls faulting, while other faults, silt and a decline in rainfall left the Okavango as the last surviving remnant of those times. The uncertain future hints at a fragile and diminishing water miracle, with sometimes only a vegetation trail left to tell the tale.

LEFT: Camel Thorn (*Acacia erioloba*).

Matetsi Game Lodges
Zimbabwe

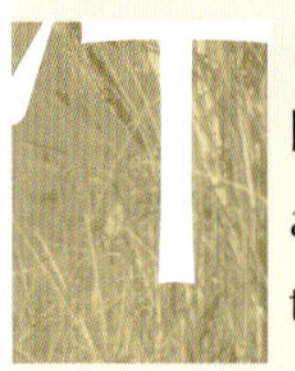

'The whole scene was extremely beautiful; the banks and islands dotted over the river are adorned with sylvan vegetation of great variety of colour and form – no one can imagine the beauty of the view from any thing witnessed in England,' wrote David Livingstone in 1858, when he travelled along the Zambezi River in search of the Victoria Falls.

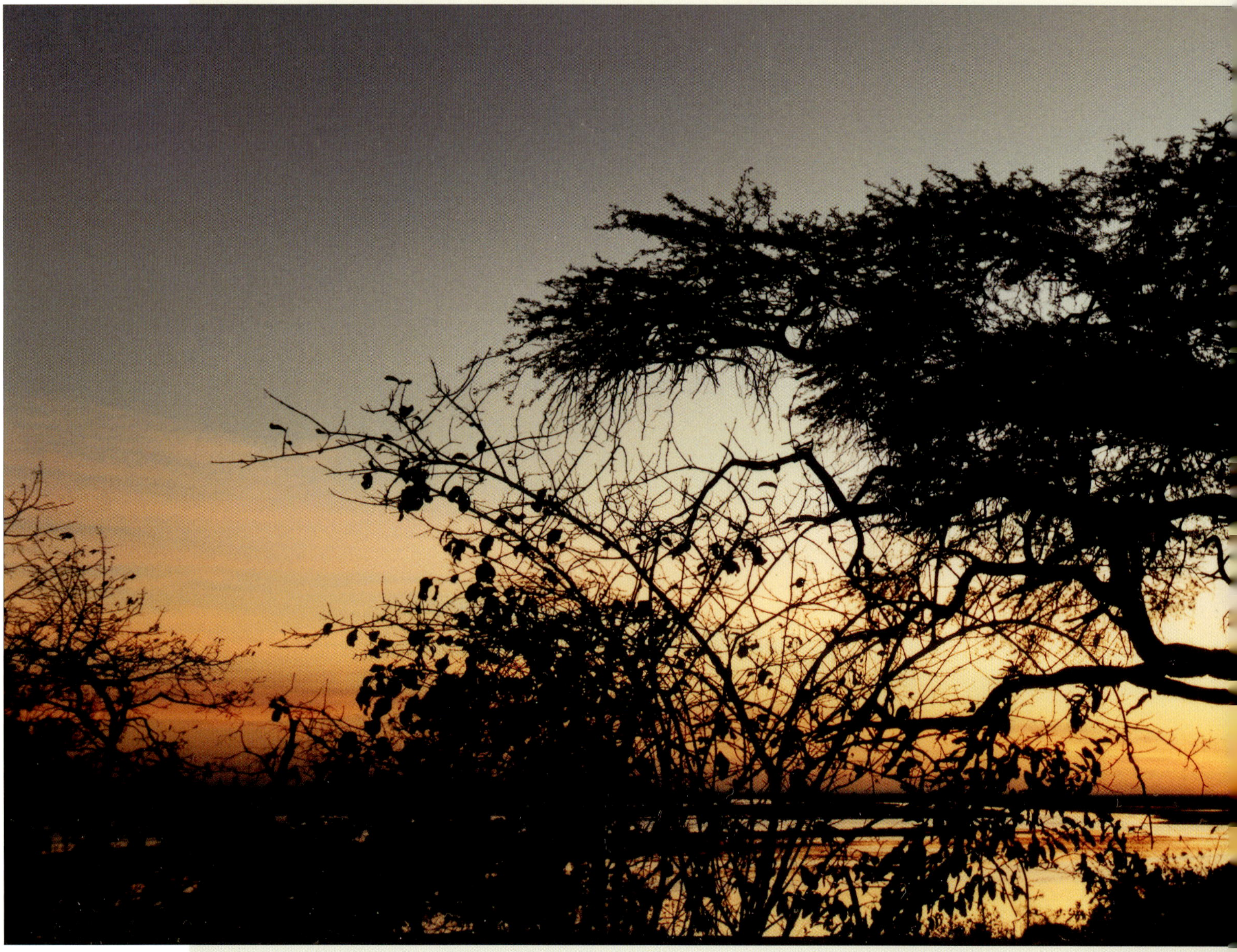

Some 150 years later, the riverine forest along the banks of the mighty Zambezi reminds us of early explorers as well as radical change in the twenty-first century. Great Jackalberry (*Diospyros mespiliformis*), African Mangosteen (*Garcinia livingstonei*), Leadwood (*Combretum imberbe*), Sausage Tree (*Kigelia africana*) and Camel Thorn (*Acacia erioloba*) thrive along one of the few remaining perennial rivers in Africa marking the border of Zimbabwe, Botswana, Zambia and Namibia. Although the trees are sparse in many places, they are well cared for and appreciated along the 15 kilometres of river frontage in Matetsi. From northwestern Zimbabwe to Botswana, animals roam freely across borders. Matetsi is part of a huge unfenced conservation area that includes Hwange National Park, the Zambezi National Park, and Botswana's Okavango Delta and Chobe National Park.

Cutting through the safari area in Zimbabwe is the well-travelled road straight from Victoria Falls to Kasane. In autumn, bare branches of the Wild Seringa (*Burkea africana*) Scotsman's Rattle (*Amblygonocarpus andongensis*) and Manketti (*Schinziophyton rauta-nenii*) stretch their branches to the sky and show off their different forms of growth that were hidden by green leaves in the summer months. The Kalahari sand is covered in a mosaic of orange, brown and yellow. All along the grassy verges are perfectly formed False Marula Trees (*Lannea schweinfurthii*), tempting the photographer to walk out into this Eden were it not for regular sightings of buffalo and lion nearby.

BELOW: Camel Thorn (*Acacia erioloba*). Insensitive development along the banks of the Zambezi River is threatening trees that have existed here for up to 1 000 years.

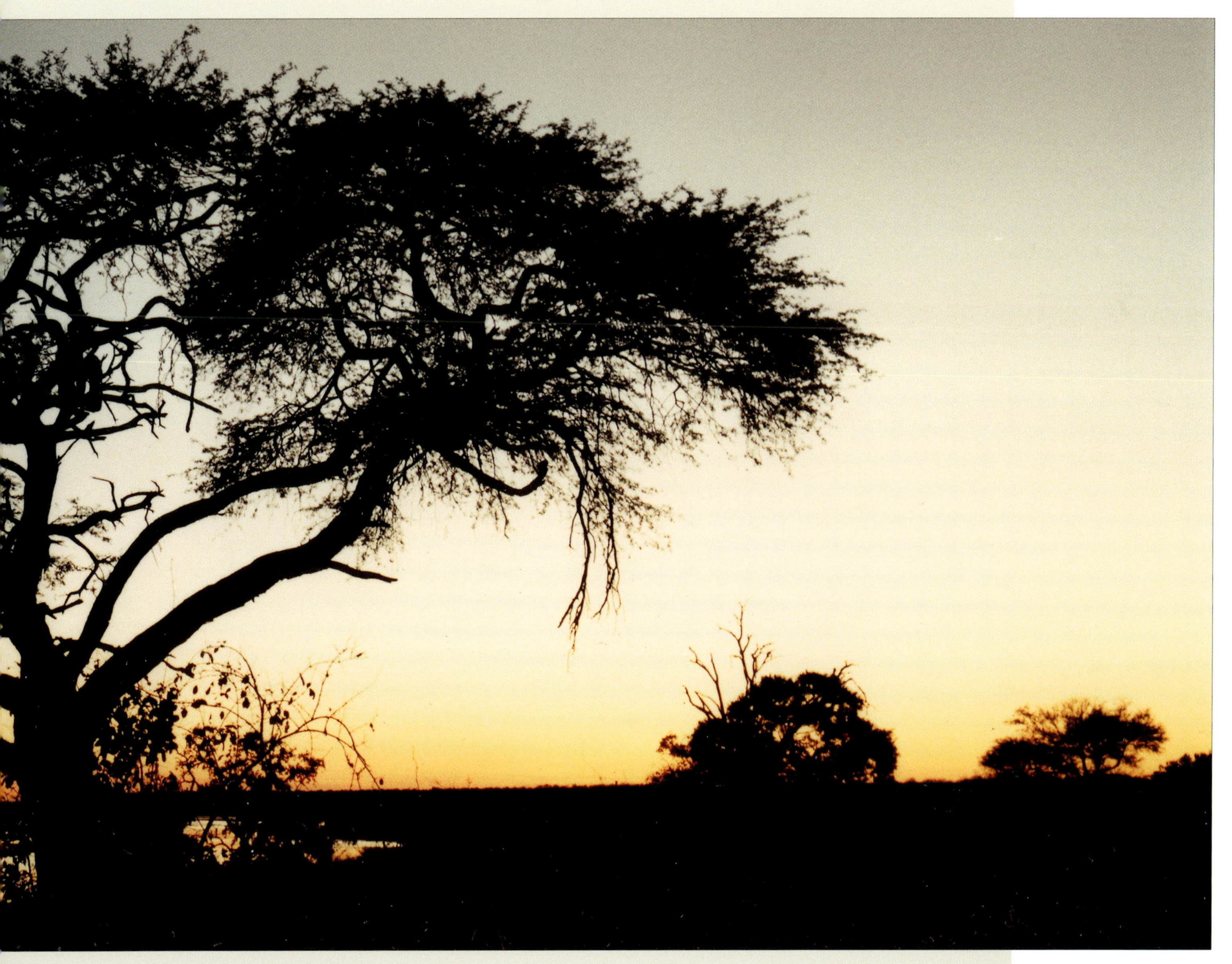

BELOW: Floodplain Acacia (*Acacia kirkii*). The pods of this acacia, which contain segments that protect each seed, break up very easily as they hit the ground.

OPPOSITE: Baobab (*Adansonia digitata*). The trunks of Baobabs often dry out from the inside and the hollow cavities have been used over time as toilets, jails and bars.

We were awoken long before dawn to catch the morning sun lighting up showy acacias in deep Kalahari-type sandy soil. This is their favourite environment. A bulky Camel Thorn marking the turnoff to the River Camp was our first challenge. It takes up so much space, making it almost impossible to fit into any camera format.

We came across an Umbrella Thorn (*Acacia tortilis*), the epitome of an African tree, from which the local people believe the Ark was made, and then an Ana Tree (*Faidherbia albida*). Each specimen seemed better than the last and we realised this place had more to offer than we could ever have imagined. In contrast to the bare trees all around us, the Ana Tree had just developed fresh green leaves for the winter months.

The leafless Baobab (*Adansonia digitata*) our guide Vitalis showed us on the road back was full of dangling fruits resembling a heavily decorated Christmas tree. It is a pleasingly pretty specimen, unlike some of the grotesque individuals we have seen on our travels, and referred to by David Livingstone as 'that giant upturned carrot'. I was tempted to pick the furry green fruit of the Baobab, which yields one of the highest known contents of Vitamin C and which can be used as a substitute for yeast. They have a sweet fragrance that lingers for months like a divine bush pot pourri. Matetsi, which was once a hunting concession area, is dominated by an upland plateau lying 1 000 metres above sea level. It has a range of habitats including miombo and mopane woodland that suffered from a serious drought in 2002. Unfortunately, the environment in countries ravaged by political greed is often further neglected. We can only hope that butterflies, supported by healthy flourishing vegetation, will be there for an eternity.

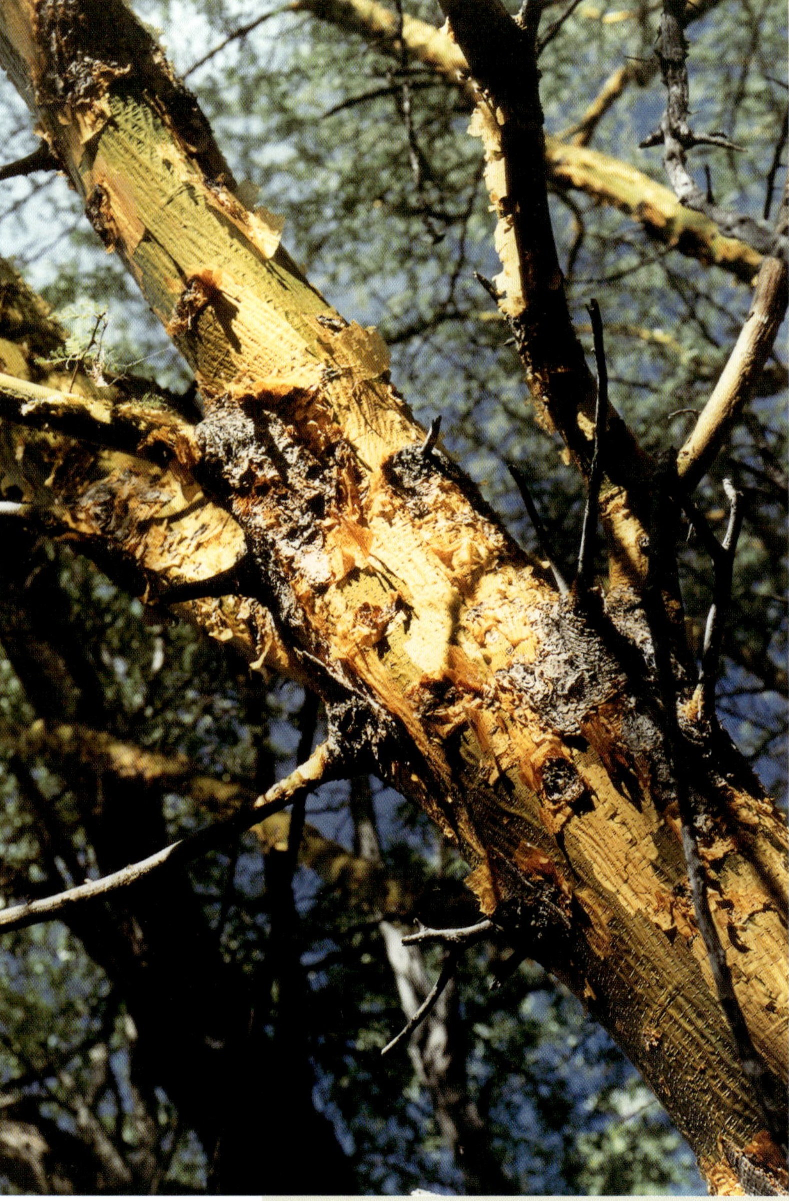

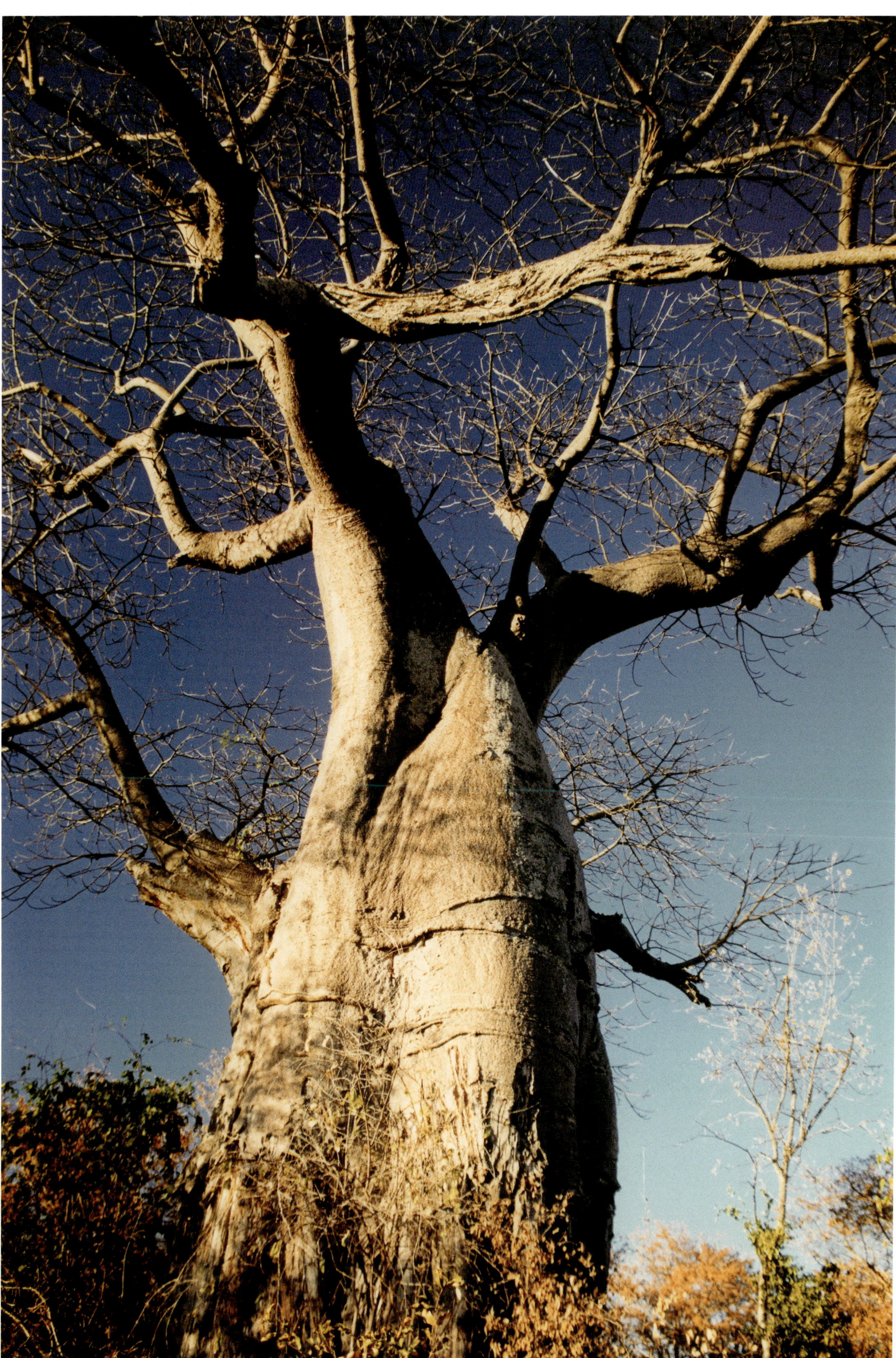

Matetsi | Zimbabwe

BELOW: Umbrella Thorn (*Acacia tortilis*). The shape of this tree differs across Africa, but this particular tree on the fringe of Matetsi represents the most classic of Umbrella Thorns. These trees attain great heights and ages, but can be stripped and destroyed by elephant that are particularly fond of the bark. It is sometimes necessary to preserve the very old specimens by wrapping barbed wire around the trunk to protect them from elephant.

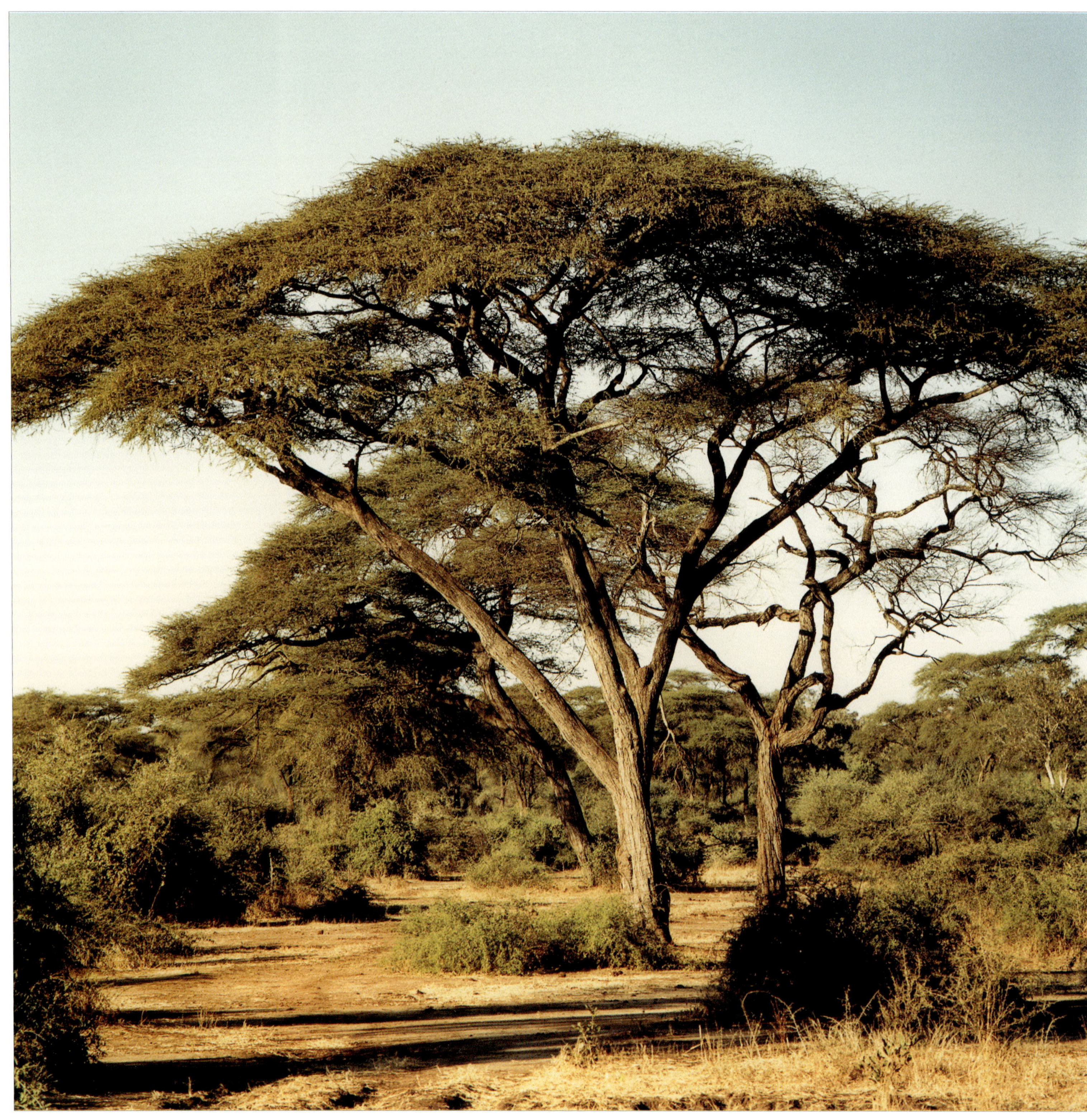

BELOW: Baobab (*Adansonia digitata*). The wood is very soft, spongy and fibrous. When drying out, the volume decreases by 40 per cent, making it worthless as timber.

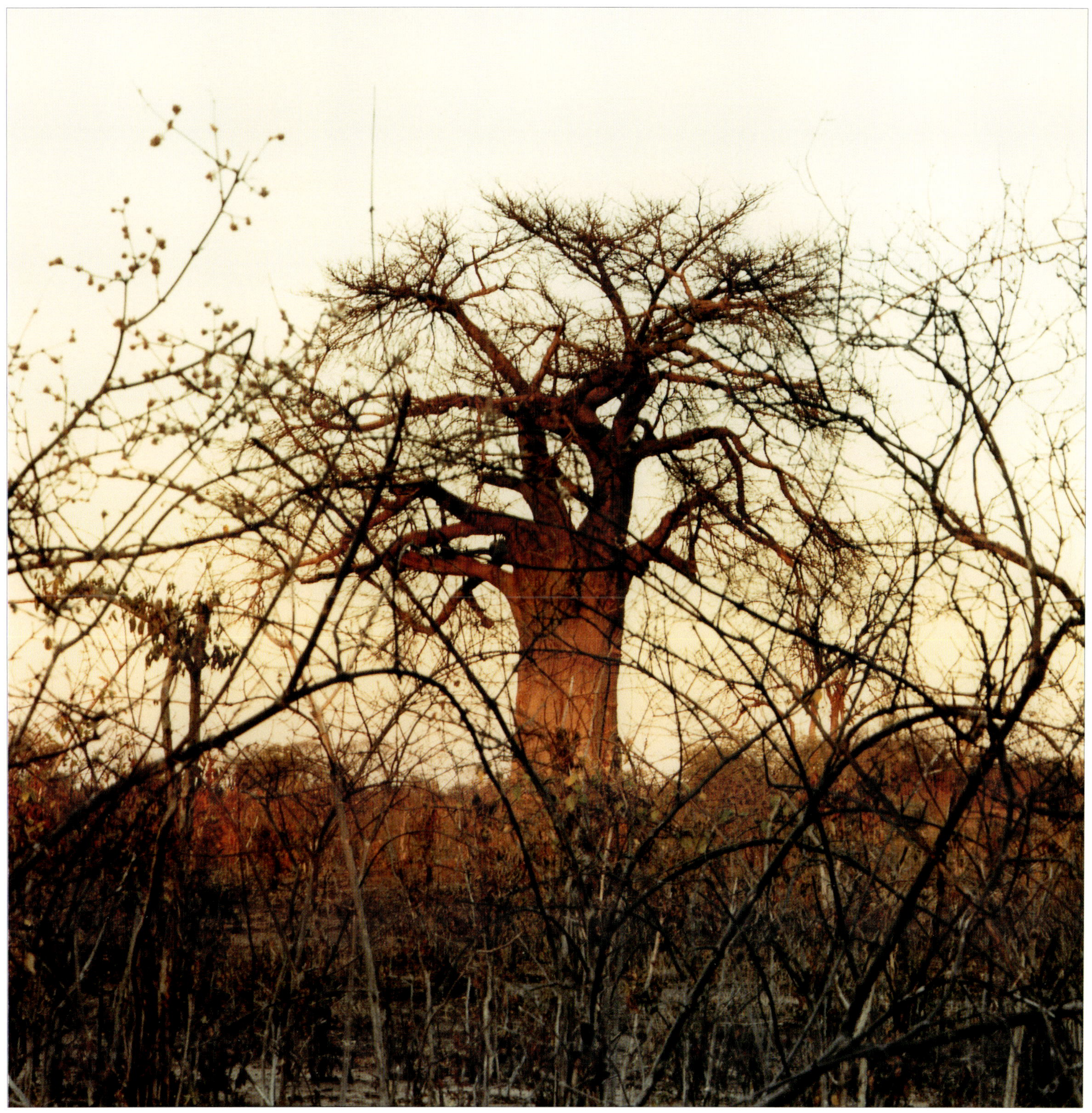

RIGHT: This Apple-leaf
(*Philenoptera violacea*) has
taken on the typical contorted
shape of the species.

Matetsi Zimbabwe

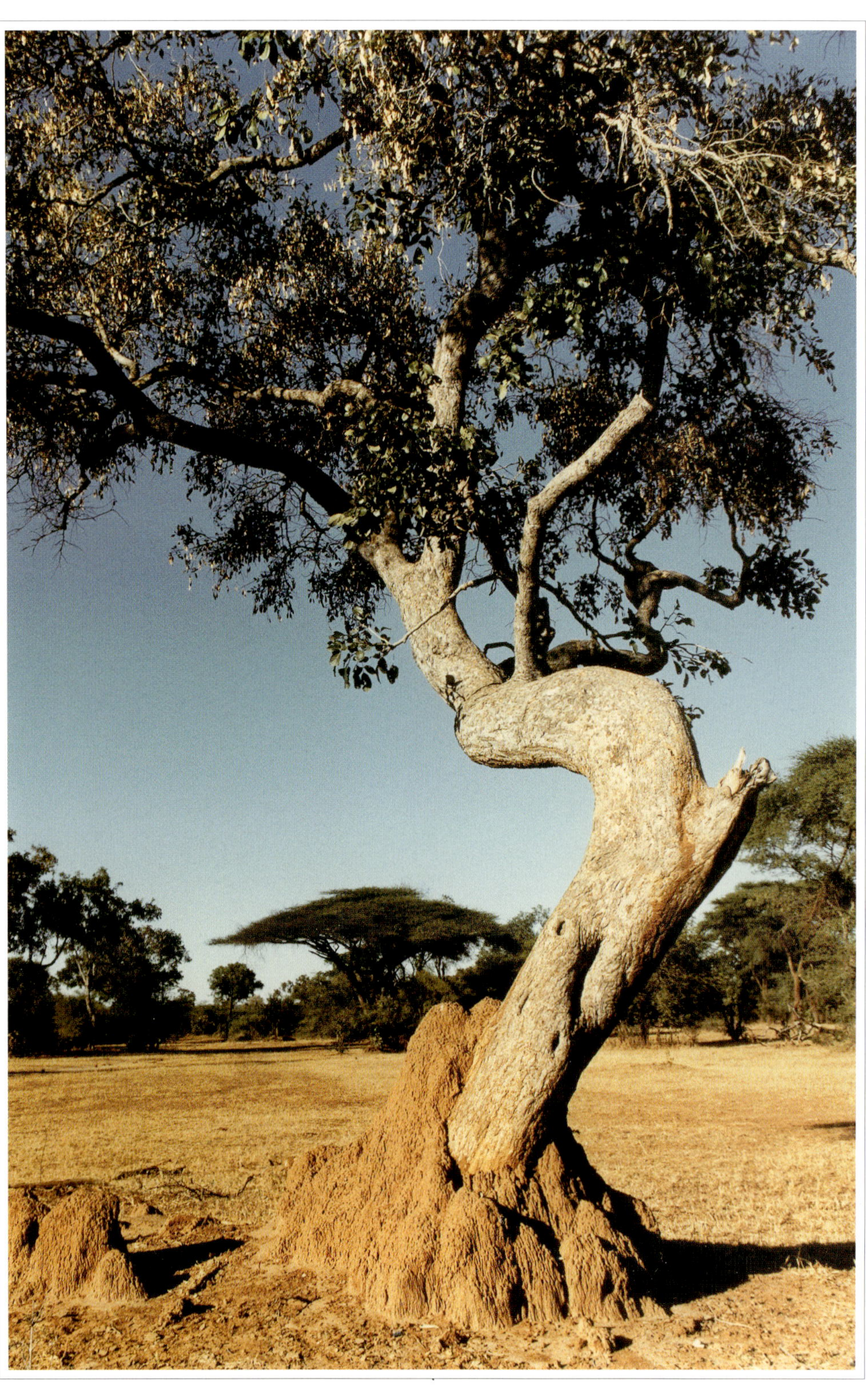

OPPOSITE: Leadwood
(*Combretum imberbe*). The
heartwood of this tree is so
hard that it is not often used to
make furniture as it damages
tools. Blades for hoes were
made of this wood before
metal became available.

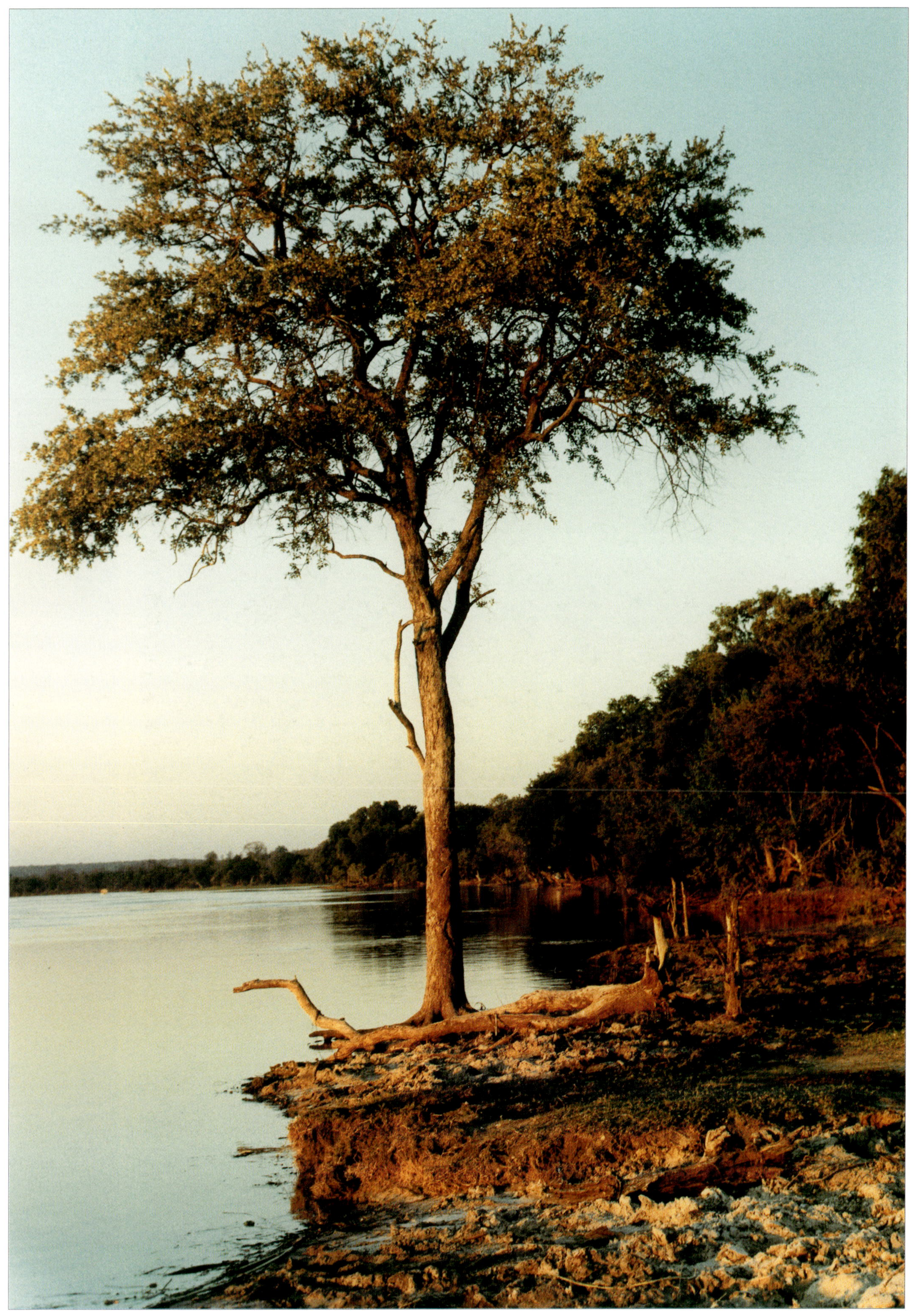

Matetsi Zimbabwe

BELOW: Mopane (*Colophospermum mopane*). When a Mopane stands as tall as this one it is known as a 'cathedral tree'. The natural tendency of the wood to form holes provides an ideal habitat for a variety of hole-nesting birds and the tree squirrel.

OPPOSITE: Common Wild Fig (*Ficus burkei*). Rope is made from the bark of these trees.

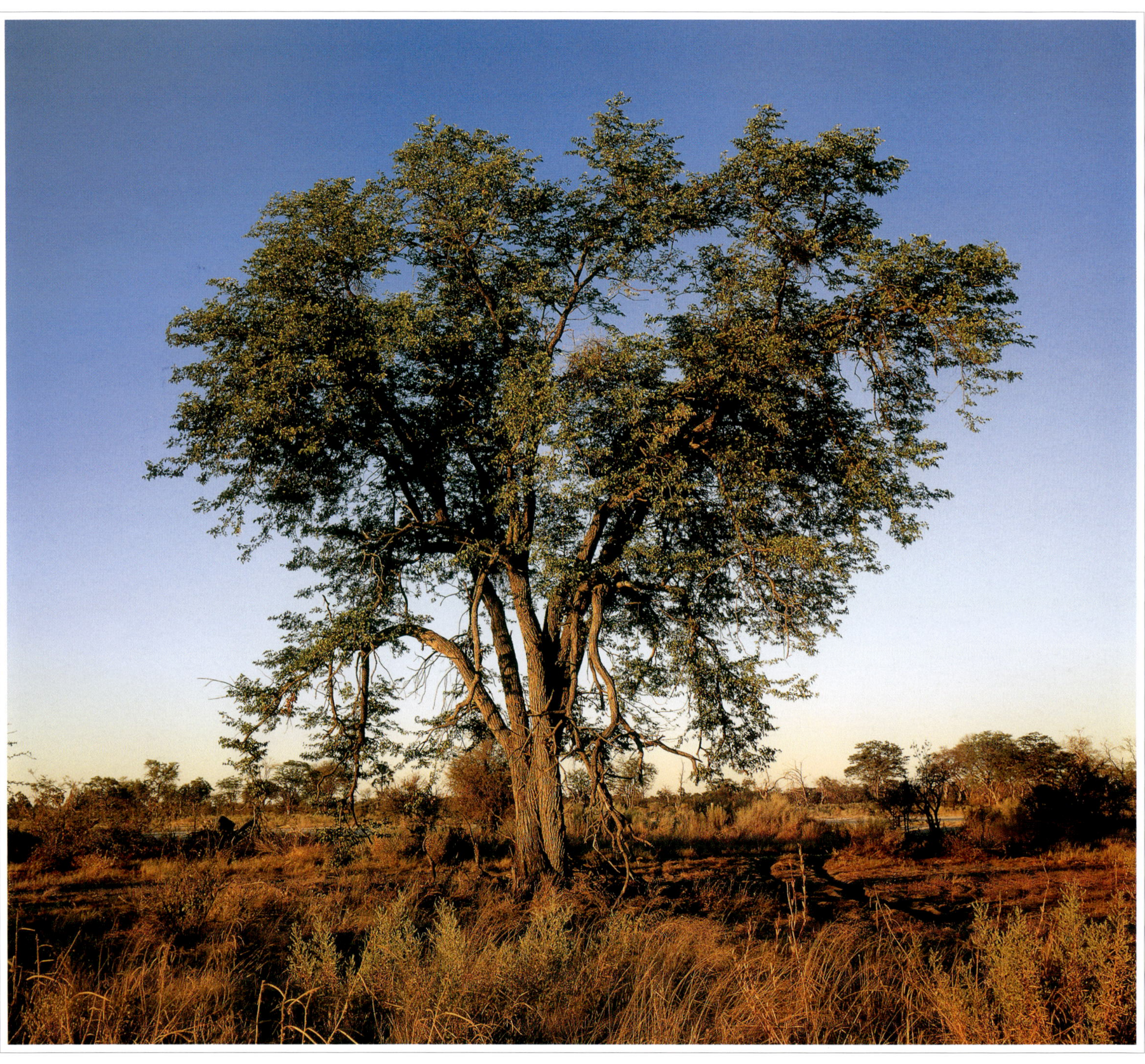

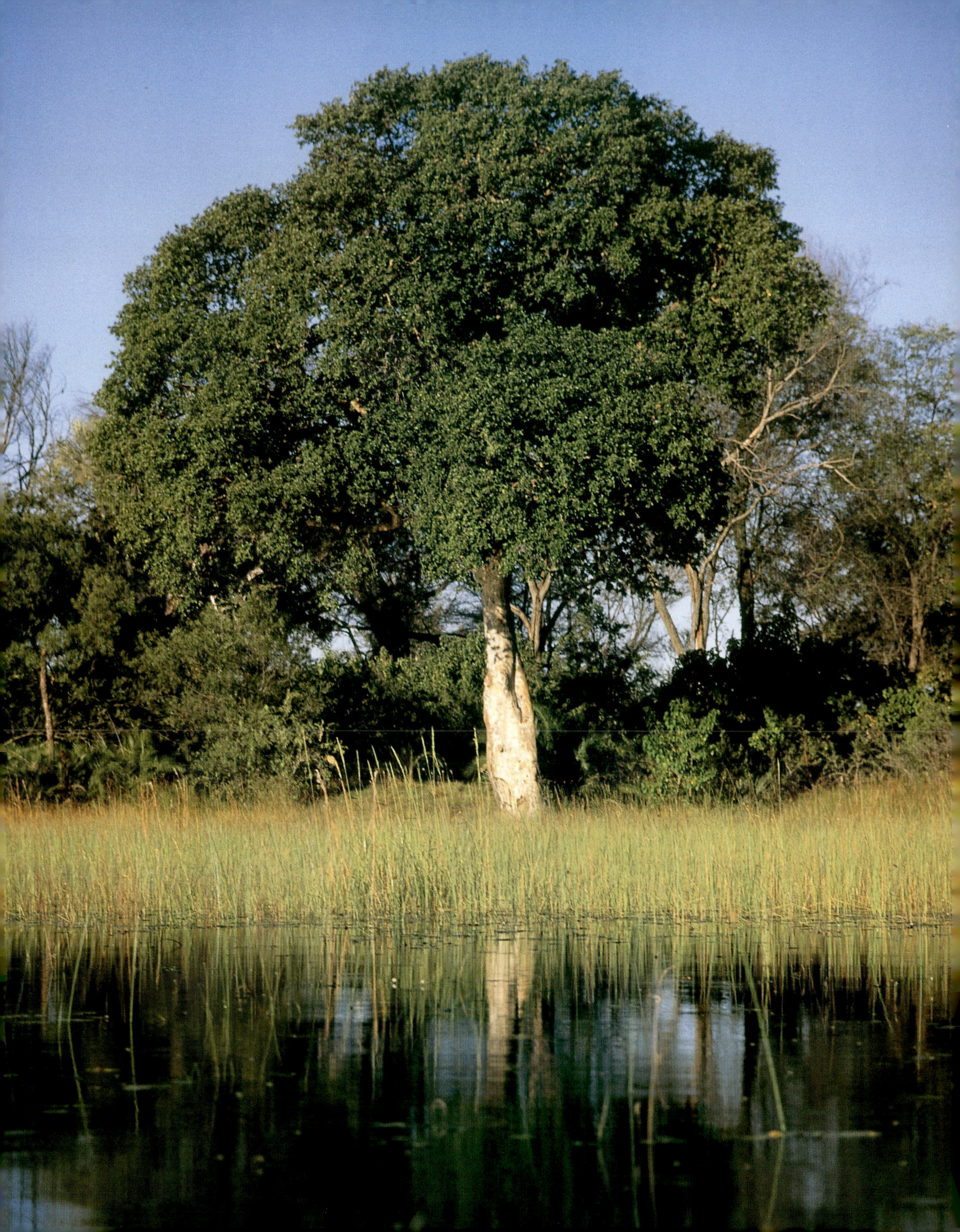

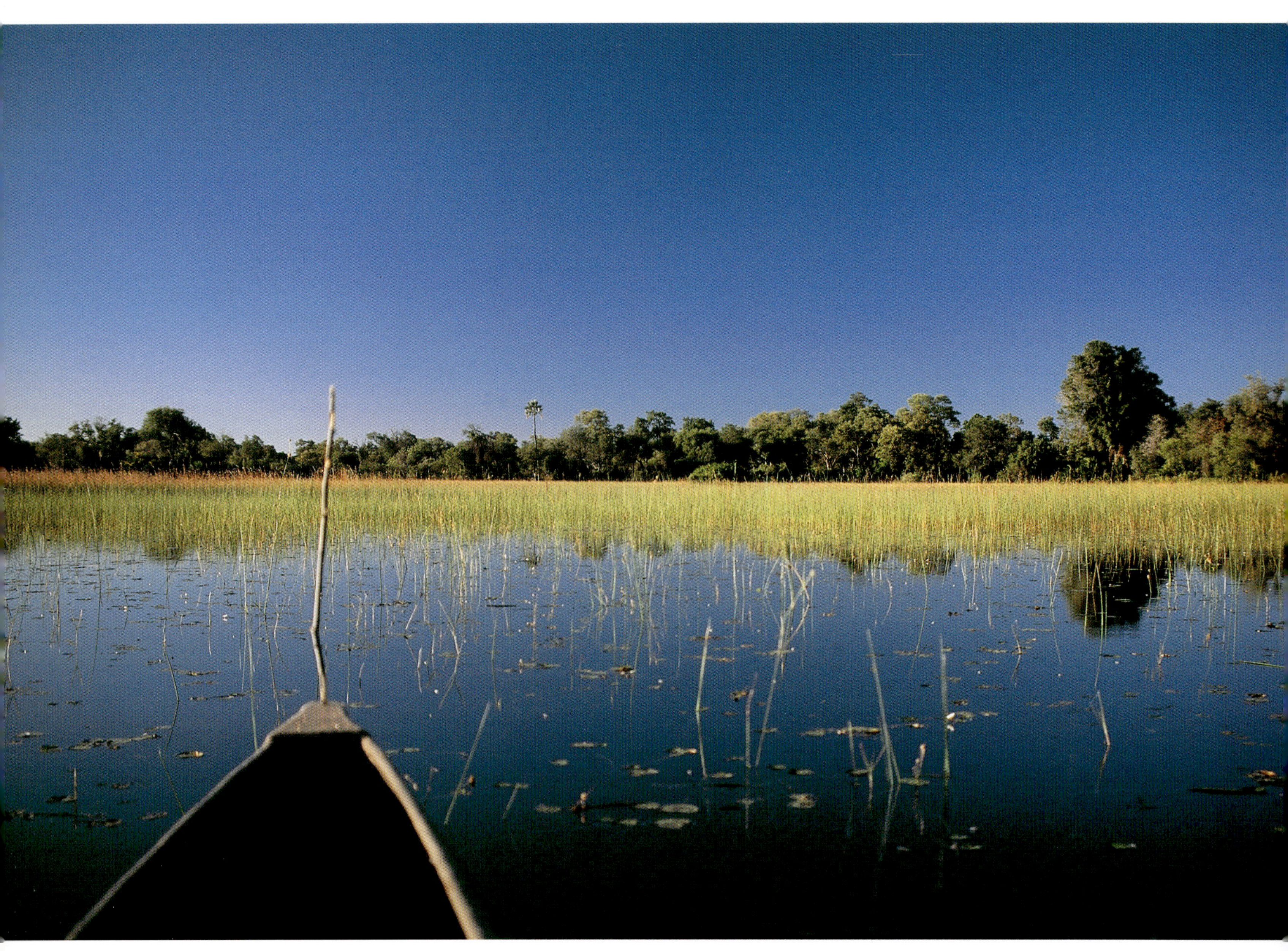

ABOVE: Mokoros were first made in the delta by the Bayei tribe who came from the Zambezi River area in the 1750s. The presence of tsetse fly forced them to abandon their livestock and become expert fishermen. Jackalberry (*Diospyros mespiliformis*) and Sausage Tree (*Kigelia africana*) trunks are used for carving out dugout canoes or mokoros – one of the best ways of experiencing the delta.

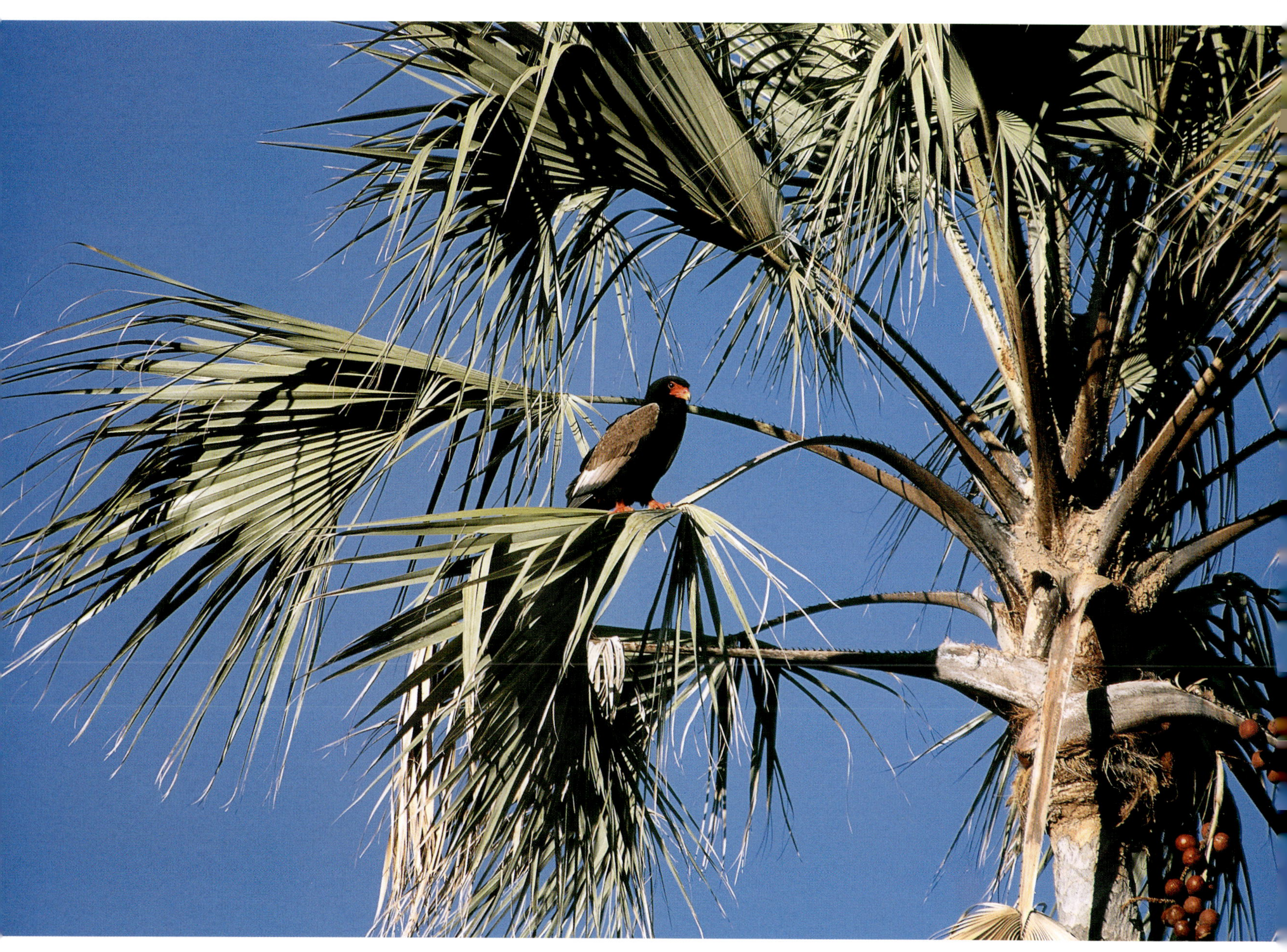

ABOVE: Northern Lala Palm (*Hyphaene petersiana*) with bateleur eagle. These trees not only stand out as landmarks of the Okavango Delta, but also play an important role in sustaining both humans and animals. They are the source of a popular wine, the new leaves are a source of food, the crown-heart of the stem is eaten as a vegetable, and the fruit pulp is quite palatable to baboon and elephant.

INDEX

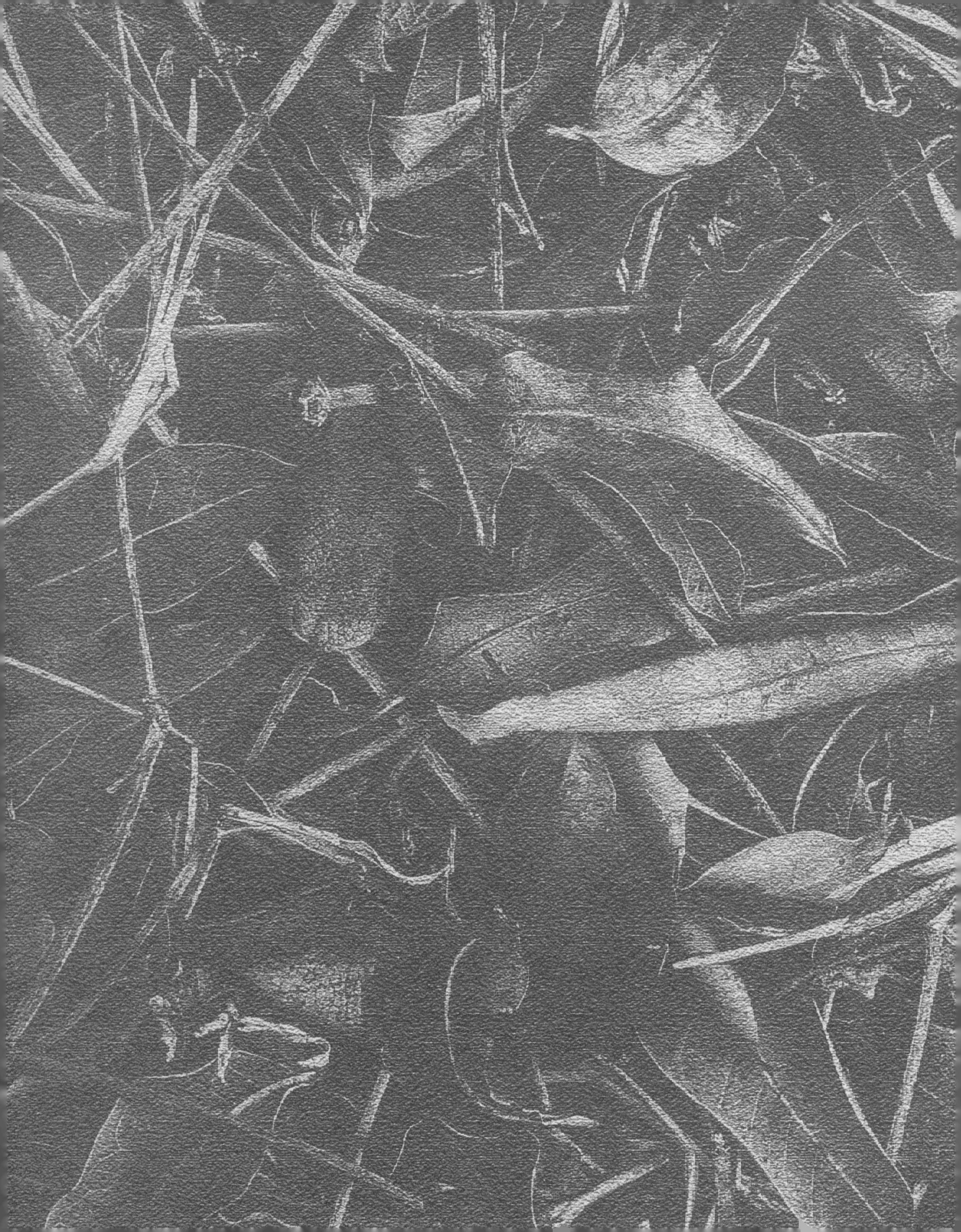